Praise for
UNTRUE
by Wednesday Martin, PhD

"Scientifically literate and sexually cliterate...An exuberant unfettering of female sexuality."

—Ian Kerner, sex therapist and author of *She Comes First*

"For centuries, men have been telling the story of female sexuality. Unsurprisingly, it was riddled with condescension, bias, and sheer ignorance. With *UNTRUE,* Wednesday Martin sets the record straight, shining a light on some of the female researchers reshaping our understanding of what turns women on and why. This is an important story, beautifully told. Highly recommended."

—Christopher Ryan, coauthor of *Sex at Dawn*

"Wednesday Martin understands female sexuality—from the #MeToo movement and polyamory to women's prehistoric and cultural heritage. She goes far beyond our current psychological understanding of women's infidelity to tell the real story of women's ubiquitous, tenacious, and primordial sexual strategies. And her writing is not only informative, timely, and refreshing but wonderfully engaging. Brava."

—Helen Fisher, author of *The First Sex* and *Why We Love*

"If you have ever felt different, other, or just weird when it comes to love, sex, or intimacy, read *UNTRUE.* Wednesday Martin bulldozes the sexual stereotypes that have silenced and constrained us for centuries, bringing the voices of women who love in a range of ways to the surface. Dazzling."

—Rachel Simmons, cofounder of Girls Leadership and author of *Enough As She Is* and *Odd Girl Out*

"Combining Barbara Ehrenreich's immersive reporting style and Carrie Bradshaw's savoir faire, Wednesday Martin dispels many myths about female desire."

—Michelle Hart, *O, The Oprah Magazine*

"At times playful, the narrative teems with fascinating commentary about everything from bonobos and Paleolithic gender roles to Craigslist ads, as Martin examines how female sexuality continues to be shaped and stigmatized by artificial social constructions, sociopolitical values, and economics, all under the guise of 'natural' female biology and desire. A timely take on femininity and sexuality."

—Emily Bowles, *Library Journal* (starred review)

"Revolutionary…A book that may very well set off nuclear bombs in bedrooms and boardrooms."

—Deborah Copaken, *The Atlantic*

"A simultaneously frothy and substantive tour of female sexual desire… An indispensable work of popular psychology and sociology."

—*Kirkus Reviews* (starred review)

"Probably the best and most up-to-date overview of the latest research on female desire, cheating, and the question of whether women have an 'innate' proclivity toward polyamory and/or sexual variety…A must-read if you want to understand why monogamy might not always feel 'natural.'"

—Rachel Krantz, *BuzzFeed News*

"Martin offers a provocative read—based on the latest research studies and interviews with experts in human sexuality—that challenges us to think differently about women and sex."

—Justin Lehmiller, *Vice*

UNTRUE

Why Nearly Everything We Believe
About Women, Lust, and Infidelity Is Wrong and
How the New Science Can Set Us Free

WEDNESDAY MARTIN

Little, Brown Spark
New York Boston London

Copyright © 2018 by Wednesday Martin

Little, Brown Spark
Hachette Book Group
1290 Avenue of the Americas, New York, NY 10104
littlebrownspark.com

Originally published in hardcover by Little, Brown Spark, September 2018
First Little, Brown Spark trade paperback edition, September 2019

Little, Brown Spark is an imprint of Little, Brown and Company, a division of Hachette Book Group, Inc. The Little, Brown Spark name and logo are trademarks of Hachette Book Group, Inc.

The publisher is not responsible for websites (or their content) that are not owned by the publisher.

The Hachette Speakers Bureau provides a wide range of authors for speaking events. To find out more, go to hachettespeakersbureau.com or call (866) 376-6591.

"Eula" on pages 195–97 first appeared in *Apogee*.

ISBN 978-0-316-46361-4 (hc) / 978-0-316-46363-8 (pb)
LCCN 2018941914

10 9 8 7 6 5 4 3 2 1

LSC-C

Printed in the United States of America

CONTENTS

We do not even in the least know the final cause of sexuality... The whole subject is as yet hidden in darkness.
—Charles Darwin, "On the Two Forms, or Dimorphic Condition, in the Species of *Primula*, and on Their Remarkable Sexual Relations," 1862

Our worldviews constrain our imaginations.
—Patricia Gowaty, distinguished professor of ecology and evolutionary biology, UCLA

Every sensible woman got a back door man.
—Sara Martin, "Strange Lovin' Blues," 1925

UNTRUE

INTRODUCTION

MEET THE ADULTERESS

Adulteress.

The word is charged. It scandalizes and titillates. The *adult* makes it sound grown up and serious, somehow, the territory of those with enough life experience and agency to know better than to do what they are doing. The *ess* is all crackle and hiss, the long, low whistle of femaleness and dishonesty rubbing against each other, a silk dress against a suit, creating a conceptual commotion. The adulteress has a noirish cast; she has stepped out of a 1950s divorce proceeding, perhaps. She wears seamed stockings. She is no kid, and no angel. And while we may judge her harshly, we have to admit she is anything but boring.

In contrast to adulteress and adultery, "monogamy" sounds… well, it literally sounds like monotony. Monogamy also has the ring of something cozy to sit on—"Come on over and join me on the monogamy"—which, after all, it is. Monogamy is our society's emotional, cultural, and sexual baseline, the place that comforts us. Sexual exclusivity is the turf, we tell ourselves, of the well-adjusted, healthy, and mature. Adultery and the adulteress are a wild swing away from this place we know, this reference point of security and safety. Seen this way, "adulteress" is not just sexy and interesting; it has a taxonomical, diagnostic ring to it, more than a tinge not only of the illicit and immoral but of illness. For good reason. Many psychologists, anthropologists, and scientists have virtually fetishized monogamy and the pair bond over the last several decades, insisting that it is "naturally" the purview of women, even going so far as to assert that the heterosexual dyad is the reason we humans came to rule, where other hominins bit the dust. From the notion promulgated by biologists that a woman's egg is costly and finicky while sperm are a randy dime a dozen; to primatologists' long unchallenged presumption (since Darwin) that males who benefit from having more than one partner compete for sexually passive females who seek one great guy; to mental health professionals and social scientists maintaining that human males and females are "wired" or destined or have evolved to do that very same gender-scripted dance—just about everything tells us that for women especially, infidelity is off the map and out of bounds.

And yet.

Women lust and women cheat. And it sets us aflame. Shere Hite took a hit, received death threats, and eventually went into exile in Europe after suggesting that 70 percent of us do. Other statistics range from as low as 13 percent to as high as 50 percent of women admitting they have been unfaithful to a spouse or partner; many experts suggest the numbers might well be higher, given the asymmetrical, searing stigma attached to being a woman who admits it. Who, after all, wants to confess that she is untrue? What's clear is that several decades after the great second wave of feminism, with increased autonomy and earning power and opportunity, and now with all manner of digital connections possible, women are, as sociologists like to put it, closing the infidelity gap. We're just not talking about it.

At least not in a voice above a whisper.

"I don't think you really even want to talk to me, because I'm really—unusual..." most of the women I've spoken with begin by saying when we meet to talk. *Why's that?* I wonder.

"Because I have a really strong libido. And—I don't think I'm cut out for monogamy," they tell me, haltingly, one after another. We chat over coffee, in person, or on the phone. They fear they are going to "throw the data" with their freakish singularity. They think they are outliers. They are foreign to the tribe of women, they suggest and believe. But when woman after woman in a committed relationship tells you she is unusual, sexually speaking— because she wants more sex than she's supposed to, because she feels compelled or tempted to stray—you can't shake the feeling that in matters of female desire, sexuality, and monogamy in particular, "unusual" is normal, and "normal" desperately needs to be redefined.

Untrue is a book with a point of view—namely that whatever else we may think of them, women who reject monogamy are brave, and their experiences and possible motivations are instructive. Not only because female infidelity is far from uncommon but also because the fact of it and our reactions to it are useful metrics of female autonomy, and of the price women continue to pay for seizing privileges that have historically belonged to men. This book is not an exhaustive review of the literature on infidelity, though it does reference the dozens of articles and books I read in a range of fields in an attempt to get my arms around the topic. But for the many studies I cite that suggest female "extra-pair" sexual behavior is a social and reproductive strategy that has served females in particular contexts well over the millennia, there are other studies that argue or suggest otherwise. I am only your guide to my view— informed by the social science and science to which I was drawn and to which I was referred by experts whom I believe are correcting bias in their fields—that what we today call female promiscuity is a behavior with a remarkably long tail, so to speak, a fascinating history and prehistory, and a no less intriguing future. And that it merits open-minded consideration from multiple perspectives. For too long we have handed our sexual problems and peccadillos exclusively to therapists and psychologists, presuming the issues to be personal, even pathological—rooted primarily in our emotional baggage, our families of origin, our "unique difficulties" with trust and commitment—and presuming they have solutions. But these ostensibly most personal matters—how and why we have sex, why we struggle with monogamy—have deep historic and prehistoric underpinnings as well. Biological factors, social control, cultural context, ecologies—female sexuality and our menu of options are shaped by all these factors and more. Rethinking topics as complex as female infidelity and our often heated responses to it arguably requires multiple lenses—sociology, evolutionary biology, primatology, and literary theory are just a few discourses that can enhance our understanding, reframing the adulteress in ways that facilitate greater empathy and understanding of her—and of ourselves.

This book, then, is a work of interdisciplinary cultural criticism. It distills and synthesizes the research of experts on female infidelity in a range of fields, melding it with my own opinions and interpretations of everything from articles in academic journals to studies by social scientists to pop culture songs and movies. I interviewed thirty experts in fields including primatology, cultural and biological anthropology, psychology, sex research, sociology, medicine, and "lifestyle choice advocacy and activism." I also wanted to include the perspectives of those who have experienced female infidelity firsthand. To that end there are anecdotes and longer stories from women and men I interviewed, who ranged in age from twenty to ninety-three, as well as insights and observations from those I spoke to more informally about infidelity (see the Author's Note for details). There was not a single dull conversation. Women who refuse to be sexually exclusive can't be pigeonholed—mostly they struck me as profoundly normal. But what they all have in common is that they dared to do something we have been told is immoral, antisocial, and a violation of our deepest notions of how women naturally are and "should be." As the sociologist Alicia Walker has suggested, in being untrue, women violate not just a social script but a cherished gender script as well.

The women I spoke to were obviously not a representative sample—that wasn't and isn't the point. They were storytellers—sometimes remorseful, often guilty or ambivalent, occasionally defiantly unrepentant and even enthused about what they'd done—who added vibrant color and detail to the realities of female infidelity I read about in academic studies and journals and learned about from experts. They were the flushed faces of statistics and the protagonists of their own narratives, as well as the larger narrative of our culture's ambivalence about women who cheat.

I come honestly to my interest in our culture's obsession with women who are untrue. In my twenties, I struggled, like a lot of young women, with monogamy and the specter of the adulteress. I moved to New York for the vibrant intellectual culture, the vivid nightlife, the like-minded people—and the large pool of potential romantic and sexual partners. Yes, New York seemed like a great place to find a boyfriend, or a few of them. And I did. I intended to date these guys one at a time, to break it off neatly with one before moving on to another, until I found The One I would marry, in the semi-accepted tradition of serial monogamy. That's what people *did*.

But on the ground, things were somehow more complicated. I fell into a pattern: date a guy, have great sex, fall for him, get serious, get very serious, get bored. The next step was always to try to resuscitate a foundering, floundering thing, to convince my libido that we could and should make this work. What nice girl wouldn't? What kind of young woman would just get psychosexual ennui and move unsentimentally, unromantically on? "C'mon, he's a great guy," I would coach myself and my libido. But my desires were hard to convince and even harder to bargain with. They took no prisoners and had other plans. These were: notice another guy, feel a tug of mutual attraction, and act on it. There were invariably messy, painful scenes when I was discovered, or when I just came out with it. Which I quickly learned was not the solution I had hoped it would be. Being direct about my desires, it turned out—"I really love being with you, but I'd like to be able to see other people" or "I'm into you, but monogamy is not easy for me"—was something my gay male friends, who had advised it, could get away with (as experts who work with them have pointed out, many gay couples were "consensually non-monogamous" *avant la lettre*). But my beaus were hurt, as I might have been in their position. They would say or do something hurtful in retaliation—imply I was a slut or just walk away, wounded and upset, as I might have done. Still, I couldn't bear making them feel that way, any more than I could tolerate the sting of judgment, the feeling of having done something bad, of *being* bad. And while I felt the urge to play around on the side and couldn't sustain interest in one man for as long as I felt I should, I didn't want to be subjected to non-exclusivity myself. Hypocritically, I wanted to have affairs, but I didn't want my partner to. As one vivaciously beautiful and intelligent woman in her late thirties told me, "I don't want to be with a player, even though I want to *be* one." Of course she added, "What the hell is wrong with me?!" She also lamented finding herself single and childless, pinning it on her "inability to settle down," by which she meant "be monogamous." While she wasn't religious or politically conservative, she had her own catastrophic narrative about the Consequences of Female Infidelity. Don't we all?

Like her and a lot of women I interviewed, I learned to be indirect in these matters. I didn't ask and didn't tell. I tried to keep my pretexts straight. I had heart-pounding close calls. For a time, I decided to just stop being in a relationship, because trying to be true and allowing myself to be untrue were both so stressful. I was sure something was wrong with me. How come the more I knew a young man who was in theory and in reality so right for me, and the closer we got, the less I wanted him? Everybody knew women wanted intimacy and closeness. And commitment.

Meanwhile, not a few of my boyfriends cheated themselves, and it hurt me profoundly. But I didn't question the fact of their straying on any deep level. That was what men did, wasn't it?

Over the next decade or so, I worked, socialized, and had relationships and sex. I thought I would grow up and grow out of my "crazy" libido, that non-monogamy was perhaps a developmental stage for the twentysomething, and that once I was in my thirties, things would change. I would calm down and figure it all out, and life would get easier. It didn't. When I was in a long-term relationship, the sexual spark died within a year or two, and I felt defective that it had happened—and that I cared enough about it to move on or look for other excitement. When I wasn't in a relationship, I longed for sex and sought it out. This too made me feel like a freak, since everyone knows men want sex more than women.

But more and more, I was learning that my peers were struggling too. Older now, my girlfriends and I had more perspective and less apprehension about talking. Even those of us in sexually exclusive relationships were not exactly true, at least in our minds. We fantasized about other men, and some of us fantasized about women. And struggled with the fact that we did. Some of us stepped out. We were bored, all of us, with coupled sex after a year or two, but what could we do? Cheating was a lot of work, with a lot of stigma. But when we thought about or experienced the passion and excitement of being with someone new, or considered trying something we'd never tried before, it felt worth the risks. In fact, it felt urgently *necessary* sometimes.

Why? If only we had known. According to primatologist and evolutionary biologist Sarah Blaffer Hrdy, my girlfriends and I were facing some typical quandaries of the bipedal, semicontinuously sexually receptive, higher-order female primate living in the shadow of agriculture. Our age didn't matter so much; our *gender* did. Contrary to everything we had learned and been told, many of us craved variety and novelty of sexual experience and had a hard time with monogamy precisely *because* we were *female*. On the one hand, we had evolved appetites and urges that were once highly adaptive. Under particular, not uncommon ecological circumstances, promiscuity was a smart reproductive strategy, a way for a female early hominin or human to increase the likelihood of getting high-quality sperm and becoming pregnant while maximizing the chance that numerous males might be willing to support her during pregnancy and help provision her and her offspring once she gave birth. On the other hand, these very same deeply evolved predilections now put us in conflict with a culture that continued to tell us, even post-second-wave feminism, that women were naturally choosy and coy and sexually passive. And monogamous. Men wanted sex; women wanted to put on the brakes. Right?

It was a relief when, in my mid-thirties, I found someone I lusted for and loved and could imagine settling down with, someone with whom I could have children and a life. Someone to whom I could stay true. It calmed the sexual static in my brain for a time. I was soon pregnant, and then exhausted by the demands of caring for an infant, who became a toddler, who became a preschooler, and then the whole thing began again with a second child. But when the heaviest lifting phase of motherhood subsided, when the nursing and the late nights were over and I came back to myself, a grown-up in command of her own mind and body again, I discovered that, although I wore a wedding ring on my left hand, not much had changed. My husband and I were thankfully back to having sex—sex I enjoyed, and plenty of it. So why, in my mind, was I faithless? I had fantasies I did not want to share, daydreams that were more graphic than soft focus and romantic. I liked sexually explicit novels and movies as much as I had before, maybe even more so. And I entertained crushes on wholly inappropriate objects—men who were married, or too young for me, or too old for me. I had crushes on women too, even though I was pretty sure I wasn't gay or even bisexual. *What kind of a wife and mother felt this way?*

I was older now, and my work as a writer afforded me some autonomy in my intellectual and professional pursuits. I queried therapists and open-minded mommy friends and experts, and turned again to anthropology and primatology, particularly the writing of feminist anthropologists, and the new, game-changing sex research being done by women. *What was sexually normal for women? Why was it so hard to be true?*

My list of questions was long. I wanted to know: Who *is* the woman who steps out? And why does she do it? Are her motivations different from a man's? What separates the woman who actually cheats from those who merely think about it? How do women who stray experience their infidelity, and live with it? And why do we as a society feel the way we do about these women—riveted, triggered, convinced that they must be contained, corrected, and punished, that something must be *done* about them? Finally, I wondered, what larger lessons can the adulteress teach us—about female longing and lust, about our fixation on women we deem "deceptive," and about the past, present, and future of partnership and commitment?

I also wanted to know how things had changed for young women since I had been one. And how those changes were impacting the lives of women across a range of ages, socioeconomic groups, and identities. Even as I write these words, the ground is changing beneath our feet. #MeToo and the backlash against it dramatize, in real time, how much is at stake in narratives about female sexual autonomy. The media, at this writing, continues to frame #MeToo by reducing its human players into two neat categories: women as victims and accusers (they are) and men as either villains (some are) or potentially falsely accused victims themselves. But this simplistic framing leaves out what I understand to be perhaps the most important aspect of what women are saying with their #MeToo stories: men are not allowed to tell women anymore, in words or with deeds, that sex is for men alone to choose to have. Men like Harvey Weinstein, Matt Lauer, and Charlie Rose curated ecologies where men were entitled to women who were decorative, as a way to disempower those women and empower themselves. Meanwhile, men who do not abide by or who trivialize affirmative consent assert a worldview in which female permission is extra or an obstacle to find a way around. In this mindset, female desire is mere icing on the cake of the real thing: what men want. The practices of these men effectively quash female sexual agency. #MeToo doesn't. It responds, "I am not an extension of your sexual desires." Now comes the next wave: women who say, "Sexually harassing me, sexually assaulting me, and not operating within the rules of affirmative consent are no longer options because I refuse to accept what you tell me when you do those things—that sex is not mine to want but yours. I have my own sexual desires and sexual agenda." As of this writing, saying so may feel at once too dangerous and too complicated—what would happen to women who challenge our facile and reductive media categories and the thinking that subtends them with this defiant assertion? Better, for now, to take cover behind the hulking, protective, and familiar notion that women don't want It; men do.

There has been much hand-wringing about #MeToo turning women into "victims" who need "fainting couches." And complaining that consent is unromantic and will be the death of flirtation. And that #MeToo is somehow robbing women of desire and agency. I see it doing precisely the opposite. Its logical horizon is that we start thinking about *female*-centered sex and sexuality, focusing on women's desire, women's pleasure and privilege. Perhaps in the coming months and years #MeToo and #TimesUp will open the cultural space for a new reality: female sexual entitlement. Could women come to see ourselves as just as inherently deserving of and equally driven to seek the thrill, exhilaration, and pleasure of sexual exploration as men? And if we did, what else might change? How might this new view of female sexuality—"naturally" autonomous, assertive, and adventurous—alter the larger Order of Things? What might it mean to close the "sexual entitlement gap"? In many ways, the adulteress has been waiting for us all to catch up with her. For better or for worse, women who cheat often do so because they feel a sense of bold entitlement—for connection, understanding, and, make no mistake about it, sex.

A shift—not toward all women cheating but toward women writing our own sexual destinies and being the protagonists of our own sexual stories—might eventually be abetted in part by social media and tech, everything from selfies to apps like female-friendly Bumble and Pure, which helps you find a sex partner within minutes of your location. (Pure's tagline is "Problems are for therapists, Pure is for fun" and its splash page suggests, "Pretend like you're strangers afterwards—no calls, no texts, no approaching in public." Sex tech expert Bryony Cole told me a surprising number of users are women.) "My whole life changed when I got an iPhone," one woman in her twenties told me. "And I didn't have to have a text blazing across the front of my phone. Or a comment on my Facebook that everybody could see, or a tweet my boyfriend could look at and say, 'Who's this guy liking your tweets?' I could use apps—Snapchat, DMs on IG or wherever else—to reconnect with people I hadn't seen in a long time, and to set up my hookups." These technologies are changing the sexual ecology women live in. For example, this young woman lives in a tight-knit Dominican community where neighborhood men "keep watch" over women; apps make that harder to do. They also demand that we revisit the question of what counts as cheating in the digital age. Sexts? Flirty texts? Intimate emails without physical contact? A bit further into the future, will there be sex robots for women as well as men? What will we want from them? Will using them make us cheaters?

Another new wrinkle: the polyamory movement, which has blossomed in the last decade or so and is in large part driven and led by women, according to experts. Polyamory—being involved with more than one person at once, and being honest about it—is an option that, like open marriage and swinging before it, allows women new freedoms. But might it also recapitulate old roles and stereotypes, and open them to the same forms of stigma, slut-shaming, and interpersonal violence that have long plagued women who "step out of line"? A woman with access to resources and power or celebrity, such as Tilda Swinton—who at one point reportedly occasionally lived with both her ex-partner and her current partner but denied that she was in a "dual relationship" or "ménage à trois"—may be able to get away with having an intimate relationship with two men at once. But what about regular women with average incomes? What about women of color, whose sexual lives, longings, and predilections have long been subjected to extraordinary scrutiny and social control? Will polyamory change their lives too?

And what does "female infidelity" even mean in a context where, increasingly, millennials may identify as post-binary—rejecting the neat distinction between antinomies that previously defined our lives and created meaning, including heterosexuality and homosexuality, male and female, true and untrue? I was surprised to hear the phrase "I'm non-binary" from so many of the people in their twenties and thirties I spoke with, and impressed by the conviction with which so many people now live it.

Finally, the book looks at "female sexual fluidity," a term coined by the psychologist Lisa Diamond to describe both a tendency among many women to feel and sometimes act on attractions outside their orientation, and a growing social acceptance of that reality. When Elizabeth Gilbert, author of *Eat Pray Love,* left her husband for her female best friend, she was breaking the mold while also fitting a profile of women loving in ways that are more flexible than the categories we currently use to describe them. How is female sexual fluidity impacting our marriages, partnerships, affairs, and friendships? Is a woman who discovers she'd rather be with a woman than with her husband "cheating"?

Conversation by conversation, article by article, expert by expert, I learned things that enriched the picture of what it is to be female and sexually autonomous, and chipped away at my suspicion that my friends, my interview participants, and I were somehow pathological or extreme in our sexual desires, fantasies, and, in some cases, practices. The things I learned also challenged my deep and unexplored presumption that there was one right or best way to be part of a couple or a relationship. The experts and participants I interviewed for this book, the literature I reviewed, the fieldwork I did, the anecdotes others shared with me, gave me a wholly new sense of how and why women refuse sexual exclusivity, or just long to; how they live with it; and what it means to be true.

CHAPTER ONE

FREE YOUR MIND

I wasn't sure what to wear to an all-day workshop on consensual non-monogamy.

It was a typically disappointing early spring morning in Manhattan, rainy and colder than you'd hope. The program I was attending was designed for mental health professionals but open to curious writers and everyday citizens like me who paid the $190 fee.

Maybe I was overthinking things as I stood in front of my cramped closet, considering my options. But this keenly felt need not only to find something appropriate to wear but to *be* appropriate, and at the same time a little rebellious, reminded me of all the bargaining we do with ourselves about monogamy. I stared at blouses and trousers and dresses and thought of the big concessions we make and the little ones, and of the greatest trade-off of all, in which we surrender complete, dizzying sexual autonomy and self-determination for the security of the dyad. This conundrum— I must extinguish the part of me that lusts for a universe of Others in exchange for the ability to raise kids, get work done, and sleep through the night without obsessing about what exactly You, my One and Only Other, are up to while we're not together—is the beating, bleating heart of Freud's *Civilization and Its Discontents* and much else written on the topic of coupling for life. Relinquish your libido, or tame it, for stability. Somehow we presume this is a developmental imperative of sorts, the hallmark of maturity and health, and that it will be easier for women, that it comes "naturally" to them.

Was there any way around this particular compromise, with its implicit assumptions about gender and desire? Maybe today I would learn something new from people trying to circumvent it. I imagined them—the pointedly and deliberately non-monogamous, and those there to support them—as ninjas in sexy black jumpsuits and aviator style sunglasses, stealthy, well versed in self-defense, and exceedingly limber.

I settled on a floral blouse, a red coat, and black jeans. At the last minute, I also put on some bright red lipstick, because it was Friday, and I was going to a workshop on consensual non-monogamy, even though I kept transposing it, every time I told someone about it, into a workshop on "non-consensual monogamy."

"You just told me a *lot*," a psychoanalyst friend had quipped when I flipped things around just so as we chatted. A heavy patient load had prevented her from signing up for the workshop. "Have lots of anonymous encounters for me!" another shrink friend who couldn't make it for the same reason texted me the morning of, winkingly conflating shrinks who help swingers with swingers. And sex addicts. "Poor Joel," my literary agent ribbed in faux sympathy with my husband when I told him of my day's mission. I was learning over the course of many months of talking to people that infidelity, promiscuity, non-monogamy, whatever terms we use to describe the practice of refusing sexual exclusivity, fascinates and flusters pretty much across the board.

And I knew from prodding and poking and reading and interviewing and from just being female that the specter of a *woman* who is untrue still raises hackles and blood pressures and outrage especially, all along the spectrum. For social conservatives, female infidelity—seizing what is generally believed to be a male privilege, doing what you want sexually speaking—is symptomatic of larger corruptions and compromises of the social fabric. ("Madam: What a decadent, pathetic woman you are. You don't have to wonder why the west [*sic*] is in decline; just look in the mirror," a self-described "traditionalist media personality" emailed me after I had written a piece on female sexuality.) Among progressives, especially those who describe themselves as "sex positive," female sexual self-determination may be tolerated, even lauded. But in their world, a woman who has an affair is still likely to be considered or called something much worse than "self-determined" for having done so. (The echo chamber of obsessional Hillary hatred from supporters of both Sanders and Trump demonstrates that the Left can be as triggered by the idea of female autonomy in general as the Right.) Meanwhile, many advocates of "disclosed" non-monogamy believe transparency is best, and that cheating by men and women alike is unethical. But with the accreted layers of history and ideology, it's hard to carve out a space where there isn't a particular pall hanging over the *woman* who creeps and lies, even within these apparently enlightened arrangements. Everyone, I learned, seems to have a point of view about the woman who refuses sexual exclusivity, whether she does so forthrightly or on the down-low.

Talking about my work could up the awkwardness quotient at cocktail parties. Plenty of people were eager to ask me about and discuss female infidelity. About as often, it brought the conversation to a halt. After a few uncomfortable exchanges, I decided it was easier to tell people that I was writing a book about "female autonomy." It seemed considerate to deploy a half-truth about an uncomfortable reality in order to spare those who might not really want to discuss it. And to sidestep any ire or judgment directed at me by association when I said the "I" word. "Some of us have been on the receiving end of that," more than one man told me dourly, as if it were reason enough for me to write about square dancing instead. A colleague with whom I could be frank about my work and whose opinions I trusted looked at me across his desk and offered, "A shrink I know told me all women who cheat are crazy." At a dinner party, I asked an until-that-moment perfectly charming couples therapist for his informed view on non-monogamy. "Those people are ... *unwell*!" he sputtered. Those around him—well read, well thought, considered and considerate—agreed, citing "disease" and "instability." "He studies healthy people, and your topic is unhealthy people," a woman said amiably, as if this were a given. And this was a *friendly* crowd. When I spoke about my work with female friends and acquaintances, I often floated the notions that compulsory monogamy was a feminist issue, and that where there is no female sexual autonomy, there can be no true female autonomy. This was met with everything from enthusiastic agreement to complete confusion—what did monogamy and infidelity have to do with feminism?—to denunciations of women who stepped out as "damaged," "selfish," "whorish," and, my favorite, "bad mothers." By self-described feminists.

But the most common responses by far when I spoke about my topic were "Why are *you* interested in *that*?" and "What does your *husband* think about your work?" The tone ranged from pointedly curious to accusing, and the implication was clear: researching female infidelity made me, at the very least, a slut by proxy.

But I suspected that these people today, the ones at the workshop, would be different.

"Working with Non-Monogamous Couples" was held at a nondescript family services center in a nowhere neighborhood between Midtown West and Chelsea. (I later learned that it fell within what was once called "the Tenderloin," Manhattan's entertainment and red-light district in the late-nineteenth to early-twentieth centuries, and that the particular street had once housed a row of brothels. Reformers had referred to the area as "Satan's Circus" and "modern Gomorrah.") The center's building was near a sushi restaurant and a handbag wholesaler. Having attended a talk in the same series ("Sex Therapy in the City") in the same venue about a year before, I knew I would be surrounded by therapists who were there for certification credits and to learn from an expert in their field about the best approaches to issues that were likely to come up in their work. I also knew a little bit about consensual non-monogamy: I knew that it was for people who didn't want to be monogamous, and who didn't want to lie about it. It was presumably for "consenting adults," which made it sound a little sexy and a little unsexy and clinical at the same time.

As I checked in with Michael Moran, one of the program's organizers—a high-energy, friendly psychotherapist with chic, short salt-and-pepper hair—he observed that whereas in previous years he had mainly worked with gay men for whom non-monogamy "was often more or less a given," he had recently noted an uptick in his practice and in general of heterosexual couples seeking solutions to *their* monogamy quandaries.

"It's pretty incredible that people commit for life, that they get married, without even *discussing* the issue of sexual exclusivity," I offered by way of chitchat, realizing as I said it that my husband and I had committed for life, that we got married, without even *discussing* the issue of sexual exclusivity. Monogamy and marriage, for straight people in much of the US, go together like a horse and carriage. Or they used to. Or maybe not. After many months of research and interviews, seeing headlines like "Is an Open Marriage a Happier Marriage?" on the cover of the *New York Times Magazine,* attending Skirt Club parties where avowedly straight, frequently married-to-men women had one-off sexual encounters with other women, and chatting at Open Love cocktail parties and other mixers for those in the polyamory community, I was no longer sure. Things were changing, but it was hard to gauge how much and how fast and how comprehensively. After all, the signs can seem bewilderingly contradictory. For example, a single niche, TV, has seen a quick uptick in series on non-monogamy. These include Showtime's *Polyamory: Married and Dating;* TLC's *Sister Wives,* about a polygynous patriarch and his four wives; HBO's *You Me Her;* and the web series *Unicornland,* about a young female divorcee in New

York City exploring her relationship options with different couples. Then there's a counterpoint, the seventeen-season success *Cheaters*. The latter show's premise is irresistibly simple, like *Candid Camera* for the not so candid: "dispatch a surveillance team to follow the partner suspected of cheating and gather incriminating video evidence. After reviewing the evidence, the offended party has the option of confronting the unfaithful partner." This roster of shows dramatizes a contradiction: our country's enduring emphasis on policing and enforcing "fidelity" precisely as it comes up against an impetus to redefine it.

A glance at the bookshelves in the "relationships" section of any bookstore confirms that something is indeed afoot. Reads like *How Can I Forgive You?*, *Getting Past the Affair*, *When Good People Have Affairs* (a title that suggests we generally think they don't), and *Transcending Post-Infidelity Stress Disorder* long predominated. But of late, there are books providing alternatives to the Ultimate Devotion/Ultimate Betrayal narrative we Americans cleave to when it comes to monogamy and infidelity. And they are popular. *Opening Up: A Guide to Creating and Sustaining Open Relationships* by Tristan Taormino is a perennial seller. So is *The Ethical Slut,* a how-to for the woman who wants to get sex outside of monogamy in a way that is principled, nay *virtuous* (it seemed all my divorced girlfriends and friends in their twenties were reading it). In *The New Monogamy,* Tammy Nelson, a guru for those who struggle with the issue of sexual exclusivity, deftly redefines monogamy as a frequently difficult *practice,* like yoga, that requires commitment. She also suggests we think of monogamy as a continuum, encompassing everything from "You can't look at porn because that's a betrayal" to "You can sleep with others, but our relationship has priority." Esther Perel's *Mating in Captivity* and *The State of Affairs,* along with the work of psychoanalysts Michele Scheinkman and Stephen Mitchell, all challenge our expectation that our partners can and should be everything to us—co-parents, companions, confidantes, and lovers. Scheinkman suggests that rather than presume we are failing at marriage when we can't make this "being all things" business work, we might consider the "segmented model" of marriage that exists in Europe and Latin America, where it's understood that marriage will fulfill some needs but not others. Affairs and marriage are separate domains in some of these contexts, and affairs are more likely to be presumed "private" than "pathological." Scheinkman critiques what she calls the "dogmatic no secrets policy" that tends to prevail in our fifty states of affairs and in the therapy sessions where we try to work things out with partners.

As if to describe this recent shift in our thinking, the emerging idea that lifelong sexual exclusivity might be up for reconsideration, sex and relationship advisor Dan Savage, the openly gay and unsparing critic of what he sees as the hypocrisies of compulsory monogamy in the US, coined the term "monogamish" to describe a committed relationship that allows for forays with others. Savage asserts that monogamy is a tough racket, that we need alternatives, and that gay men gentrified non-monogamy for straight people, sort of like they did the Upper West Side and all of San Francisco. But how extensive are the renovations to the house that monogamy built, really? In 2000, experts reported that roughly 95 percent of respondents in a nationally representative sample of cohabiting and married American adults expected monogamy of their partners and believed their partners expected it of them. Australian researchers presented a nearly identical statistic in 2014. Sociologist Alicia Walker, who has studied infidelity extensively, observed that in spite of changes in the sociosexual landscape, "studies and polls routinely find that Americans disapprove of infidelity for any reason . . . [and] the cultural mandate against it is so strong that no one wants to admit to being cheated on, or to be the person who publicly says we don't think cheating is so bad." Will there ever be Starbucks and Bugaboo strollers in the edgy, exciting neighborhood of Monogamish?

I wondered. For some reason I had decided not to wear my wedding ring to the workshop and had slipped it into the front pocket of my jeans on the trip downtown. Now it dug into my hip, asserting itself, as Moran checked in more attendees and I joined several dozen therapists milling around a table laden with coffee, tea, and oranges. At the front of the room sat featured speaker Mark Kaupp, LMFT (licensed marital and family therapist). When I introduced myself, he hopped up to shake my hand, nodding and laughing amiably as we chatted about his work and mine. Raised in California, Kaupp—who I learned teaches couples therapy to master's and doctoral students at San Diego State University and also has a thriving private practice—is lanky and affable. In his bright blue short-sleeved plaid shirt and gray chinos and sneakers, bouncing up and down on the balls of his feet, he brimmed with a kind of polite, keyed up enthusiasm that reminded me of the midwesterners among whom I was raised—if they had devoted their energy to supporting "triads" and "quads," groups of more than two who are committed to one another emotionally, romantically, and sexually, sometimes for life.

As we took our seats and Kaupp began his talk, I noted that, like my dad, he frequently refers to women as "gals" and says "gosh" a lot. But utterly unlike my father, he says, "A gal called me to ask me how comfortable I felt treating people in 'the lifestyle'...by which she meant swingers. And I said sure!" He makes pronouncements like "At a certain point, I decided that, while I do not have any photos in my office other than of my dog, and I don't wear a wedding ring in sessions with clients because I don't want them to be distracted by my own choices, I was just completely *over* not being able to go to the gay nude beach because I might see a client or former client there." He does so in such a pragmatic, sensible tone that you find yourself automatically nodding in agreement, as if you too have such options and are just completely *over* self-imposed limitations. Kaupp is impassioned, persuasive, and has an approachable, vaguely goofy quality—something to do with his height, perhaps, combined with his self-effacement and easy chuckle. All this belies his vast clinical experience and impressive commitment to a subfield of marital and family therapy submerged in mystery and misunderstanding for many practitioners. Mark Kaupp is what we might think of as an expert's expert—the one called on to teach the teachers.

Kaupp is certified in Emotionally Focused Therapy (EFT), a type of psychotherapy pioneered by Dr. Sue Johnson, author of mega bestseller *Hold Me Tight.* The goal of EFT is to help couples in therapy construct a healthy, secure emotional attachment to each other. This not only improves our intimate partnerships, the thinking goes—it can heal our very selves. Complicating matters for Kaupp, Johnson, whom he greatly admires, believes that monogamy helps strengthen healthy attachment and that non-monogamy disrupts it. In his impassioned support for those who choose not to be sexually exclusive, Mark Kaupp, all his gregariousness aside, is a bomb thrower. And today he wasted no time in getting down to it.

"Most therapists will tell you that working with couples on consensual non-monogamy is like rearranging deck chairs on the *Titanic,*" Kaupp told us. "'Non-monogamy does not work. It is going to take you down!'" He waved his arms histrionically, parroting the views of many clinicians in the country and perhaps not a few in the room. He pointed out that people for whom non-monogamy *does* work are probably not the ones coming to therapists for help. He said he believed therapists should get out into their communities in general, and into non-monogamous communities in particular, to educate themselves and expand their points of view. Too often they were seeing non-monogamous patients only when the patients were in crisis, which skewed their view of the issue, making them unnecessarily negative. "Non-monogamy *can* work," he insisted.

"I don't really think it can," a hip-looking, curly-haired therapist behind me said very quietly.

Kaupp defined consensual non-monogamy for us—it was, he said, an umbrella term for relationships in which all the partners involved agree that having romantic or sexual relationships with other people is acceptable. This makes it the opposite of what experts call undisclosed or non-consensual non-monogamy, in which someone does it without telling or discussing it before-hand. He described his time as a group facilitator of the gay men's coming-out group at the San Diego LGBT Community Center. He also discussed his later work with gay male clients in open rela-tionships. He then described his own evolving relationship with commitment and non-monogamy, and told us that he and his partner were currently experimenting with introducing what he called a "Third," a new person with whom they would both have a relationship. This had been Kaupp's idea, and he told us that while he was here running the workshop, his partner and this new person were getting to know each other back in San Diego. He said he hoped it was going well and that he was a little apprehen-sive. I was taking notes on my laptop, and at this point I typed, in all caps, "HOW THE HELL CAN THIS MAN CONCENTRATE RIGHT NOW?!"

Kaupp instructed us to break into groups of three or four, so I turned around to join two women in the row behind me. One looked as if she very much wanted to be somewhere else—she kept staring at her phone. The other was the one with curly hair and doubts about non-monogamy. I knew her partner, we figured out after some chitchat, and we both had teenagers. Kaupp put a slide up on the overhead projector. I craned my neck around to see. There were four bullet points, each ending in a question mark.

- What would it be like to watch your partner/spouse have sex with someone else... and see them really enjoying it?
- What feelings would come up?
- What meanings would you make from their enjoying the sex?
- What if they fell in love?

I turned back toward my group. We stared at one another in si-lence. I thought for a moment of the thrill I used to feel when the possibility of sex with someone new opened up before me like some kind of interpersonal Serengeti, vast and replete with deli-cious possibilities and potential peril. Then I flashed on how, on the kind of day when I am on a deadline, the dishwasher breaks, and I get a phone call that one of my sons is having an issue at school, it brings me to my knees. I imagined adding to the mix an evening of watching my husband having sex with someone else.

"You go first," I said to the woman who had said she didn't believe non-monogamy could work.

Our group was more like two of us since the other participant did not join in readily, apparently uncomfortable with the topic at hand. The curly-haired woman and I decided to forge ahead as our "Third"—I couldn't help thinking of her as that and chortled to myself—hung fire. We decided that if we watched our partner having sex with someone else and really enjoying it, we might feel jealous, turned on, hurt, angry, curious, excited, gutted, and more. We might derive meanings from it, including: I am not good enough; he/she is bored with me; something is wrong with me or our relationship; being with someone new is exciting and that's no reflection on me. If our partner fell in love with this other person, we might feel confused, sad, threatened, and devastated. I added that I might also feel homicidal. ("You should have an affair if you need to, for research for your book," my husband had offered nonchalantly when I first set out on my project. He is steadier and more self-confident than most people I know, certainly more so than I am. "If you're fishing for permission yourself, you *can't* have it," I had snapped at him in response.)

When Kaupp asked each of our groups what we had discussed, I ended up going first. Kaupp listened attentively, seizing on what I shared about feeling murderous and turned on. He explained that the opposite of the jealousy that feels like a stab to your heart and a stone in your gut is "compersion"—a sensation of excitement in witnessing your partner enjoy himself or herself while having sex with someone other than you. In the beginning stages with this new person, you might experience "NRE," or new relationship energy—that rush of feelings and hormones and neurochemical changes that comes when you are connecting with a person sexually and emotionally and it's all giddy and hopeful and passionate. This might also be called "limerence," which sounded delightfully like "limerick" to me but refers to wanting, sometimes almost desperately, to be in the presence of the new person and to have your feelings reciprocated. Then there is "CNM"—because saying "consensual non-monogamy" over and over gets to be a mouthful.

Others in the room had insights and observations and questions. "The gender of the person—" one man said, "I'm interested in how this would affect things." I presumed he was straight—I don't know why—and guessed he meant that for him it would be different to see his wife have sex with another man than it would be to see her with a woman. But it seemed rude to ask.

"People might reenact issues from their family of origin in a triad like this," another therapist ventured.

"Does fairness come up?" a man with a European accent wanted to know.

Nobody seemed to really want to talk about how it would make them *feel*, which made me feel gauche and out of my league among these mental health experts, the tourist who gawks up at the tall buildings in New York in amazement.

The room went silent. Kaupp waited.

"It could be amazing, or it could be a complete train wreck," a female therapist with dark hair finally blurted.

We all laughed uncomfortably, and Kaupp nodded.

He wasn't done with us yet. There was another exercise: "Come up with some rules or guidelines that you might put into place if you and your partner decided to see others."

We went back to our groups. "No seeing somebody we already know. And no seeing other people on the weekend," I suggested, suddenly territorial about my friendships and protective of the sanctity of my Saturdays and Sundays with my hypothetically non-monogamous husband. The third nodded, her arms crossed in front of her chest. The curly-haired woman said firmly, "You have to terminate it if I ask you to." Why hadn't *I* thought of that? I had to admire her foresight.

Then the groups shared their rules.

"Use good oral and genital hygiene."

"No documentation. No photos and nothing on social media."

"No scratches or bite marks."

"Only penetrative sex. No gazing into each other's eyes or kissing."

"You can have sex but not an orgasm."

"If we have kids, don't come out to our community about our lifestyle."

"You can only see this person three times."

"You can only see this person once. Then find another person."

"You can't talk about me or our relationship with this person."

"You have to come home and tell me about it after."

"You have to have sex with me after."

"You can't have sex with me after."

"Don't tell me about it after."

That seemed to be it. Kaupp asked whether there were other rules that made sense to us. There was a pause.

"Bring home a trophy. Like a pair of underwear," a woman who looked to be in her sixties deadpanned.

"Your new person doesn't get to meet the dog," the man sitting next to her said.

Kaupp quickly got to work puncturing our sense of what, exactly, might help us feel in charge of the imaginary situation we were confronting—us or our life partners seeing others, with all parties consenting and in the know.

"I very rarely see that rules create security in these situations. How can we possibly anticipate all the possibilities? It's an attempt to control, but it might make people feel more *out* of control," he said. He told us that in his work with couples practicing CNM, he kept the focus on their attachment bond and let them come up with the rules without getting too involved in that himself. In his experience, he said, the rules might change or even fade out in time if the relationship security is sufficiently strong. "My job is to help people who have decided not to be monogamous keep turning back to *each other* if they feel insecure or flooded with fear. That way a negative becomes a positive. What might weaken or sink a relationship strengthens it."

Kaupp then told us there are three types of non-monogamy, and while they might overlap, their practitioners belonged to quite different tribes. There are people in "open relationships," arrangements in which the couple agrees to see others but might not want to talk about it, or even know. "You go play, but I don't want to hear about it" is how Kaupp summarized this practice, putting his hands over his ears to make his point. Meanwhile, swingers—I couldn't help thinking of the 1970s and kept flashing, for some reason, on the fireworks display in the opening credits of *Love, American Style,* a show I watched as a kid—are committed to having sex with others, both individually and as a couple. They talk with each other about what they are doing, they do things with others together and sometimes separately, and they might go to conventions, cruises, or sex clubs where they can meet like-minded others committed to what they call "the lifestyle." As with open relationships, the dyad is the primary relationship for swingers; they invite others into their established relationship whose boundaries, while sometimes malleable, are more or less clear. The hierarchy is unambiguous: the established pair bond is the home base.

Then there are the polyamorous, or poly, people. Polyamory is the practice of having multiple romantic, sexual, and/or intimate partners with all the partners' full knowledge and consent, Kaupp explained. Those who practice polyamory believe they can love more than one person and be in more than one relationship simultaneously. They tend to go for deeper emotional connection with their partners than those in open and swinger relationships do, sometimes without privileging any one connection or partnership. The "hierarchy" may be that all the connections matter equally. Polyamory can be time-consuming and complex, both logistically and emotionally. Sometimes those who practice it have verbal or written contracts—drawn up by lawyers and therapists who specialize in such matters—to keep things clear and fair. And polyamory requires conversation, ground rules, and plenty of disclosing and "checking in." As Kaupp put it, "People in poly configurations tend to process the crap out of everything!" Although there is no hard data, polyamorists and the experts who work with and study them seem to agree that poly relationships are most often driven by women. And poly peeps, as I came to think of them, are likely to emphasize that their relationships aren't "just" sexual, that the emotional component is as, if not *more*, important than the physical one. (How disappointing, I thought, that in this sense even the poly movement recapitulates our culture's insistence that women—who are at its forefront—are less sexual.)

Polyamorous people may live in "throuples," or triads, quads, or larger groups. For all their well-intentioned, earnest, and thoughtful talking things through, like Kaupp, they are basically bomb throwers, taking aim at something no less sacred than the US flag or the belief in God. In essence, while they are accepting of people who want to do things their own way, they want to blow up the heterosexual dyad and the dyad more generally, which even swingers and those in open relationships, not to mention everyone everywhere in the industrialized West, tend to prize, privilege, and believe in so fervently, albeit with local variation. Plenty of poly people concede the couple works for others. But as a compulsory reality, they say, it is dated as well as the source of much pain and discontent, because it is predicated on and promulgates limited, limiting old think: that women are the property of men; that we "evolved" to be pair-bonded; that refusing sexual exclusivity is sinful or simply bad for society, a gateway drug that leads to other forms of corruption that compromise the very foundation of our culture. ("The best thing for gender equality and relationships will be for all the old people to die," one young woman joked at a panel on sexuality I later attended. She was only kind of kidding.)

And whereas the rest of us may view love as water in a well, and feel that there comes a point where we scrape the bottom of the well and there is nothing left—call this a "scarcity model" of love and desire—the polyamorous believe in what they call a "bounty model." As polyamory activist and educator Mischa Lin asked me, would we say of our children "One has to go. There isn't enough room in my heart for two kids"? When we make a new friend, do we send the others packing with the explanation "Sorry, I only have enough energy and bandwidth for one"? We do not. And this is evidence enough for poly practitioners that love, lust, and feelings of connection are nearly endlessly plentiful, not finite, and can and do grow expansively, even exponentially, if we let them.

Kaupp was saying that when someone calls him and says, "We're poly. Can you help us?" he responds, "Sure. Why don't you all come in?" Sometimes, he noted, the couch in his office was very crowded.

I wrote on my laptop, in all caps, "BRAVE OR CRAZY?" I meant the people themselves, and Kaupp.

When I returned to the center after a break, the attendees were several minutes into watching a video of a therapy session Kaupp had done a year or so earlier with a throuple. The man, perhaps in his early forties, had dark hair and sat on a sofa between a wiry brunette and a rounded, sad-looking blonde. My immediate impression was that the woman with dark hair was on the outside in a way that made me feel almost despondent on her behalf. As the man and the blonde woman held hands and stared into each other's eyes, the dark-haired woman said things like "I want us to be rooted and sustainable. I want to build our bond, and I want to keep opening." The man and the blonde continued to gaze at each other and seemed to me to almost be doing a pair-bonded eye roll as the brunette went on. The brunette placed her hand on the man's shoulder, and he turned toward her briefly. I wanted to take a swipe at him as he said, "I don't know what the hell is going on."

Kaupp asked the blonde woman how *she* was feeling.

"I'm afraid of getting pushed out again," she said. "I'm confused about what you both need and scared about the future. I don't know what the boundaries are and what we want this to look like."

Kaupp paused the video. He asked for comments and reactions. One therapist said she thought the brunette was insincere. Another hypothesized that the brunette saw that the blonde was getting the man's attention by being vulnerable, and she wanted to have his attention by being vulnerable too but couldn't actually *be* vulnerable. I wanted to say I hated the man for sitting in the middle and having it all, for being showered with attention by two women, but it seemed unproductive so I didn't. It didn't matter. Kaupp seemed to sense what we were all feeling.

He told us that the married couple—the man and the brunette—ultimately ended their relationship with the blonde, the third in their triad. In my mind I did a little fist pump. Then I wished the blonde and the brunette had gotten rid of *him* and become a couple themselves, which struck me as somehow a just outcome. But a young and beautiful African American therapist sitting in front of me had the opposite response. "Oh no, that's so upsetting!" she said of the couple's return to monogamy. She was rooting for a concept, the triad, that I could barely wrap my mind around.

"Hang in there and try not to get triggered," Kaupp advised as more of the workshop attendees spoke up. Then, perceptively, to everyone and no one in particular, he advised that in a situation like this, as a therapist, "you'd better get your shit together and figure out how to like them and understand what they're going through."

In his experience, Kaupp told us, what we have to give ebbs and flows with our attachment security. The less attachment security we have to begin with, the less connected we feel to our love object, and the more threatened and threatening others seem. The more attachment security we have, the more we have to give not just to one but to potentially myriad others. And the more we can tolerate our loved ones doing the same. In this rather startling reframing of non-monogamy, limiting ourselves to dyadic sexuality and romance is restrictive, stemming more from anxiety than from a moral or even pragmatic stance.

When I thought Kaupp's point through, it made sense that there was a parallel universe where I might feel secure enough in my relationship with my husband that I could endure him being with someone else. And so confident in our mutual attachment that I could do what I wanted with others without it intruding on or diminishing my marriage. Kaupp's view that consensual non-monogamy is a solution of sorts, allowing people "to stop lying and start living their lives and relationships a little or a lot more authentically," as he put it, seemed utterly reasonable. "People have a hard time keeping it in their pants. Why don't we give them a way to live without sneaking around and being hypocritical and feeling like failures?"

Still, I couldn't help imagining jealous scenes and drama. I was wrong; I later learned that polyamorous people, swingers, and those in open relationships "generally report high levels of relationship satisfaction and happiness" and "do not experience any more jealousy in their relationships than do monogamists." But what about the practical aspects of a life lived polyamorously or even "just" openly? Polyamory is an underdog when it comes to institutions as concrete as those that issue marriage licenses and as abstract as the monogamy-industrial complex, which produces dozens of books and thousands of therapy sessions and many conferences every year on how to survive the searing betrayal of an affair. Parents feel exhausted. Mothers of young children are still more likely to be primary caregivers and have less access to the field of play, so to speak, than fathers of young children do. How can we possibly balance the demands of careers with the demands of our unleashed libidos? And the emotional complexity of multiple involvements? The psychiatrist, sex therapist, and author of *Love Worth Making*, Stephen Snyder, MD, later told me that of the people in his practice who had open marriages over the years, most were either gay men or "older couples with the time, energy, and maturity for such [complicated negotiations], and whose kids have left the house." (He winkingly added that he had no doubt the next sexual revolution would be fueled by retirees.)

Polyamory, consensual non-monogamy, and open relationships might be nice for idealists with flexible schedules and time on their hands, I found myself thinking. But for the rest of us, it hardly seemed realistic. And all this stuff about transparency and being honest, about ethical non-monogamy and its standard of relentless candor, which *Atlantic* columnist Hugo Schwyzer notes is "the non-negotiable admission price to liberation" in CNM, raised red flags for me. My inner graduate student, a 1990s Foucauldian, saw and still sees mandatory disclosure—principled and ethical as it may be—as a form of social control. What made it any better, in the end, than telling women they had to be monogamous? It smacked of puritanism too: in embracing consensual non-monogamy, which a recent study found more than 20 percent of single US adults have done at some point, it was as if we Americans needed to repent and confess at the very same time we were sinning. It also offended my sense of privacy, somehow, in ways I wasn't sure I wanted to consider too deeply, and in ways that were related to my sense that if I was going to be a slut, I didn't want someone telling me how to do it ethically. Isn't part of the whole point of sluttiness the thrilling freedom of saying "Fuck you" to ethics? Why didn't these people just get out of my bedroom already, I wondered crankily.

Just talking about polyamory and CNM was making me feel threatened and defensive. I wondered how people actually lived it. And I had to admire the polyamorous in particular. Not only for their commitment to finding another way and making it work but also for the pointed radicalism of their stance. To them, binary thinking and the dyad—the guiding principles of our entire thought system about sex, intimacy, and relationships—are relics. They reject our Northern Star.

How did we get here? To the point, as a culture, where we conduct and attend workshops on consensual non-monogamy? And to the point where consensual non-monogamy is a thing? According to researcher and historian of CNM Elisabeth Sheff, the "first wave" of intentional non-monogamy experiments was initiated by Romantic poets and then refined by transcendentalists, who brought their ideas about group living and group sex to life in experimental communities, including the progressive Brook Farm, a free-love community founded by a former Unitarian minister with the help of Nathaniel Hawthorne; John Humphrey Noyes's Oneida Community, which emphasized group-based "marriage" and sexuality, and where kids lived together in a communal children's house; and the Nashoba experimental community, founded by Frances Wright in 1826, which brought together freed blacks and whites "to work and make love" on a large farm as a way to confront racism.

And yet what Sheff calls the "second wave" of CNM—the fringe-y free love, communal living, open relationships, and swinging movements of the 1970s—seemed like a radical break with tradition. There was a lot of fuss in the mainstream about "living together," which seems quaint today. And most people who weren't "free lovers" were likely to keep it to themselves if they fumbled monogamy, in part because couples therapy itself was not really even a "thing" until recently (there were only three thousand family and marital therapists in the US in 1970, whereas by May 2017, the official figure was nearly forty-three thousand). Anyone with marital problems, and anyone interested in issues of sexuality and infidelity, let alone openly discussed and agreed-upon sexual non-exclusivity, did not have the sheer number of advocates, expert voices, or experienced practitioners and advisors that they do today. Indeed, the term "consensual non-monogamy" seems to have been used for the first time as recently as 2000, when academic psychologists writing a paper on the swinger lifestyle introduced it, almost as an aside. Sure, the phrase was coined because it described something that was actually going on, but it was going on in a stigmatized subculture (well, in two of them—as Kaupp, Moran, and Savage all point out, gay men and swingers were into CNM long before we called it that).

Kaupp's workshop was happening that gray spring day and drawing not a few therapists who thought it important to attend because non-monogamy of all stripes—consensual/disclosed and non-consensual/undisclosed, male, female, and transgendered, straight and gay—is happening. From some angles, interest in it seems to have reached a critical mass or tipping point. On thinky/newsy platforms like *Psychology Today,* CNN, *Salon, Slate,* and NPR, smart writers and experts are giving us provocative pieces like "Maybe Monogamy Isn't the Only Way to Love," "Rethinking Monogamy Today," "A Cultural Moment for Polyamory," and "Black Folks Do: A Real Look at Consensual Non-Monogamy in the Black Community." There are service-y pieces too—like "Is Consensual Non-Monogamy Right for You?" and "Dating Experts Explain Polyamory and Open Relationships"—presumably to help us figure it all out. Meanwhile, consensual non-monogamy is not just a plotline but practically a character on various shows: in season two of the wonderful *Insecure,* in which creator Issa Rae imbues her female characters with desires and sexual agency rarely seen on the little or big screen, Molly gets involved with a man in an open marriage (at one point he must leave abruptly during a sexy moment in the bathtub because his wife has locked herself out of their house). On *House of Cards,* all lugubrious lighting and power plays, the First Lady has lovers with her husband's full knowledge and consent. If our Google habits are any indication, these shows and articles on the topic have stoked our curiosity. Sex researcher and Kinsey Institute fellow Amy Moors discovered that from 2006 to 2015 there was a dramatic uptick in searches for terms like "polyamory" and "open relationship." Sheff calls all this CNM's "third wave."

To state the obvious, non-monogamy is exercising a pull on us because monogamy isn't working for everyone. Sure, in 2008, four-fifths of Americans polled in the General Social Survey (GSS)—a comprehensive sociological interview instrument that tracks social attitudes and changes—said infidelity is "always wrong." And 91 percent of over 1,500 adults responding to a 2013 Gallup poll rated it "morally wrong." But research that relies on the GSS and other representative samples also suggests that over our lifetimes, anywhere between 20 and 37.5 percent of us will cheat. The real percentage may well be higher, experts tell us, because we under-report our cheating. One source suggests that up to 60 percent of men and 50 percent of women in the US "reported sexual inter-course with someone who was not their spouse while married." Ask-ing about infidelity over a lifetime—"Have you *ever* cheated on your spouse or long-term partner?"—is likely to yield higher numbers than questions about the previous year or decade, experts note.

Accurate stats are tricky to come by not only because we don't like to disclose stigmatized behaviors but also because our defini-tions of infidelity and cheating have shifted over the decades. Is forming a tight bond with someone without ever having sex, some-times called "microcheating," actually cheating? Is it cheating when you aren't married? Is sexting, including sending or receiving nude and seminude photos, infidelity? (One survey found that roughly two-thirds of men and more than half of women had sexted; half of respondents were married.) To keep up with our morphing be-liefs and practices, experts now divide infidelity into several types: sexual intercourse; sexual activity without intercourse; "emotional infidelity," which doesn't involve sex at all but is still perceived as a betrayal; and "cyber infidelity," in which sexy messages and photos are exchanged digitally.

Experts like Marianne Brandon tell us that while our cultural norm is monogamy, we have high rates of undisclosed non-monogamy. However we define infidelity, what is clear is that it happens, and not infrequently. One study characterizes infidelity as a "secret, but widespread (and widely acknowledged) social prac-tice," while sociologist Eric Anderson, author of *The Monogamy Gap*, says it plain: "Cheating is as common as fidelity...although society cherishes monogamy." In other words, the baseline we cling to as the measure of whether we are healthy and moral—monogamy—is arguably no baseline at all.

And yet the difficulty of monogamy and even the fact of struggling with it can create tremendous pressure. "People wonder, *What's wrong with me that I can't do this?* That's something my patients, particularly my female patients, struggle with a *lot*," author of *The New Monogamy* Tammy Nelson told me. The stakes are high: numerous studies tell us that infidelity is the most commonly cited reason couples divorce.

If monogamy is so hard and we're so bad at it, why do we keep doing it? Not a few anthropologists, taking the long and unsentimental view of these things, tell us monogamy and monogamous marriage are neither in our blood nor in our DNA. They are rather a relatively recent, imperfect, species-wide compromise, a good enough way to find companionship and raise kids in our current ecological circumstances, in which we're far from extended family and without easy or high-quality childcare options. Some data suggest that long-term, committed relationships are good for us physically and emotionally. But there is also research indicating that marriage brings health benefits for men, not for women. And one sixteen-year longitudinal study of a representative sample of more than eleven thousand adults showed not only that marriage has little impact on health or happiness but that any positive effects of marriage are likely attributable to a more positive evaluation of one's life rather than improvement on concrete measures. While there may be some psychological benefit to being exclusively coupled in a culture that pathologizes singleness, that hardly seems cause for dancing in the streets or buying a ring.

In fact, two-fifths of Americans polled in 2010 said marriage was "becoming obsolete," and that year found a mere 51 percent of US adults married, an all-time low for our nation. Marriage has been losing "market share" in the US for half a century, regardless of the state of the economy, and across all age groups, the same Pew Center research tells us. And yet today we are less tolerant of infidelity than we were in 1976, when less than half of highly educated GSS respondents said infidelity was "always wrong"—75 percent of them agreed with that statement in 2008. Hugo Schwyzer notes with some surprise that we think cheating is worse than "suicide, human cloning, and polygamy," and that while polls show we are more forbearing than ever of divorce, premarital sex, homosexuality, and gay marriage, infidelity remains, in a sense, "our last sexual taboo."

We may think marriages are ending or not being entered into and monogamy is under pressure and infidelity is upon us because of men and male behavior. Isn't that what we were always taught? That men, who have "stronger sex drives" than women, step out on their wives and female partners because what choice do they have? That men need to conquer and spread their seed? That men are wired to seek new partners, while women are wired to seek the comforts of companionship and the security of the cozy couple, which we crave more than the thrills of orgasm? Right?

We might be surprised to learn just how many of our assumptions about the whos and hows of infidelity are wrong. In fact, it turns out that when it comes to our sexual selves, women have been sold a bill of goods. In matters of sex, women are not the tamer, more demure, or reticent sex. We are not the sex that longs for or is more easily resigned to partnership, to sameness, to familiarity. Nor are we goody-goodies relative to men when it comes to fidelity, after all.

CHAPTER TWO

WOMEN WHO LOVE SEX TOO MUCH

Imagine a total stranger asking you, among other things, whether you'd had sex with someone other than your spouse since getting married.

In 2013, some new data emerged from the GSS: women were roughly 40 percent more likely to be cheating on their husbands than they had been in 1990. Meanwhile, their husbands' rates of infidelity hadn't budged. The finding wasn't unique, and it wasn't such a new development, it turned out. In 1993, across the Atlantic at Cambridge, a British academic had realized that if she threw out the men in her infidelity study who claimed to have had twenty or more sexual partners (these are called "outliers" in a sample), the ratio between male and female infidelity was nearly even. And in four national surveys conducted between 1991 and 1996, women and men under the age of forty-five were basically neck and neck in the cheating game, while a 1992 survey found that American women aged eighteen to twenty-nine reported even *more* affairs than their male peers, and a more recent GSS found the same thing. Meanwhile, a 2017 study shows that among women aged twenty-five to twenty-nine, group sex and threesome experience equaled that of men the same age, and women were nearly twice as likely to have gone to a dungeon, BDSM, swingers', or sex party, challenging the easy assumption that men are the naturally more sexually adventurous sex.

Some experts believe this new gender parity in sexual autonomy and sexcapades, often referred to more broadly as "closing the infidelity gap," might be due in part to more women being out in the workforce. There, they have increased exposure to a greater number of potential sexual partners, more time apart from their spouses or partners, and more travel opportunities (people tend to have flings when they travel), not to mention greater financial wherewithal and independence, which can make getting caught seem like less of a potential catastrophe and more like a risk worth taking. Technology may also be giving women a leg up when it comes to sexual exploration, with various social media platforms and apps affording them the opportunity to couple outside the couple discreetly. But using technology or leveraging your financial wherewithal or physical separation from your spouse in order to have an extra-pair experience or simply act on your desires requires *wanting* to. And *having* desires.

What if women of all ages are uncoupling sex from monogamy simply because of who and what we are? The recent work of several female sex researchers suggests it may be so. Over the last decade, a triumvirate of academic experts—Meredith Chivers, biopsychologist at Queen's University in Kingston, Ontario; Marta Meana, professor of clinical psychology at the University of Nevada, Las Vegas; and Alicia Walker, a sociologist and expert on female infidelity at Missouri State University in Springfield—have all peeled back what science writer Natalie Angier has characterized as "the multiple sheaths of compromise and constraint" that cloak and contort female sexuality so thoroughly as to make women strangers to ourselves and our own libidos. What these experts have unveiled shakes up many of our most deeply ingrained and dearly held assumptions about who women are, what motivates us, and what we want. Our sexual selves are being rethought, reexamined, and perhaps finally revealed.

TRAILBLAZERS

Sex researchers are a friendly tribe. At least the ones who attended the 2017 annual SSTAR (Society for Sex Therapy and Research) meeting in Montréal are. It was unseasonably cold and relentlessly gray when I arrived in Quebec's largest city in late April—the conference's theme was "Healing Relationships and Fostering Sexual Well-Being"—but I found the sexologists, sex researchers, sex therapists, and sex educators there warm and welcoming to a person as I bumped from presentation to presentation. These included "Dialectical Behavioral Group Therapy for Out-of-Control Internet Porn Users," "Impact of Persistent Genital Arousal Symptoms on Women's Psychosocial, Sexual, and Relationship Functioning," and sessions on "Kink Awareness." No one rejected my requests for interviews or even put me off, an occupational hazard for writers dealing with experts. Instead they offered copies of their books, their contact information, and advice about journal articles I might find helpful. Questions posed to speakers by their colleagues were collegial, even when they were challenging. I began to suspect that being open, curious, and matter-of-fact about sex—a subject many of us consider shameful and private and, like those newly discovered creatures who inhabit the deepest parts of the ocean, perfectly suited and inherently appropriate to its indigenous darkness—correlates with a sunny disposition and bright interpersonal style. The hotel's bar was convivial at 5 p.m., when the sexperts repaired there to unwind, the kind of detail that tells an observer a lot.

I was lucky enough to have set up an interview with Dr. Meredith Chivers, who suggested we meet there one evening. Earlier that day, a hundred or so other attendees and I had watched her take command of the dais with rock-star-like self-confidence in her black jacket and black jeans to explain her recent work. Chivers spoke quickly about topics familiar to most of her listeners, including Rosemary Basson's concept of "responsive desire." This "desire style" is more common among women than men, according to numerous sex researchers and therapists, and describes a tendency to feel sexually excited *after* erotic stimulation, versus in anticipation of it (that's called "spontaneous desire," based on an experience that sexual desire is an appetite like hunger that just comes upon us). I found myself at sea as I struggled to keep up, but thankfully, I already knew something of Chivers's work. I had read about how, as founder, director, and principal investigator of Queen's University's Sexuality and Gender Laboratory, Chivers has her study participants sit in what looks like a La-Z-Boy to watch porn. But first, they hook themselves up to a machine called a plethysmograph. This tiny instrument is inserted into a woman's vagina or attached to a man's penis, allowing Chivers and her students to measure blood flow—precisely how much of it rushes to fill the participant's vaginal walls or penis, or to engorge her clitoris. This helps Chivers and her team better understand what does and does not trigger a physical response in participants.

Chivers shows the study participants explicit photos or movies—of women and men having sex, of women and women having sex, of men having sex with men. That's when things get interesting. The women who describe themselves as heterosexual have physical responses to just about everything they see—a man having sex with another man, a woman going down on a woman, a man and a woman doing it. They are adventurous, at least in their minds, un-finicky and indiscriminate omnivores. They take it in with category-blurring gusto, liking what they see regardless of who they presumably are. In a detail the media has loved around the world, they even respond physically when Chivers shows them images of bonobos—close relatives of chimps—getting it on. The self-described straight men, on the other hand, have desires that are more predictable: they respond to images of men and women having sex, and of women having sex with one another. Watching two men may get their blood flowing, but they have the strongest responses to the movies and images that match their reported sexual attractions and interests, and bonobos leave them flaccid. Unlike the women, the men's desires are mostly what we would expect based on how they identify—that is, their arousal patterns are more category specific.

What does it all mean? It seems our libidos don't give a hoot about the boxes we check. Perhaps we are sexual anarchists, in the formulation of Daniel Bergner, the author of *What Do Women Want?*, who spent time observing Chivers at work, and whose assertions about women's unexpected appetites basically suggest we might quite fairly be described as the "largest group of sexual deviants" in the world.

As we sat and talked over drinks, Chivers explained her recent work, which suggests female desires don't just confound categories; they're also *stronger* than we've been told. In a 2014 study, Chivers told me as she sipped her Negroni, she had participants watch sexy films and then report their responses and desire to have sex with a partner and masturbate. Remarkably, men and women reported essentially identical degrees of desire. "There is this fairly monolithic idea about a gender difference in sexual desire...it's like a sacred cow [in sex research]." She paused and then went on, her tone measured, to describe how the findings had created controversy in her field and at the conference itself. "It's frustrating to hear it repeated over and over that men have stronger [libidos] than women do, as if that's a simple fact. Let's consider that maybe we've been measuring desire incorrectly." She pointed out that there were a few other papers with preliminary findings like her own and told me she expected there might be more if researchers measured triggered or responsive desire rather than spontaneous desire.

Chivers has a composed, elegant, and almost patrician bearing, making her at once an unlikely and ideal bomb thrower. Like Kaupp, she seemed philosophical about upending the order of things in sex research, where the notion still prevails, as it does in nearly every corner of our society, that men want sex more than women do, and that testosterone and androgens are the main drivers of sexual desire. "That people like to hang their hats on certain presumed truths doesn't mean they're true," she noted. For her, the science is the thing.

A third experiment in Chivers's lab suggested yet another surprise: that straight women were not as turned on by the idea of sex with a male friend as they were by the idea of sex with a long-term partner or a total stranger. In fact, she explained as the bar got louder and people crowded around us, female study participants were just as turned on by the idea of sex with a stranger as straight men were. When it comes to fantasies about partners, they enjoy novelty every bit as much as the guys. Not to mention having those restless, category-confounding desires we might think of as more of a "guy thing."

Chivers told me that one of the highlights of her career was when a woman stood up at a conference where she was speaking to tell her, "What I love about your work is that you are showing us there is more on the buffet than anyone ever thought." Women don't necessarily want what they fantasize about, or want to do what turns them on, of course, and Chivers is careful to emphasize this. But if her work destigmatizes the range and variation of female sexual fantasy, and the sheer force and strength of some women's desires, she's delighted. She hopes her work "might give women permission to enjoy this internal playground." And help other women feel validated in their actual experiences—such as those who have had sex with other women and enjoy it but identify as straight. "They say, 'So you're saying I'm not weird or abnormal?' And I'm like, 'Nope, you're just another woman,'" Chivers said with a laugh.

When it comes to women and monogamy, and monogamy more generally, Chivers points out that it isn't her area per se. But she believes that just as kink was destigmatized over the last decades— hair pulling, spanking, biting, and handcuffs during sex are virtually mainstream, she points out—CNM may well also gain acceptance. This could lead to even larger social shifts in institutions like marriage and partnership. "Why do we think that two people—versus people who are poly—should have some kind of corner on the market for all the legal protections and benefits that are available? I think in the next couple of decades we're going to see more folks arguing for the broadening of the definition of what legal marriage should look like," she mused. She understands that plenty of people want to work to stay in monogamous relationships, and she wants to see them supported, too, by a culture-wide acknowledgment that it's not easy or necessarily "natural" to stay sexually exclusive over time. "The very idea that people could form long-term pair bonds and be equally sexually exciting to each other from day one to day seven thousand makes no sense. It doesn't fit any psychological model we have of how people habituate over time," she observed with a shake of her head. "I'm going to guess that it is a minority of people who live out a truly monogamous relationship with zeal." Certainly there are things to do about that—porn, fantasy, and other strategies to "spice things up," she mused. But from her perspective, knowing what she does of what turns women on and how strongly we desire, Chivers says of sexual exclusivity, "It's *work*!" The simple acknowledgment that women struggle with monogamy as much as men do—something implied by her years of research proving that women are not who we thought they were, and in many respects are not so different from men—is as radical as it is logical and data driven.

IT'S NOT YOU, IT'S ME

Like Chivers, Marta Meana is an exacting and meticulous researcher whose discoveries may nevertheless strike us as bold and freeing. When I sat with her in Montréal, at the same hotel lounge where Chivers and I chatted, the petite, energetic, and formidable brunette stood up more than once to "act out" a point. Unlike many researchers, she has a wonderful proclivity for a sound bite and an engaging playfulness as she explains her work (she even allowed me to snap a selfie of us together, like the fan girl I am). But Meana studies an unhappy topic, and takes it very seriously. In a qualitative study of nineteen women in long-term partnerships and marriages they describe as otherwise satisfying, Meana zeros in on the women's low desire. We think of it as a classically female problem, one we hear interpreted in a certain way over and over, with the explanation generally being "Of course, what do you expect? Men have stronger sex drives than women do."

Meana is open to that possibility, but she thinks, based on her research and clinical experience, that something else may be at play. She has found that the institutionalization of roles and the familiarity of a spouse or long-term partner—the fact of being in a relationship, basically—is especially challenging *for women*. "We have plenty of data telling us that long-term relationships are tough on desire, and particularly on *female* desire," she told me across the small table where we sat as the sun temporarily broke through the clouds outside. She asked me to think about how, when we get dressed for an evening out, women often discount the opinion of our long-term male partners. And not just because our partners are afraid to tell us that the dress does, in fact, make us look fat. "He just doesn't have a lot of credibility. You're all he's got. He doesn't see you the way you want to be seen! But admiration from someone you know less well, or from a stranger—*that* has an impact!" She laughed. Something similar was going on with the women she had worked with and sex and sexual desire, she told me. Being desired by someone whose desire for us is a given doesn't confer the same thrill we feel when we get that lustful glance from a stranger on the street.

Long-term relationships are particularly tough on female desire. I rolled it around in my head like a noisy marble. The thought was uncomfortable. After all, Meana's work contradicted just about everything I had been taught since childhood about relationships between men and women—that women need intimacy and familiarity to feel sexy, for starters. And yet her reframing made intuitive sense. I thought of the woman in her early sixties who, upon learning about my project, had told me with a frankness that took me aback, "I want to have sex all night long. Just not with my husband!" And the dozens of other women who had said a version of the same thing over the many months of my conversations and interviews. The women who said, "My marriage is pretty great. But I think about other guys all the time," and the ones in long-term partnerships who said, "Maybe I'm just bored with sex," but then, later in the conversation, said that if there were no consequences, they'd really love to have sex with X, Y, or Z. Meana's work and her survey of the work of others suggested these women might be the rule, not the exception. As did a 2017 study of more than eleven thousand British men and women, aged sixteen to seventy-four, which found women who lived with a partner were twice as likely as cohabiting men to lose interest in sex. The same held true for women in a relationship lasting more than a year. "Moving in with Your Boyfriend Can Kill Your Sex Drive, Study Finds," a headline in *Newsweek* declared. One interpretation is that women are just the less sexed sex. Another is that they are suffering from what ails Meana's study participants: a kind of sexual listlessness from which they might well be roused if circumstances were right. So much, then, for the old canard that women need to be in cozy and emotionally intimate long-term relationships in order to thrive sexually, in ways men don't. So much for a woman necessarily requiring the familiarity of a partner she can count on in order to be turned on. In Meana's careful analysis of her cohort of female study subjects who desire to once again feel desire, and her attention to the additional research on the subject, that very closeness and familiarity are often the problem (Meana wanted to make sure that I understood that she had thus far only worked with heterosexual women).

Meana was not the first or only expert to tell me that while straight men are likely to report that they are sexually satisfied if they get sex regularly from their long-term partners, women are another story.

"Marriage itself tends to routinize what was once transgressive and sexy in ways that especially impact us," she explained, "overfamiliar-izing" our spouses in a fashion that we struggle with. In a talk she gave, Meana had also mentioned that "crude initiations" (a husband or partner who doesn't bother trying to be seductive) and being exhausted from mothering and "wife-ing"—being in charge of the domesticated this and that of coupled life—also tended to push fe-male desire underground.

When I asked Meana whether any of her study participants had talked to her about seeking sex outside their marriages, she shook her head no, explaining that they wanted to get sexual satisfaction and excitement with their life partners. "But so many women expe-riencing low desire in long-term partnerships know that if they did step out, their desire would probably be back like *that*," she said, snapping her fingers.

Meana has of late been homing in on "female erotic self-focus," which sounds like masturbation but isn't. Acting on a hunch that women were deriving arousal from their very own sexiness as much as or more than their male partners', she asked a group of men and women, "Would you want to sleep with you?" *Hell yes*, many women basically said, in a way that suggested to Meana that in some sense they already had. Men, on the other hand, mostly didn't even know what she was talking about. "There's this way in which seeing them-selves desired is the ultimate turn-on for women," Meana told me, "which suggests that female sexuality has a kind of wonderful auton-omy that people miss all the time." She said she had titled the paper she and her graduate student wrote on the topic "It's Not You, It's Me," and we laughed at the play on a familiar apology reframed as an unapologetic declaration about what women want and need dur-ing sex: to see themselves as sexy and desired. Meana likes to refer to pop culture to bring her points home, and now she mentioned song lyrics like "You make me feel like a natural woman," and Sha-nia Twain pronouncing, "Man! I feel like a woman!" and Katy Perry singing, "Put your hands on me in my skintight jeans." "What's going on with these lyrics? You're a woman so of course you feel like a woman, right?" Meana noted gamely. "But what it's telling us is that the singers are a lot more focused in these songs on *themselves*. See?"

To test the hypothesis that women find themselves being sexy *sexy*, she asked male and female study participants another hypothetical question: Imagine you're having sex in front of a large mirror. How much time do you spend looking at your partner's body and how much time looking at your own? The women, it turned out, would be looking at themselves a lot more than would the men. In certain moments, it's like he's not even there. "That doesn't mean she's not turned on by her partner. My stuff is so easily misinterpreted," Meana was quick to point out. It's the *independent* aspect of female sexuality that she wants to underscore, the fact that the women in her studies "are not always looking into their partners' eyes and experiencing whole person transcendence. Sometimes, they're just really focused on a hot body part." Or the hotness of themselves. "Women's arousal may depend on their erotic relationships with themselves to a greater extent than is the case among men," Meana summarized. This can be good or bad, depending on how we're feeling about ourselves, she says. But there it is, that unique sexual autonomy and self-regard, demanding we deal with it.

As to the notion that women get off on eroticizing themselves because they've been objectified so much and so often, Meana shakes her head impatiently. "Ideology and sex make terrible bedfellows!" she exclaims, really warming to her topic now. To her, there is something much more profound going on than false consciousness, and if it is false consciousness, or narcissism, well then, so what? "I don't really care what we call it. But the minute you try to put ideology on sex—whether it's progressive ideology or conservative ideology—sex rebels! Sex is by its very nature transgressive." Meana doesn't want women to be judged or pressured from either direction. What matters to her is the finding: that to a certain extent heterosexual women are their own erotic targets, and that their arousal emanates to some significant degree from their erotic re-lationship with *themselves*. Its mind-blowing quality aside, Meana's work has plenty of practical applications. Understanding what turns women on, helping women understand it, might just turn back the tide of low female desire that plagues so many otherwise happy marriages. We're used to women being the lower desiring partners in hetero marriages and long-term partnerships, but Meana's work suggests surprising, previously unconsidered *whys*. In her SSTAR talk, she said she had noted that many women in her study seemed to feel very little sense of agency in addressing low desire in their relationships; to me, that sounded a lot like women were feeling hopeless and resigned to no longer wanting sex. To counter this, Meana urged the clinicians in the audience to help women not only have realistic expectations but feel a sense of ownership of and responsibility for their own sexual excitement. Taking notes, I imagined a sudden uptick in the sale of large mirrors and their in-stallation in bedrooms. I considered that if this were Marta Meana's legacy, it would be a pretty damned good one.

THE "INFIDELITY WORKAROUND"

Like Chivers and Meana, Alicia Walker—an assistant professor of sociology at Missouri State University—does research that forces us to rethink not only female sexuality but our most cherished and basic beliefs about what women do and are, what they want and how they behave, and the role that context plays. In her extensive review of the sociological and psychological studies on female in-fidelity, and her own study of forty-six female users of the Ashley Madison website before its infamous hack and shutdown in 2015 ("Life is short. Have an affair," the company's tagline suggested), Walker explodes several of our most dearly held notions about fe-male infidelity: that women cheat only when they are unhappy in their marriages; that unlike men, they seek emotional connection, not sexual gratification, from affairs; and that like Diane Lane's character in *Unfaithful,* who literally falls and skins her knee, thus attracting the attention of the man with whom she has tryst after hot tryst, women "just" stumble into affairs. For Walker's cohort, this was no case of having one too many at the holiday party and then somehow sleeping with a coworker. "These women weren't just falling into it or seeking out *companionship,*" Walker told me flatly when we spoke on the phone one morning after she had bustled her daughter off to school.

Walker, who has blonde hair, favors red lipstick, and speaks with a touch of a Southern drawl, is well aware that her findings demolish certain familiar stereotypes. She is also conscious of the profound discomfort this might cause and more than once told me she hoped that readers of the book she wrote based on her study of female infidelity, *The Secret Life of the Cheating Wife,* would not shoot the messenger as they took in just how different women who commit infidelity are from our comforting clichés about them. But her email signature includes a quote from the French sociologist Pierre Bourdieu, one she lives: "My goal is to contribute to preventing people from being able to utter all kinds of nonsense about the social world." Walker wanted me to know that the women she interviewed were funny, smart, and insightful, and most of all, they struck her as very normal. They worked quiet jobs and enjoyed being mothers, having friendly conversations with neighbors, and, in some cases, going to church.

They were also dead set on having affairs.

"The women I studied went on the [Ashley Madison] site. Created a profile. Checked back in for responses. Vetted candidates. And then met them in person. Then they 'auditioned' them. This was a very *intentional* process," Walker emphasized. They undertook it, they told Walker, because they wanted to find partners. For *sex.* Most of Walker's study participants, who ranged in age from twenty-four to sixty-five, reported being in sexless or orgasmless marriages and told Walker they simply wanted and needed what they couldn't get at home. But perhaps most surprisingly, the majority of women in Walker's sample reported that they were otherwise happily partnered or married, and that *these affairs were a way for them to remain in their primary relationships.* They were not looking for an exit strategy or a new husband. They did not seek emotional connection or companionship. They wanted a solution to a dilemma: they felt unable or were unwilling to end their sexless or sexually unsatisfying partnerships or marriages, but they also wanted great sex. After years of sexual deprivation and dissatisfaction and struggling to stay monogamous, the women, who described themselves as otherwise unremarkable, decided to do something about it. Erica (forty-six and married) said, "One day I had just had it. I really wish I could remember what exactly caused me to search online for 'someone' because that is not like me at all." Regina, thirty-eight and also married, added, "I tried very hard to just ride it out. I held out as long as I could. Once I gave in, I wondered what took me so long." "[A] lack of sex drove me crazy," forty-seven-year-old Tiffany told Walker simply. "I finally decided [after many years of no sex] that I deserved to have my needs met," fifty-three-year-old Georgie said.

And once they crossed that line, they were focused, unsentimental, and strategic in finding partners for what Walker calls "concurrent relationships." Avery, forty-five, explained what she sought in an OP (outside partner) and how she vetted candidates: "I ask penis size, availability, and what kind of associations they are looking for, what sex acts they enjoy. And that's all in the first email." Heather, thirty-three and partnered, told Walker, "In an OP, I want (this sounds shallow) a big cock, stamina, knowledge of female anatomy, and discretion." The women also had clear ROE (rules of engagement). They avoided men who seemed emotionally needy or who seemed to want relationships rather than liaisons. They had complicated primary partnerships and wanted to keep their affairs simple and purely sexual. "I want the [penis] but not the [complications] that go with it," thirty-three-year-old

Trudy explained to Walker. "I strongly identify with an approach to sex stripped of sentimentality," Priscilla, thirty-seven, said. Finding a man who was clear on these boundaries was an important task for these women. Heather noted, "I try to find guys who won't be clingy, and just want great sex."

If things did start to get serious, or even if the feeling of exhilaration about being in a new sexual partnership faded, the women ended the affair with no apparent regret and found *another* outside partner. And if a guy misrepresented himself? Walker chuckled and told me, "Oh, they felt no compunction about moving quickly on when someone was not what he had promised!" Having chosen a husband or life partner who did not satisfy them sexually, they were not going to make the same mistake in their affairs. Why not simply end their marriages? Mostly because doing so would be far from simple. The women told Walker they didn't want to divorce for various reasons. Many said they loved their husbands and did not want to hurt them. Except for the lack of sex or the unsatisfying sex, they enjoyed their lives together. Others said they did not want to unsettle their children's lives and routines. Still others said divorce would be too costly or complicated.

Their concurrent relationships were pragmatic and rather ingenious strategies to remain, on the surface, good wives and partners while getting the sex they felt they needed, not to mention a heady dose of novelty, variety, and excitement. As Darcy, forty-eight, explained, after years of being sexually deprived, "some of the fun... [is] sampling from the parts of the menu I wouldn't normally order." Jordan, thirty-four, said, "I'm looking for that feeling when you first meet someone and...your stomach is all wobbly and every time they touch you, you about jump out of your skin." The majority of the women expressed guilt, Walker told me, but none were so remorseful that they stopped having affairs. Indeed, many "found they enjoyed the boost in self-esteem, empowerment, and sexual fulfillment an outside partnership brings." And not a few had several partners simultaneously, so they would not be subjected to any one outside partner's whims or schedule. These women, like the calculating and unsentimental dames of film noir, were thinking through all the angles; Walker describes the women's outside partnerships as "relationships of sexual utility." Their sole focus was their own pleasure. "That's very different from all the other relationships in their lives," Walker observed, adding, "The amount of power and freedom the women exercise in their outside partnerships is much more than we see them employ in their marriages."

Walker notes that these women were rather creatively inventing a space in which they could get their needs met while avoiding the stigma, inconvenience, financial strain, and emotional pain of divorce. She calls their strategy an "infidelity workaround," a way to have your cake and eat it too. Of course the women of Walker's sample were taking considerable risks. Should their husbands find out, the marriages they were trying to preserve would surely end (because women who used Ashley Madison were not required to provide as much information as male users were, they were not affected by the hack of 2015). They also knew they were likely to be shamed and shunned in their communities if they were caught. And on the site itself, they were often subjected to male rage and retaliation for ending a liaison, or even for not messaging back after an invitation to do so. "You're a fat cow no one would fu*k anyway" one man wrote to a woman (who had not posted a photo) when she didn't respond to his online overture. Men sometimes also left information on the "feedback" section of the women's profiles, falsely suggesting they had slept with them and rating the experience unfavorably, as "payback" for the women not responding to them. Slut-shaming apparently exists even where men and women come together to cheat. Such consequences for simply being on the site and exercising the right not to connect with male users who desire it were common, the women told Walker.

But the participants in her study wanted sex badly enough that they willingly took these chances. They had run the calculus and considered the options: cheat for sexual satisfaction and accept the risk it entailed; don't cheat and continue to live without satisfying sex, or any sex at all; be openly non-monogamous and risk almost certain stigma in their communities and blowback from their husbands, including, possibly, divorce; initiate divorce, thus, in the words of one woman, "dismantling my life and breaking my husband's heart as well as my own." Divorce could mean custody issues, financial hardship, and the loss of social and family support. In Walker's formulation, "These women were unwilling to toss the dice a second time on marriage and risk ending up with a lesser hand than the one they currently held." They efficiently pursued what they wanted and confounded our received script that women don't care about or need sex the way men do, and that women who have affairs fall in love and inevitably "destroy their marriages" because "women who have affairs want emotional connection, not sex." As Walker says, "These women enjoyed the time spent with outside partners but were not left pining for them to ride in on a white horse and sweep them away into the sunset." Walker's study subjects challenge just about all our received notions of female sexuality, fidelity, and motivation.

Walker openly acknowledges that her sample was relatively small and not intended to be representative. The study does, however, mesh with the findings of a pilot study she did in 2014. " 'I'm Not a Lesbian; I'm Just a Freak' " sought to understand the experiences and motivations of a group of thirty-four assumed-monogamous, married-to-men women who went online to seek out in-person sexual encounters with other women. These female study subjects identified as straight but longed for the variety and novelty of a new, one-time-only same-sex partner. And acted on it. They did not seek companionship, a relationship, or emotional connection. They did not think they were "actually" gay or bisexual. Rather, they described themselves as having "strong" and impossible to categorize lusts. They were "freaks" in their own parlance, a term that underscores how aware they were of the stigma they would encounter if they were "out" about their practices. And so they remained "undercover," as one study participant put it.

Walker's findings are also supported by ample sociological, social psychology, and sex research data. Numerous studies, for example, have found that men and women alike have affairs even when there is no perception of dissatisfaction in their primary relationship. Others suggest that when women are guaranteed a pleasurable experience and no safety issues, they are just as likely as men to participate in casual sex, and that women choose potential mates based on sexual attractiveness as often as men do. Studies in 1997 and 2018 found no difference in rates of non-exclusivity in men and women under the age of forty. And while men outnumber women on online sites for those seeking extra-pair partners, it turns out that women are more likely to go through with meeting in person for sex. Men create profiles; women follow through. The data suggest that the eighty women Walker studied, women whose behavior many are likely to find shocking, even appalling, not to mention deeply "unfeminine," are far from exceptional.

The findings of Chivers, Meana, and Walker point to possibilities that are at once freeing and disquieting. What if it's women, not men, who struggle especially with monogamy? What if *women* are the comparatively decadent sex, asphyxiating in sexually exclusive relationships, whereas men in the aggregate are more amenable to it? If the routinization of sex and institutionalization of roles within a long-term partnership dampen us in ways they don't men; if women, too, crave variety and novelty of sexual experience and partners, perhaps even more than men do; if women's sexual excitement is autonomous and disconnected from their partners in fundamental ways, rather than contingent on staring deeply into a soul mate's eyes; if self-described happily married women are having affairs and doing so not for emotional but for sexual gratification, then nearly everything women have been taught about our sexual selves is patently untrue. It is as if Walker, Meana, and Chivers were the unbelievably skilled tricksters who pulled the tablecloth from under the polite and perfect place settings, and we stand marveling that our lives and silver service and plates remained miraculously undisturbed.

I had heard from Mark Kaupp and other poly advocates and experts, including Open Love NY co-founder Mischa Lin, clinical psychologist and consensual non-monogamy expert David Ley, and polyamory practitioners I met at panels and social events for the poly community, that women, not men, were leading that movement. It tends to be women, I was repeatedly informed, who are telling their partners that they want open relationships and marriages, or that they want a sexual and romantic life unbeholden to the dyad. Women, not men, are the relationship radicals in this recent rearrangement of our intimacies.

Now, however, I began to consider that women like the ones Meana works with might themselves be driving a social movement. But this movement has no slogans, and women drive it from the backseat, in the muted voice of discontent, by simply not having sex in long-term partnerships. In a profound sense, these women are on strike. They're saying, "I'm not doing this." Not because they don't like sex, or because they don't love or care for their partners, but because the same old sex with the same old person isn't working for them. Rather than throwing "female Viagra" at these women, what if we told them the truth? That it's normal for women to get bored? That it's normal to want to have sex in lots of different ways, with many partners? And that women too, and perhaps especially, have cheating minds and hearts and bodies?

In this case, women who refuse monogamy are not pathological and unrelatable and unlike us. They are, rather, versions of our deepest selves, exemplars of autonomy, perhaps even teachers with valuable lessons to impart. What if we entertained the notion that Alicia Walker's adulteresses—and the ones in film noir and novels of the nineteenth and twenty-first centuries, and the ones who live as hunter-gatherers in Botswana and nomadic pastoralists in Namibia, and the ones who are married to men and go to all-women's sex parties in New York and London and Shanghai—might be able to show us the way? The way to more satisfying partnerships and enhanced self-esteem and even to happiness? This would go against everything we're taught and much of what we feel, to say the least. But I vowed to consider, as I sat down to talk with two women I'll call Sarah and Annika, that they might be not just peddlers of cautionary tales about cheating and its price but Sherpas of sorts, guides with intimate knowledge of a fascinating, thrilling, and potentially treacherous but ultimately rewarding terrain.

Sarah and Annika live only a few towns away from one another, but their experiences of infidelity are continents apart. Nonetheless, they both bring the findings of Chivers, Meana, and especially Walker vividly to life, showing us just how intensely some women want sexual excitement, the risks they will take in pursuing it, and the price they may pay, even in our ostensibly enlightened culture, when they seize the opportunity. Mostly, Sarah's and Annika's stories underscore the interplay of female sexuality and context— the culture women live in, the company they keep, the material circumstances of their lives—and beg the question: How free are we, really, if we are not sexually autonomous? How real is our self-determination if exercising it is occluded by "belonging" to a man? And just how deeply and unthinkingly do we continue to accept as "natural and right" certain ideologies that hold us obediently (though perhaps not always willingly) in place? Namely, that femininity is about restraint, about being wanted rather than wanting; that good mothers and women are asexual; that women who step out are essentially unfeminine while men who do so enhance their masculinity, even if we judge them. Annika and Sarah attempted an end run around these beliefs.

CHAPTER THREE

HOW FREE ARE WE?

A no-nonsense, hard-driving financial asset manager in her early forties who is surprisingly vulnerable once you get past the guarded, hyper-competent facade, Sarah seemed wistful as we sat at a diner not far from her office. We had first met several months earlier, and when I told her about my project, she said she'd like to share her story with me, explaining that she hoped doing so might help her make sense of it. But in the end, it was Sarah who helped me make sense of quite a bit. Her story challenges us to re-think what it is to be female and self-determined, and to consider all the factors that present women in the US with a series of false choices rather than real options when it comes to negotiating—with ourselves and the world—how we will be sexual.

Sarah had been married for nearly a decade when she met Paul one evening at a restaurant halfway across the country from the town she called home. They were both traveling on business, and as she waited for her coworker to show up, Sarah and Paul discovered they lived within a few miles of each other, had kids about the same age, and had attended the same school. They said their good nights when Sarah's colleague arrived, but Paul emailed her the next day. Sarah felt a thrill she hadn't experienced in years as she read it. The message itself was tame, but, she told me, "the fact that he was basically telling me, by being in touch, that he was interested in me—that was exciting."

Sarah has three children and described her marriage as unhappy. She felt her husband was "sometimes more like another child than a partner," as she put it. Their sex life was listless, it seemed—Sarah said it was "rote but okay." Soon she and Paul were emailing several times a week, and then daily. They began to text. Things got very intimate very fast: details about their children, their work, their days and evenings, quickly segued into confidences. He was being treated for depression. She felt stalled in her career. Every email, every text, brought them closer. They met a few times for lunch, Sarah explained as she stared down at the Formica table, "because lunch seemed safe and collegial. It was sexy, but I could tell myself it was aboveboard too."

Sarah was smitten with Paul's easy confidence and charm, and by his interest in her. He was the first man she had encountered in years who really seemed curious about her, who asked her questions about herself and her life and her thoughts, and who seemed fascinated by her answers. "I felt like someone worth knowing around him" is how she put it. "I felt *wanted* and exciting. Whereas with [my husband]...there was no mystery or..." She searched for the right word and then said, "*discovery.*" Sarah wanted to be discovered. She wanted to be new to someone, and be with a new someone. She wanted to know all about Paul too. "I fell for him hard," she explained simply, wiping the beads of water off the side of her glass.

Within several months of meeting, Paul and Sarah decided to act on their mutual attraction and arranged to meet at a hotel one late afternoon. Sarah thrummed with erotic energy in the week leading up to their date, feeling ebullient at work and at home as she thought about what she and Paul would do. But she was also a nervous wreck and felt tremendously guilty. "I had the voice in my head saying, *This is wrong and you know it.*" Still, Sarah told me, for reasons she couldn't exactly articulate, she felt she deserved to follow through on her attraction to this man. Maybe it was that she felt she had been taking care of not just her kids but her husband for years. Maybe it was that she worked hard and felt she deserved some fun. Maybe it was just curiosity and lust. Whatever was motivating Sarah to step out and allowing her to justify it to herself, she was "probably the best wife and mother I've ever been, whatever that means, in the days before my meet-up with Paul." She paused and thought for a moment, then explained, "I felt happy and desirable—that's the best way I can describe it." And being in the nimbus of being desired by Paul buffered her from frustration with her marriage and the day-to-day stresses of mothering.

But, Sarah told me with a shake of her head, she hadn't dared to cross the line once the two of them were alone. She just felt too nervous and guilty. When she began to cry, Paul told her not to worry and seemed to understand her anxiety about having sex. But in the end, he felt wounded and perhaps rejected, she surmised after the fact, or maybe just annoyed, because he cut off all contact with Sarah.

Two years later, she still missed him in her inbox and in her life.

And she was still trying to understand how she could feel so bereft when what she'd had with Paul had mostly been "just" a digital relationship. Why exactly, she wondered, had she been unable to consummate their intimate connection in person? "I think I was still holding out hope for my marriage," she suggested as she stirred her coffee. That seemed understandable, and wise. But Sarah was clear: she regretted not sleeping with this married man while she was married. She had been good, and it felt bad, and if she had it to do over again, she would go through with it and do the thing she thought was wrong.

Sarah was far from the only woman I spoke to over the course of researching this book who pondered this apparently inescapable, fundamental contradiction: while doing what was supposed to be natural for a woman—refuse sex outside monogamy or marriage—she was profoundly remorseful and resentful about the enormous sacrifice she felt she had made. Our deeply ingrained social script about female sexual reticence—a script that persists right alongside and in spite of assertive anthems of female sexual autonomy by CupcakKe, *Cosmo* articles about how to get what you want in bed, and episodes of *Veep* in which the female president has sex when she feels like it, "like a man"—ensures that women like Sarah won't get credit for exercising self-control and self-abnegation about something that, after all, they're not even supposed to desire. It's as if there isn't room in our culture for Sarah's wants. We are far more comfortable with the narrative of a woman who regrets with every molecule of her being having had an affair, or whose life is destroyed or nearly destroyed by one—Emma Bovary, Anna Karenina, Patty Berglund—than we are with the woman who regrets *not* having one. Or has one with few or no regrets. Or simply refuses monogamy *a priori.* Or struggles with it in a long-term partnership. Over a century and a quarter ago, Ibsen's precocious creation Nora Helmer walked away from her entire life in the name of autonomy and self-respect in *A Doll's House,* and the inscrutably complex Hedda Gabler killed herself rather than be exposed to a scandal involving a former lover. Nearly half a century ago, the pill was legalized for unmarried women, decoupling sex and reproduction as well as sex and marriage; a year later, Isadora Wing pined for and sought out the zipless fuck in *Fear of Flying.* But today, Sarahs everywhere expose the bedrock of lies that so much of what we cherish continues to rest upon: the notion that healthy women don't want as intensely as men do, that they don't long for more than what they have, which implies they are somehow essentially less likely (not to mention fundamentally less entitled) to act on that longing once they have committed to someone.

Consider one such assertion, on no less an arbiter of mainstream scientific ideas than PsychologyToday.com, where an article blares, "It's official: Men are hornier than women." The piece purports to prove that women "aren't quite so driven by strong urges and cravings as men are" because they supposedly masturbate and fantasize about sex less often (some data contradict this).

The piece, as many such pieces do, refers to a study conducted at Florida State University between 1978 and 1982 that found women propositioned by handsome male strangers are less likely to say yes than are men propositioned by attractive female strangers. But as critics of this study have already pointed out, women are more likely to get murdered by strangers with whom they have sex than men are. If they aren't killed, they are more likely to become pregnant, get an STI, not have an orgasm, and be called names and looked at askance by neighbors and even friends who find out they've had casual sex.

Context is everything. If women were told, "Imagine you are propositioned by this guy, and there is no way he will kill you and there is no way he'll be a jerk and it's guaranteed that he'll be skilled enough to give you an orgasm and you won't get pregnant or get an infection or disease, and your mom will never know and neither will anyone in your dorm or neighborhood. He won't make disparaging remarks about your body or gossip afterward. He will text you after or not, and want to see you again or not, depending on what you wish he would do." And so on. These are the kinds of conditions we would have to engineer in order to get an accurate sense of what a woman's sex drive might be like under circumstances conducive to actually feeling entitled to have and admit to having a sex drive. Until such a test exists, we need to consider the likelihood that we are only measuring men's willingness to admit they are sexual compared to women's willingness to do the same. Guess who wins that contest?

D-I-V-O-R-C-E AND THE DOUBLE STANDARD

Some studies suggest that men who find out their wives are cheating are more likely to divorce them than are wives who discover their husbands have stepped out. Other experts tell us that *female* infidelity can be especially destructive for a marriage or partnership. These findings make sense when we consider the gendered double standard that has long prevailed in matters of extra-pair sex.

Along with life, liberty, and the pursuit of happiness, the sexual double standard is one our country's foundational concepts. In *The Times of Their Lives,* a history of Plymouth Colony, Patricia Scott Deetz and James Deetz tell us that in that place and others where pilgrims first carved out their hardscrabble, pious lives, sanctions against adultery were severe—and severely skewed. In the first codification of the law in 1636, they note, adultery was a capital crime, punishable by death (no one was executed for adultery in Plymouth, but the Massachusetts Bay Colony took a harder line, and three people there were put to death for the offense). In 1658, it was decreed that adulterers could count on at least being whipped and compelled to wear the capital letters *AD* sewn onto their garments.

The Deetzes tell us that when Mary Mendame of Duxbury, wife of Robert Mendame, was accused of having sex with an "Indian" named Tinsin in 1639, she was whipped, compelled to wear an *AD* on her garments, and told that if she failed to comply, she would get her face branded. (Tinsin was, like Mary, "whipped, but at the post.") Had Mary been Mark, how differently things would have gone. For in the colonies of this period of the seventeenth century, a man, even if he were married, could have relations with an unmarried woman and be accused of the lesser crime of fornication. This was punishable by either a whipping or three days in prison and a ten pound fine. But having sex with a married woman was adultery: "adultery was viewed as the breaking of the marriage bond by the fact that the woman was married. The husband was not bound by the same constraints." Having sexual relations with another man's wife violated not just moral beliefs but his property rights, the Deetzes explain. (While some historians suggest this belief originated in medieval Europe, as we will see, it was much,

much older.) As property, women like Mary Mendame were not only their husbands' concern but wards of the entire community. Their trespass was a trespass against their husbands, God, and law and order itself. And a man trespassing with such a woman was violating more than his individual vow to goodness and to his own wife, if he had one—he was tramping all over his neighbor's possession while demeaning a social contract. But whether he was married or not, he was somewhat freer to indulge.

Mary would have gotten off in more ways than one had there been no double standard.

Nearly two hundred fifty years later, Richard von Krafft-Ebing was moved to write a justification of the sexual double standard in *Psychopathia Sexualis* that would have made a Puritan proud. "The unfaithfulness of the wife, as compared with that of the husband, is morally of a much wider bearing, and should always meet with severer punishment at the hands of the law. The unfaithful wife not only dishonors herself, but also her husband and her family, not to speak of the possible uncertainty of paternity." Such hypocrisies were baked into us; we still live in the shadow of this belief that a woman cheating on a man is just that much more outrageous and inexcusable.

Cacilda Jethá, a psychiatrist and co-author with Christopher Ryan of the game-changing bestseller *Sex at Dawn,* told me a story that illustrates the intractability of the double standard, its ability to flourish in different ecologies. Over dinner on a fall evening, Jethá—who has a dancer's bearing, and speaks six languages with what can only be described as animated elegance—recounted how during her early career she undertook a study on HIV and STI transmission and prevention in Marracuene, a southern district of Mozambique. Her work, funded by the World Health Organization in coordination with the government's health ministry, involved interviewing both men and women about their sexual practices and, not infrequently, their extra-pair involvements. "Once they were engaged," Jethá told me, "it was common in the region for men to go off and work in mines to earn money for their weddings and married life. During this long period of absence, the women who were engaged to be married often had affairs. It was a known thing. And since there were cultural beliefs that you shouldn't have sex for two years after a baby was born, during this period it was common for husbands to have sex outside the marriage." In spite of the relative cultural openness about these practices, Jethá quickly noticed an asymmetry in how her interview participants talked about their infidelities. "The men were much more forthcoming. Much more!" Jethá observed, shaking her head. "Whereas the women were very, *very* reluctant. You had to ask in many different ways. They were notably more hesitant. Even in an environment where people knew this was happening, they felt they couldn't say! Whereas men were not hesitant at all. They were almost proud, you could say."

Thousands of miles away, several of the women I spoke with in the US told me that infidelity was likely to "stick to [them]" in a different way than it would a man, explaining it to me as if it were the most obvious point in the world when I asked them to elaborate. Yes, too many women die at the hands of jealous husbands and lovers, and in some countries this is still excused as a "crime of passion." But here it is often the linked fears of reputational assault and of being caught and divorced that inform women's decisions about monogamy. These fears also inform a male partner's decisions about sexual exclusivity. However, there is an important difference underlying the choices heterosexual men and women make when it comes to risking infidelity.

Even in regions of the world with "no-fault" type practices, divorce can be an emotional and economic trauma, but it is most especially so for women. In spite of a widely embraced stereotype of the gold digger taking her hapless husband to the cleaners, women tend to fare markedly worse financially than men in the breakup of a marriage. In a 2008 study, the Institute for Social and Economic Research found that 27 percent of women fall into poverty post-divorce—triple the rate of men. Much of that has to do with women having left or never having entered the workforce in order to raise kids. But even those who work before, during, or after their marriage experience a 20 percent drop in income when their marriages end, on average (the poverty rate for women who are separated is a staggering 27 percent, just under three times the rate for separated men). And effects of this drop are long-lasting and profound: across the board, women's incomes tend never to reach pre-split levels post-divorce. One Australian report found that divorced women had assets valued at 90 percent less than their married peers. Women are no fools—they see these numbers and statistics and realities played out in the lives of their sisters, girl-friends, and female colleagues, and they take note: divorce costs plenty. Such concerns can reinforce what comes to look more like compulsory monogamy than a choice to remain sexually exclusive.

For Sarah, divorce would mean sacrifices, everything from struggling to pay a mortgage and run a household on her own to forgoing relative luxuries like the summer sleepaway camp the kids loved. These considerations, big and small, and the idea that her own desires, including her sexual desires, meant she and especially her kids might have less, had prevented her from initiating a divorce, or having an affair and risking getting caught, which she felt would certainly drive her husband to divorce her. "It seemed selfish and at the same time almost masochistic" to initiate a divorce herself, Sarah summarized as we sat there, even though she had long considered it.

In other words, Sarah wasn't just exercising restraint when she decided not to sleep with Paul. She was encountering what anthropologists call "constraint"—those ecological and environmental realities that determine our options and roadblocks. In general, constraint includes factors like predation, disease, or the relative difficulty of procuring calories. Sarah didn't have to fear being eaten by a jaguar, of course, and vaccines kept her and her kids safe from pathogens. And living in the industrialized West, she didn't have to hunt or gather—she could buy food from the grocery store. In the parlance of anthropology, Sarah, like most of us in the United States, lives in a state of ecological release. Nonetheless, she faced tremendous constraint—both internal and external—when it came to her sexual autonomy.

The fear of "blowing things up" with her husband was just one of her considerations when it came to Paul. She added that she would find it especially humiliating if her community—the other parents at her kids' school, for example—thought she had had an affair. "The Scarlet Mom," she joked as she picked at a piece of toast. Sarah was no prude—she had slept with a number of men before marrying and didn't pass judgment on a friend who'd had a fling with a coworker while her husband was out of town. But like many of the women I spoke with, Sarah also felt certain—and she wasn't necessarily wrong—that not only her peers but also family and divorce court judges were not always immune to bias against "cheating wives and mothers" and that a custody hearing might not have gone her way had she been accused of infidelity, even though her state's "no-fault" divorce law was supposed to protect her from such prejudice.

In addition, Sarah had the kind of shoddy social safety net typical of many women in the US. Her parents lived all the way across the country. She couldn't count on them if her husband, say, tossed her out as Sarah Jessica Parker's character's husband attempted to do in an early episode of *Divorce*. (Sarah had plenty of friends, but living with them with her kids was simply out of the question in a culture where we live in nuclear families and privacy is highly valued.)

These were the reasons, Sarah explained, that she had "wanted" to remain in an unnourishing marriage and hadn't been able to have sex with Paul in the hotel room that day. She had, albeit largely unconsciously, run a kind of mental calculus about upsides and downsides—anthropologists call these "life-history trade-offs"—and decided that, no, she wouldn't. The burden of "what if" was everywhere. *What if my husband finds out? What if Paul's wife finds out? What if I fall for him even harder and it complicates my life terribly?*

And then after her divorce, as she contemplated getting in touch with Paul again, her trade-offs morphed into another form of balancing the pursuit of satisfaction against risk. She wanted to have sex with Paul, still. But he hadn't responded to her emails since that disastrous Friday afternoon at the hotel. And, she told me, she felt she would seem "desperate" if she reached out to him. It was "unfeminine," she said—though she said it with irony—to pursue him. Now the calculus she ran was: *What if he rejects me? What if he thinks I'm a slut? What if I* am *a slut?* Though we live in a state of ecological release, engineering a state of ideological release—freedom from censure, judgment, and self-judgment—is more complicated, particularly for women living in a culture brimming with double standards about female and male sexuality and misinformation about the hearts and libidos of women.

In the end, Sarah read her desire to be with Paul as a sign that her marriage was beyond repair. The divorce took over a year and a half and was as stressful and draining—emotionally and financially—as she had feared. Now, with hindsight as her guide, this capable woman sat under fluorescent lights in the worn booth, tearing up, lamenting not her divorce but her previous propriety, her "goodness," the way she had allowed herself to be hemmed in not only by her legitimate fears but by a code she had no role in authoring about what she might do with her own body. Sarah had dated several men since her divorce. She had great sexual and emotional chemistry with two of them. But she hadn't found the kind of connection again that she'd had with Paul—that feeling of discovering someone as deeply fascinated by her as she was by him, that awakening of the long-slumbering sense that she was desirable and capable of deep, thrilling, albeit dangerous desire herself. Maybe Paul was so important to Sarah precisely because he had been the one to rekindle that sense within her. As Marta Meana had explained, "A stranger who can desire anyone at all and desires you—*that* means something." Or maybe Paul really, truly was that special and unusual. Sarah would never know. Constraint had been every bit as effective as a leash, or a chastity belt.

As we sat there and the breakfast rush drained away, I found it easy to sympathize with her, this non-adulteress who wished she had been one. She wanted to reconnect with the man with whom she had come so close to having an affair, to be a party to his own infidelity, and here I was, wishing to hell she'd just do it already.

THE WAY WE WERE

If she were from another generation, Sarah might have conducted herself differently. In her book *Lust in Translation,* Pamela Drucker-man tells the stories of a group of women who lived in tony suburbs like Sarah's—just across the George Washington Bridge from Manhattan and in the fancier areas of Long Island and Westchester—in the early 1960s. They had moved to assisted living facilities in Florida by the time Druckerman tracked them down. But this particular clique of women and not a few of their peers across the country had sex lives that could have been written by Cheever. Their stories illustrate, among other things, that when it comes to female infidelity, we haven't necessarily become more tolerant over time.

Thrice-married Loretta, sixty-eight at the time of the interview, and Barbara, nine years her senior, reminisced about themselves and their friends and the sexual codes of their world.

"Yvonne had an affair…"

"Linda…would just have affair after affair."

"Alice was sort of happily married, sort of not. There was a surprise birthday party, and that afternoon she's screwing someone in a hotel room."

"I think most people knew Les's wife had an affair for many years."

"It was Peyton Place," Barb summarized neatly.

"We all learned from the movie stars," Loretta explained. "You met your sweetheart in New York for a drink, kind of thing. It was...Sinatra and stuff like that. The songs had words and you closed your eyes..."

Songs of the era provided a backdrop, and may also have described their yearnings and their sexual culture. They had High Hopes and believed, as much of the nation did, that The Best Was Yet to Come. They were beautiful, like the Girl from Ipanema, adorned in Pucci and Lilly Pulitzer poolside and at the club. They drank and danced at parties and stood close to men they were interested in when their spouses were in the other room. They wanted to be flown to the moon and to feel the Summer Wind year-round. But while these songs thematized their hopes and desires, "Strangers in the Night" was one that truly missed the mark. For these young married women, as they rushed to tell Druckerman decades later, seduced and were seduced by the successful married husbands of female acquaintances and friends, men with whom their own husbands worked and golfed and socialized. No strangers for them—their affairs were deeply embedded in and shaped by their social world, not rejections of it.

The story of Druckerman's interviewee Elaine is typical of affairs of the era and of her milieu. Married and in her mid-twenties, she met a man she felt an instant attraction to, Irwin, at a party at her uncle's house. Not long after, they had sex in Irwin's car ("I went down on him, in the car! I said to myself, *If I'm going to do it, I'm going to do it the whole way!*"). Irwin told Elaine that he would never leave his wife, but Elaine had an agenda of her own, and after a meet-up or two in the city, she implemented a scheme: "I got more friendly with his wife, so that the four of us were together constantly.... There were times when Irwin and I were in New York and we'd fall asleep in a hotel, and we'd both be late coming home, and the four of us [all] had [a date] that night, and [my] husband and [his] wife never put it together." Elaine would go shopping with Irwin's wife and then see him at night and say, "Ugh, what your wife bought!"

Elaine—strategic, unrepentant, calculating, perhaps even devious to our eyes and ears at this half-century-plus distance—was no outlier. She and her peers engineered trysts with precise intent. There were plenty of chances to abandon these plans and think twice about the meet-ups they plotted, as Sarah had. They didn't. Instead, they proceeded brazenly, telling their girlfriends all and even introducing their married beaus to their mothers. Nor were they embarrassed about what they'd done when they were young (or, in Sarah's case, ashamed and remorseful about what they *hadn't* done). Au contraire, perhaps because they had exercised such agency and taken such risks, they considered their affairs the best, most exciting times of their lives. "We didn't have guilt then. Everybody knew. It was exciting. It was thrilling!" they told Druckerman. Nancy described what happened when she went into the city to meet her paramour, a married real estate developer. "I'm talking about going to meet him in New York one day and having detectives follow me and…chase me!"

When things got serious, these women separated from their spouses. Their beaus put them and their children up in apartments until their respective divorces came through. There were consequences, sure, but they might strike us today as rather minimal. When Elaine told her parents she was leaving her husband for Irwin, for example, her mother was upset, but her father slipped her cash. One of her girlfriends helped her move, with the kids, out of the house she shared with her soon-to-be-ex-husband—women were granted full custody as a matter of course in those days—and she and Irwin eventually married. In fact, all the older women in the "Florida-via-northeastern-suburbs group" married the men with whom they'd had affairs. A few went on to have additional affairs and husbands. Anthropologists might characterize the Florida group's particular style of having an affair as "bridging." Among women worldwide who have extra-pair involvements, some do it as a way to test out a potential mate while still garnering the benefits— mostly material, but also companionship and partnership in child-rearing, plus enhanced social status—of being coupled. The affair is a potential exit from one marriage via another marriage. As Brooke Scelza, who studies female infidelity in Namibia but whose observations in this case have broader application, wrote in a review of women and affairs around the world, "Having an affair may allow a woman to gain reproductive access to the man of her choosing…or to assess the quality of a potential future spouse while continuing to secure investment from her current one." The description is not exactly romantic, but it underscores that even when it comes to affairs of a lifetime, ones that end in marriage and to which we might attribute great passion and excitement, the unsparing logic of the life-history trade-off ticks beneath the surface. Elaine and Nancy and Co. found their basherts by *design*. The bridging or "mate-switching" strategy is one women can use when ecological and environmental conditions are right: when they have kin or peer support to buffer them from blowback—think of Elaine's dad slipping her cash or her girlfriend helping her move out. Or when the ideology in place and the division of labor dictates that dependent women should segue from one man to another or, in Druckerman's apt formulation, from the protection of their fathers to the protection of a series of husbands and lovers. Or when a powerful figurehead—at the time, President John F. Kennedy—is doing it and so is everybody else. Indeed, one of the interviewees said that when she went to her rabbi to discuss her feelings of guilt about upending so many lives by divorcing her husband for another, he told her she was destroying lives by staying in an unhappy union. The rabbi himself was divorced. She felt not only relieved but emboldened by his advice, and by the culture where affairs—both men's and women's—were more or less a fact of life.

Duplicity and secrets were par for the course in the stories these women tell and the love lives they led; Elaine, Nancy, Loretta, and their peers were virtually unpathologized compared to our collective take on things today, when we have entire tomes dedicated to the devastating deceptions large and small that underpin infidelity.

Contemporary titles like *How Can I Forgive You?* say it all. In fact, Druckerman's interview subjects were so unabashed by what they had done in general, and their fibbing in particular, that they actually begged her to use their real names in her book, neatly inverting the sensibilities of the consensually non-monogamous, who call for disclosure, transparency, and honesty when it comes to extra-pair dalliances (Druckerman didn't). Elaine's, Nancy's, and Loretta's adult kids from their first marriages, on the other hand, are appalled by their mothers' pasts; the women complained that in some cases their children wouldn't even speak to them. The generational divide—about how mothers should behave and about the acceptability of affairs—is in this case an unbridgeable gulf.

Elaine and Nancy and Barb and Loretta, and their friends Yvonne and Linda and Alice, lived in a different sexual culture than Sarah does. They also said "I do" when young and relatively inexperienced, and proceeded to have interesting sex lives after. Today, we've reversed things: we have sexual experiences and *then* "settle down." And today these women can't believe what tremendous prudes younger people are about how things were. They might have words for Sarah—"Live a little!" "Oh, come on, everybody cheats!"—but they know to speak only to one another. And to a curious, nonjudgmental female journalist who comes to call.

ECOLOGIES

Annika is every bit the modern Manhattanite. But she has more in common with Druckerman's ladies in assisted living and the ethos of the *Mad Men* era than she does with her peer Sarah. Annika had apparently felt few of the restrictions Sarah had during *her* decade-long marriage; Annika had had numerous affairs and, another woman who referred me to her marveled, didn't seem to feel guilty about them. Why might that be? I was curious about what precisely separates women who don't pursue sex and romance outside a committed relationship from women who do. In the case of the older but far from tame ladies in Florida, it was about a particular place, and a specific era—Sinatra, Kennedy, womanizing, gaming the ethos of womanizing in your own self-interest if you were a young woman who wanted more. Are women who actually cross that line into non-monogamy today, risking being misunderstood, censured, ostracized, sometimes even killed by their husbands or boyfriends, essentially different from those who don't? If so, in what ways? Is the difference in where and how they were raised? Their economic circumstances? Their temperaments? How do they manage to slip out of the handcuffs of self-censure?

After all, self-censure is no small thing. In *Lust in Translation*, Druckerman writes about an American woman so upset by a mutual attraction she and her doctor experience but never act on that she feels she doesn't even know who she is anymore. Another woman who is engaged to be married posts online that she is nearly suicidal about having kissed a man not her fiancé at a bar. Once. We all have friends who say they simply could never have an affair, period. And friends who say they are tempted but "would never dare." What separates these women, the Sarahs who long for sexual adventure and autonomy yet hesitate to pull the trigger, from the Annikas who do not? The Florida women—who married early and then sought out sexual adventures with men other than their husbands—challenge our presumption that, when it comes to women and affairs, we have become more and more open and accepting, that sexual progress is an arrow shooting forward, unconstrained, into empty space. These women also offer a compelling model of female sexual entitlement. They desired sex and pursued it, their marital status and vows of fidelity notwithstanding. Depending on your point of view, you might say that since their day, we've had setbacks. Annika's story brings home the way many circumstances of women's lives that seem unrelated to their sexuality—childcare options, labor-force participation, family and peer networks—can actually determine the most intimate choices they make.

A few weeks after my talk with Sarah, I found myself sitting in Annika's cheerful, cozy kitchen, making small talk about our children and our work. Annika was warm, open, and engaging, with chicly messy blonde hair and an infectious sense of humor. She was Scandinavian and had moved to a wealthy suburb of Chicago with her family as a teen. The transition was jarring. "I was used to a high level of independence and maturity. At home, my friends and I could go out to lunch on our school lunch hour and have a beer," she said. "But in the US, I had to bring a note from my mother if I was late for school because I was stuck in traffic. It was so infantilizing and confusing!"

Sexual standards were just as bewildering. Back at home, Sex Ed "was practically demonstrated." She laughed. A lot of information was imparted, in great detail, beginning before adolescence. What Annika didn't learn at school, she heard from her mother, who spoke to her honestly about sex. "I remember her once saying, 'When grown-ups with kids go away to a hotel without them, it's a free-for-all!'...She gave me the sense that it was fun." Indeed, sex was "sort of in the air" wherever you looked while Annika was growing up. "Where I'm from, you see [women's breasts] in ads, on billboards. There's not the same shameful feeling there is here. Where I'm from, prostitution is legal, for God's sake, and that was always my baseline."

But in the Chicago suburb where they landed for her father's work, bodies and sex were a different animal. "In school here, Sex Ed was called 'health,' and they basically just explained how the sperm fertilized the egg and then told you not to do it."

Annika put out some cookies and made a pot of tea while we talked, and when I asked her for adjectives to describe her sex life, she hooted and said, "Colorful!" She started at the beginning.

A newcomer who struggled, initially, to find her place, Annika nevertheless managed to make some friends at her new high school. She also found a boyfriend and began having sex toward the end of her senior year, though she felt confused by the way her American peers went about it. "At home, kids my age decided to have sex and sometimes girls even had sleepovers at home with their boyfriends. Our parents knew and let it happen. But here—it was very secretive. Lots of kids were doing it, but girls especially weren't talking about it. It was a very gossipy environment. There were scary rumors about two girls at school having abortions. Well, what do you expect? Nobody talked about birth control! People went to parties and got really drunk and had sex there. It was a big change to wrap my mind around."

She moved to California for college and met Dan, a California native who found her exotic and fun. Dan was rather shy, tall and fit—"I loved his body right away," Annika recalled—and, having already graduated, had a job in their midsized college town. Annika, meanwhile, was just beginning her college adventure, so initially she turned Dan down when he asked her out. But he persisted, and she found that his maturity and competence were as compelling and attractive to her as his body. "He was a real man with a job and a life in a sea of all these frat boys getting wasted all the time." They began dating toward the end of her freshman year. From the beginning, Annika felt they were less than ideally aligned, sexually speaking. "I felt like I initiated sex almost all the time, and that made me self-conscious." She didn't bring it up, and while it progressively ate away at her feelings of worth—"I kept wondering whether there was something wrong with me"—Annika loved their time together hiking, cooking at his place, and talking. Soon things were serious and exclusive, "though it wasn't something we ever talked about; we just kind of fell into it, because that's how it was done," Annika told me, staring out the window for a moment, seemingly lost in thought.

During the summers, Dan worked while Annika traveled—and occasionally slept with other men she met. Again, she and Dan "never discussed it. I had a measure of independence even then." She was unsure what Dan did while she was away, Annika said, "but I have to guess he was seeing other people too." Or maybe not, as he didn't seem to have much of a sex drive, a fact that Annika continued to push to the back of her mind. *What kind of a woman cared about something like that?* she wondered. Anyway, a few of Annika's college girlfriends had similar non-arrangements—of the "Don't ask, don't tell, don't talk" variety—with their boyfriends. So Annika didn't feel so unusual, even as she wished Dan wanted her more and felt awkward and stressed about nearly getting caught and keeping secrets. They found an apartment together in the city after she graduated, and soon Dan began pushing for marriage.

"Maybe it's my Scandinavian background, but I was in no hurry," Annika told me as she poured us each another cup of tea. "My parents had friends in very long-term, committed relationships, people with kids, who weren't married."

Sex, specifically Dan wanting it less than Annika did, was also an issue. "It made me feel...rejected and undesirable. He said it was because he had low testosterone or because he was tired. For a while I was just occasionally having sex with guys I met through work or at a party. I would not have been sleeping with other guys if our sex life had been great, honestly. I felt like I deserved to have a sex life." But "undisclosed non-monogamy" was emotionally costly. There were several close calls over the years, once when a man she'd had over left his jacket there and Dan, suspicious, asked whose it was. Her heart pounding, Annika made an excuse—it belonged to their friend—and made a note to herself: the risks of cheating just weren't worth it.

And yet it was exciting to be with other men, and their desire was a kind of salve against Dan's sexual indifference. Like Alicia Walker's interview subjects, Annika used undisclosed extra-pair sex as a "workaround" strategy in order to stay in a sexless relationship.

When Dan proposed yet again, Annika thought it might somehow fix things, at least for him. "I figured, *He's American. This means a lot to him. Maybe getting married will make things better for us.*" She said yes, and for a while it did.

But after an initial literal honeymoon period of ardor, Dan was no more interested in sex than he had been before marriage. And Annika began sleeping with other men again. It made her feel twinges of guilt, sure, but it was also thrilling and made her feel wanted and alive.

"I remember the feeling"—here she made a frightened face and gave a little gasp—"of the phone ringing and knowing it was a guy I was sleeping with, and I'd have to pretend it was someone else because Dan was standing right there. It's exhausting, and the number of heart attacks and stress—it's complicated to keep all the lies straight. There's a whole part of it that's really difficult and tiring! Sometimes I would think, *Okay, I've got to stop. This is just too hard and dangerous.*" Such moments, the frissons of near discovery, are touchstones of narratives with infidelity plots—from *Eyes Wide Shut* to a YouTube genre called "cheaters getting caught" to Carmen Rita Wong's novel *Never Too Late*, with its storyline about high-powered, very married Latina lesbian Magda, whose happy life might be turned upside down by a one-night stand with a woman who has a taste for revenge.

Like many women in fiction and life, Annika got too much out of her affairs to stop—including the variety and novelty of sexual experience she craved. "I think no matter how hard you try and how exciting it is, even when your marriage is good—and mine wasn't, at least in the sex department—you still miss that thing where you're so excited, and it's so new, and you can't eat or sleep, you're having such an intense time emotionally and sexually with this entirely new person. That's what I kept going after, what I couldn't say no to."

Like Sarah and Druckerman's ladies in Florida, Annika was living what Marta Meana calls "erotic self-focus." When others saw her as sexy and hot, she did too. Wanting to be wanted, and withering when she was unwanted (or, in the case of Meana's study participants, wanted) by one man in perpetuity drove Annika and may drive us in ways we might not want to admit but cannot deny.

Annika had an intuitive sense of these truths about herself but believed they made her "different" from other women. Something must be wrong with her, she figured, that she wanted sex not only with her husband but with other men. But she was buffered by her Scandinavian upbringing and the girlfriend or two who shared her taste for sex outside a committed relationship. As Annika told me, framing it in the negative and as a failure, as most of the women I spoke to did, "I knew some other women who couldn't stay monogamous, and that helped me feel less abnormal." She and Dan had sex intermittently, without birth control—she always used condoms with sex partners outside marriage, she told me—and several years into their marriage, Annika was pregnant. She had a core group of girlfriends by now—from high school, college, and her work in the nonprofit world—some of whom were also expecting. Feeling sick 24/7, she drew strength from her time with them. When her daughter was born, she had a hard time nursing. Annika found herself stressed and sleep-deprived. She quit her job, as it offered no real maternal leave. They couldn't afford a nanny, and Annika didn't want to leave her newborn in full-time daycare. It was a struggle to live in the city on one salary. Dan started traveling more for work, telling Annika it would enhance his chances at a higher salary, bonuses, and a promotion.

"When he was gone, I would make a point every day to run out with the baby in the sling to see a girlfriend at a nearby café. Otherwise, I just felt very lonely," Annika said, looking miserable at the mere memory of this period.

"And when my parents—who had moved back to Scandinavia—came to visit, they couldn't believe our predicament," she told me, getting up to fuss in the kitchen, then bringing us more cookies. "In my country there's really good daycare and all kinds of support for women after they have the baby. Here, in comparison, there's nothing."

Less than a year after her daughter was born, "just as I was getting the hang of it and doing a little better," Annika was pregnant again.

Many things were easier the second time around—being pregnant, giving birth, changing diapers, nursing her baby boy. But Annika was more comprehensively exhausted than ever. Sometimes her friends would come over to find her sitting on the living room floor with the kids, crying from sleep deprivation and frustration. Annika thought about going back to work—but childcare would be even more expensive with two, and her potential earnings could hardly justify a nanny's or sitter's salary. She checked out daycare options she could afford but was unimpressed with the low ratio of caregivers to babies. It wasn't something she felt good about doing, given the option of staying home herself. Feeling trapped, she had good days and bad days. And "my sex drive just went into hibernation" is how she describes it. In a perfectly instructive example of how women are abetted and constrained by their ecological and environmental circumstances, the assertive and confident Annika was hobbled nearly beyond recognition by her adopted country's lack of support for families with young children and new mothers in particular, and by patrilocal patterns of residence that had her far from her parents and other kin support. Annika's girlfriends played a vital role in filling the gaps, but they had stresses and challenges of their own, with most of them as isolated and financially dependent on their husbands as Annika was on hers.

By the time the babies were toddlers, Dan had been promoted and needed to travel more than ever. He was earning more now too, and while they could technically afford to stay in the city, he suggested they move to a nearby suburb with a great public school system. Annika was skeptical, given her unhappy experience in the suburbs as a culturally dislocated teenager. But Dan convinced her life would be easier with more living space and a sizeable backyard. They could drive to the nearby town with its library and children's museum and family-friendly restaurants. They moved, in spite of Annika's misgivings about leaving the city, where there was bustle and life on the streets that buoyed her even on the bleakest days, as well as her support system of girlfriends.

In their new home, she spent most of her time isolated, alone with the kids in the house. Work was a distant memory. Dan was gone most of the time.

"For a long while we only had one car, so I literally couldn't leave the house. Then when we got a second car, I was always so tired, and the idea of strapping them in and striking out..." Her girlfriends from the city visited in the summer to lounge by the pool with their children, and Annika lived for these opportunities to catch up and feel connected and less alone—though she didn't feel she could confide in them about her difficulties, which would "ruin the fun." Mostly, she was on her own.

"The houses were really far apart, so it's not like the neighbors really had much to do with one another. So basically for several years I lived in my garage, doing arts and crafts with my kids." She paused and then summarized, "I was losing my mind."

Meanwhile, her sex life with Dan had ceased entirely. He told her the travel left him exhausted. "Once in early April I said I wanted to have sex for my birthday, which is in mid-April, because we hadn't had sex once since Christmas!" She didn't want to divorce, she told me, because she basically liked Dan and didn't want her kids to grow up with divorced parents. And like Sarah, she worried about being the odd wheel at a dinner party, the divorced one at school pickup. On another level, she said, "I just knew it would be a status drop. You're That Divorced Mom. And people might even think you're crazy. There's just a hostility and distrust for divorced women in the US." She sighed. "Damaged goods."

When their youngest started kindergarten, Annika's life was upended. Dan had a long-time girlfriend, he confessed, and he had moved them out to the suburbs in order to have more time with her. Most of the time he had been "traveling for work," he had actually been with his girlfriend.

I tried not to look shocked at this unexpected development in Annika's story.

"I guess some people could say that it was karma, or payback, or whatever, for my extracurriculars for all those years," she continued woodenly. "But the whole time we lived in the suburbs, I wasn't seeing anyone. I was lonely, raising my kids on my own while my husband 'traveled.'" She took a deep breath.

"Not having a job, not being out there in the world, just being in a house all day with my kids, no family or friends, I had zero leverage or independence." Annika told me it was important I make it clear all her affairs were before kids. After, she had less time and interest and felt more committed to making her marriage work, she said.

Listening to Sarah and Annika, I kept thinking about passages from Daniel Bergner's book *What Do Women Want?* Bergner had spent time with the neuroendocrinologist and psychologist Kim Wallen at the Yerkes National Primate Research Center at Emory University, observing rhesus macaques. Historically female macaques were often kept in cages with the males, who seemed to initiate all the sex by unceremoniously mounting them, which the females seemed to endure indifferently. This informed not just the primate literature on macaques; it served as more proof from the animal world that female sexuality is essentially passive and "less-than" male sexuality. Didn't it? Wallen wasn't buying it. He wondered, *What if the animals spend more time out of their cages? Would that change the choreography of rhesus macaque sex and, with it, some of our convictions about female sexuality?* What happened next was a stunning performance of unconstrained female macaque sexuality. In larger enclosures, females did not simply endure sex; they initiated it. Assertively and insistently. They followed the males with stalker-ish intent, and smacked the ground in a kind of Morse code that meant "Serve me sexually right now!" They also got bored and listless after a few years of having sex with all the available males. Wallen wondered, *what if we introduced new males?* Sure enough, with fresh guys on offer, the females were again suddenly bananas for sex. Out of the cage, they were utterly different than they were within it.

I also thought of the work the anthropologist Beverly Strassmann did in Mali, where women are compelled by tradition to repair to menstrual huts when it's that time of the month. In this way, Strassmann determined, men are able to "count back the days" from their wives' periods to the approximate date of ovulation. And figure out whether they are being true. It's an effective form of constraint; the rate of extra-pair paternity in this region of Mali is one of the lowest in the world.

The sexual, economic, and ecological circumstances of the lives of women could not be more closely linked or interdependent. In Annika's case, the suburban house was not so different from a macaque's cage or a menstrual hut in Mali—a container that distorted and re-formed her sexuality—as well as a way for her husband to ensure that he could do his thing while keeping track of her and keeping her isolated from other men. Sarah's hesitation to act on her sexual and romantic desires and her feelings of regret, resentment, and sadness about not doing what she wanted to do, her lack of sexual autonomy and her conflicted allegiance to a strong code of behavior that applies unequally to men and women, in spite of her feminism and achievements, are another version of constraint. And the experiences of both of these women are of a piece with a massive, overarching cultural shift, a treachery writ large, if you will, in which female independence and self-determination—economic, personal, sexual—was transformed into subservience, permission seeking, and dependence. A growing number of anthropologists tell us the pitiless and unlikely agent of this transformation was not individual men or women. It was not politics or politicians. It was not the rise of the nation-state or even organized religion.

It was agriculture.

If it weren't for farms and farming, Annika, Sarah, and you and I might be living very different lives indeed.

CHAPTER FOUR

PLOUGHS, PROPERTY, PROPRIETY

So much of a woman's sex life in the US today, so much of what happens to and is possible for and is not available to the Annikas and the Sarahs, is linked to an unlikely-seeming moment in the past. Like butterflies pinned, or bugs caught and preserved in amber, our libido and our superego, our sense of freedom and of propriety, the expansive pulsing of our desire and the contraction of our self-censure, are present-day artifacts of an unfurling of events long ago, when highly mobile foraging women were "pegged" as if onto the paper of history, literally immobilized into another way of being and thinking and living…and having sex.

The momentous change in female fortune was put into motion approximately ten to twelve thousand years ago, in the Jordan Valley of the Fertile Crescent in what is today the Middle East. There, a shift in human activity was under way. Hunter-gatherers began to domesticate plants, increasingly depending on food they grew rather than food they foraged for subsistence. This transition culminated in what we think of as a great watershed moment in human history: the rise of agriculture. The narrative goes that as humans began to focus more on crops and less on freewheeling hunting and gathering, we settled down (literally), grew up (figuratively), and created the circumstances conducive to "progress." With crops, we are taught, there was no more harum-scarum, will-there-be-enough, hand-to-mouth business. And with more food for more people, and more resource predictability, population size increased. In addition—boon of boons!—with the cultivation of crops came the unprecedented luxury of intermit-tent food surpluses. We began to store what we could—grains—for the long term, thumbing our noses at the droughts and floods and other disruptions that had previously caused catastrophic food shortages. With this steady supply of food in reserve, population levels could remain high consistently over years and years. And thus we not only multiplied, as the story goes, we "civilized." No longer needing to range far and wide for sustenance, we built per-manent villages, establishing larger, denser communities than ever before in order to be close to the crops and those who harvested them, and complexifying our endeavors beyond "merely" foraging for survival.

> As societies learned to produce, store, and distribute food, they developed the characteristics of modern civilizations: densely pop-ulated cities, centralized government, organized religion, private property, specialized occupations, public works, taxation, technol-ogy, and science. People lived as hunter-gatherers for tens of thou-sands of years before they began to plant crops and domesticate animals. Once this happened, however, the transition to modern civ-ilization was rapid and fundamental.

Storing food to stave off famine was without a doubt one of agri-culture's benefits. That did indeed lead to some significant lifestyle improvements: skeletal remains of early farmers show they had less osteoarthritis than hunter-gatherers, suggesting less repetitive joint use and hardship overall. And there is no doubt that agriculture bolstered the human population.

But our belief that agriculture was the lynchpin of our

"progress" is difficult to justify given relatively new findings by historians, archaeologists, and anthropologists. Archaeological evidence and human remains suggest that the shift from foraging to farming was anything but a straightforward improvement for our ancestors on measures like lifestyle and health. Indeed, the popular anthropologist and author Jared Diamond, pulling no punches, has called the shift to agriculture "a catastrophe from which we have never recovered" and "the worst mistake in the history of the human race." Our new diet—carbohydrate intensive, iron deficient—led to reduced growth and development. It didn't help that soil depletion and soil exhaustion eventually created crops low in nutrients. Meanwhile, neighboring farmers competed for resources, including water and farmland. Such competition and food storage birthed the concept of property; this in turn led to conflict over who controlled it. Living in close proximity to other humans, farm animals, and human and animal waste exposed our Holocene ancestors to new diseases—TB, syphilis, and nonspecific bone infections, to name a few—and polluted their water sources. Heavy dependence on a diet of grains changed facial morphology—smaller jaws meant malocclusions of teeth and infections that created serious health threats.

In fact, the agricultural, or Neolithic, revolution represents not inevitable, inexorable progress so much as a comprehensive reorganization of economic and social relations along more hierarchical and stratified lines, for good and for bad, mostly for bad. Especially for women. Simply put, a shift toward growing crops intensively for subsistence and later for profit changed *everything* between the sexes. Three linked beliefs—that a woman is a man's property; that a woman's place is in the home; and that women especially ought to be more "naturally" monogamous—are seeds that were planted in our early harvests. Stranger still, a woman's most personal decisions were transformed into a matter of public concern and her sexual autonomy subjected to social control and legislation, owing to the ox and the horse.

"BE ENVELOPED IN SEX FOR ME"

Farming made women more sedentary and easier to control than your average ranging, roaming female forager, who was likely to spend a good part of several days per week far from her husband or partner. In a more subtle but no less effective shift from female autonomy, being less active on the farm increased a woman's fat stores and jacked up her fertility, which in turn shortened inter-birth intervals. This meant having more children more quickly and even more dependence on men for subsistence for oneself and one's now more numerous dependent offspring.

Crucially, patterns of residence and social configurations also changed in the transition to agriculture. There is growing consensus among anthropologists that we evolved not as monogamous dyads but as cooperative breeders. In this way of life, loose bands of men and women raised young collectively, and very likely mated with multiple partners as well. Such an arrangement conferred many benefits. Multiple mating established and continually reinforced social bonds, so there were low levels of conflict. Enhanced cooperation meant all were more likely to look after one another and their young, thus improving each individual's reproductive fitness (the odds that their offspring would go on to produce offspring). There's ample supporting evidence of this theory among present-day hunter-gatherers and foragers, many of whom raise their young cooperatively and whose mating patterns are less strictly monogamous than our own, as well as in historical documents about aboriginal peoples everywhere from North America to the South Pacific. But it runs contrary to our cherished, 1950s-inflected notion that "early man" hunted, supplying meat for his female partner, who waited for him in the cave with their baby, whom they raised in what anthropologists call a "biparental, monogamous pair bond." Nonetheless, there is now consensus that a very different social strategy—coalitions of cooperating females, and of cooperating males and females—was favored by natural selection and characterized early *Homo* life history. Indeed, cooperative breeding may well explain, at least in part, why *Homo sapiens* flourished while earlier hominins bit the dust. What better way to survive and thrive than to have one another's backs? As Saint Louis University associate professor of anthropology Katherine C. MacKinnon told me, "We had predators. And we didn't have claws or long, sharp teeth. But we had each other. Social cooperation, including cooperative breeding, was a social and reproductive strategy that served us well."

Evidence also suggests that our early hominin ancestors, like so many contemporary hunter-gatherers who give us a window into how we likely lived in the Pleistocene, often lived matrilocally, meaning each female stayed with her kin for life. Thus highly invested relatives and other "alloparents," or helpers, who had known her since birth were there to look out for her interests, including helping to provision and safeguard both her and her offspring. Under such conditions, females contributed mightily to subsistence, had strong social support, and were relatively unconstrained by the exigencies of rearing young—others held, provisioned, and even nursed her offspring. Female autonomy was a given.

Such living practices continued among indigenous people in many contexts worldwide, giving women a measure of social and sexual autonomy that both bewildered and scandalized European settlers who stumbled upon them. Captain Samuel Wallis, who traveled to Tahiti in 1767, was agog at the beautiful women and even more shocked that "their virtue was not proof against the nail." Fascinated by the iron objects the Europeans brought with them, and accustomed to forging social bonds with sex, Tahitian women indulged with the sailors so frequently that soon Wallis's entire crew was sleeping on the boat's deck at night: they had traded all the nails from which to hang their hammocks for sexual favors. Two years later, James Cook was scandalized by the sight of Tahitians going at it in broad daylight, with neither the sense of decorum nor concerns about privacy he himself felt. The older Tahitian women apparently called out good-humored and salty instructions to a young girl who was having sex with a young man in full view of Cook's crew and an assembly of Tahitians; Cook noted, with considerable shock, that she hardly seemed to need their advice. What is clear is that, in stark contrast to Cook's own expectations, in Tahiti sex had implications for the group and was in this sense everyone's "business" to view and comment on. Nearly a century and a half earlier, in 1623, a Recollect friar (their order was later known as Franciscan), Brother Gabriel Sagard, spent some time among the Wyandot (or Wendat), Iroquois speakers who lived along Lake Huron in matrilineal, matrilocal clans. The Wyandot depended on maize cultivation, hunting, fishing, and gathering for subsistence. Women tended to the crops and were in charge of the longhouses, where groups of several families linked through the female line lived together. At one point, Sagard witnessed a traditional Wyandot healing ceremony that drew on the culture's most potent medicine: sex. He wrote:

> There are also assemblies of all the girls in a town at a sick woman's couch, either at her request according to . . . [a vision] or dream she may have had, or by order of the Oki [shaman] for her health and recovery. When the girls are thus assembled they are all asked, one after another, which of the young men of the town they would like to sleep with them the next night. Each names one, and these are immediately notified by the masters of the ceremony and all come in the evening to sleep with those who have chosen them, in the presence of the sick woman, from one end of the lodge to the other, and they pass the whole night thus, while the two chiefs at the two ends of the house sing and rattle their tortoise-shells from evening till the following morning, when the ceremony is concluded.

"Sleep" is here a euphemism. The ceremony is called the *endakwandet,* which translates as "to be enveloped in sex for me." The healing aspects of the ceremony were thought to derive from female desire, which in this cosmology was not only not to be controlled; its expression was literally lifesaving. In fact, Wyandot sex practices were basically driven by Wyandot women, who had a remarkable-seeming-to-us degree of sexual self-determination:

> The Huron considered premarital sexual relations to be perfectly normal and engaged in them soon after puberty...Girls were as active as men in initiating these liasons [*sic*]...Young men were required to recognize the right of a girl to decide which of her lovers she preferred at any one time. Sometimes, a young man and woman developed a longstanding, but informal, sexual relationship. This did not prevent either partner from having sexual relations with other friends.

Trial marriages were another aspect of indigenous life in the Americas before the arrival of Europeans (and are also typical in many present-day hunter-gatherer societies). A young woman was free to test-run a potential husband for several nights—a young Wyandot man "proposed" by presenting her with a beaver robe or a necklace of wampum—and then she would decide whether she wanted to commit or not. Either way, she got to keep the stuff. Such exchanges, like sex itself, created social adhesion and give us a clue to a worldview in which a woman had the power to choose, change her mind, and choose again. And again. Men served at their pleasure. Jesuit missionaries wrote with astonishment and sometimes horror of the agency of Wyandot women and could not wrap their minds around the fact that Wyandot parents were particularly overjoyed upon the birth of a girl. Later, missionaries sought to suppress the customs of premarital sex, trial marriages, and the *endakwandet*, but this was not easy to do; as the Wyandot were matrilineal and matrilocal, their egalitarian notions about women and the power of female sexuality and female choice were deeply rooted. Only the Indian Act of 1876, with its comprehensive imposition of European beliefs and social organization, could extinguish it, by changing underlying patterns of residence and of clan inheritance.

The pre-contact Wyandot and Tahitians were no noble savages, and their lifestyle was not some exemplary Eden. In an ecology that favored hunting and gathering, in a context where women were primary producers, cooperative breeding was in fact efficacious, and being generous—with one's food, capacity for child-rearing, and sexuality—was in everyone's individual best interest. Selflessness was, in a sense, selfish as it went the distance to ensure group cohesion, safety, and a degree of security, social and child support, and ease that present-day mothers, isolated in our suburban homes or apartments with bored children, can only dream of. And a lifestyle that anthropologists tell us was characterized by radical egalitarianism and "deliberate social intensity" meant that if men attempted to be violent, coercive, or even unreasonably possessive toward women, others would be there to see and to eventually intervene. A woman in a dense kin network could also always "vote with her feet," to use anthropologist Sarah Hrdy's phrase, and simply leave a partner she no longer wanted.

In stark contrast, in cultures more intensely agrarian than the Wyandot and their aboriginal predecessors, a woman was likely to leave the support system of her own family to live with an unrelated man—her husband—and *his* kin. And live in a situation of more or less privacy with him and his kin network. Today, nearly 70 percent of agricultural and post-agricultural societies are patrilocal. Under the watchful eye of these strangers, far from the protections of parents and siblings and aunts and uncles, female sexuality was also reorganized, as women got a clear message: you'd better behave. With the notion of property in place, and in concert with these other shifts, it was a short leap in logic to the belief that women were the property of men, and that having sex with a married woman, or a married woman having sex outside her marriage, was an act of "trespass" against her husband. Isolated from their families of origin and invested alloparents, with higher fertility rates and more dependent children than their non-farming ancestors, women had every reason to conform to these beliefs and to yield to implicit and explicit rules about female propriety. And in contexts where couples broke from larger groups to live on their own, yet another layer of protection was stripped away, rendering women more dependent than ever on the goodwill and support of their male partners. Even worse, much of the time no one with her best interests in mind was there to see. Privacy cloaked male actions, freeing men of supervision and releasing them from direct accountability to a greater social unit.

Thinkers like Helen Fisher, Natalie Angier, Christopher Ryan, and Cacilda Jethá have in recent years reiterated and expanded on the idea that agriculture played a critical role in transforming female autonomy into dependence, and in undermining female self-determination through its abetting shifts in patterns of residence and patterns of production. Part of farming's legacy is that, among other things, it "gendered" us in fundamental, comprehensive, and long-lasting ways. It sexed us as well; we are no longer Wyandot.

But putting the blame on agriculture, like putting the blame on Mame, may miss a finer, even more revealing truth about the hows and whys of more or less compulsory monogamy as experienced by women like Sarah in the US today. The more nuanced reality is that under certain forms of agriculture, women did pretty well. In fact, experts tell us that where there were hoes and digging sticks, and where there was irrigated agriculture with matrilineal and matrilocal social structures in place, women were important primary producers, contributing significantly to their families' subsistence. As far back as 1928, in an essay called "The Division of Work According to Sex in African Hoe Culture," anthropologist Hermann Baumann noted, "It suffices to state that a connexion between woman and hoe culture, nay more, between that social system where the woman rules, matriarchal society, and primitive soil cultivation is universally acknowledged to exist."

In hoe agriculture worldwide, women weed, till, and aerate the soil—all crucial steps to ensuring a successful crop. And because the hoe can easily be picked up and put down, these women could keep an eye on kids who were outside pitching in at the same time. Working in concert with men and performing the essential work of *primary* production gave women clout and a meaningful say in personal, family, social, and political matters. Meanwhile, paddy agriculture required many hands, including those of women and children. As in hoe crop economies, what women did mattered, and they did it outdoors. In both paddy and hoe fields, female labor was critical to the well-being of the entire group, and a woman's social status mirrored her indispensable contributions. Without her, no one would eat.

Economists and sociologists tell us that the agriculture practices that prevailed in a given area had a long tail. In some parts of Southeast Asia where women played such a vital part in the agricultural economy, they also retained the advantages of matrilineal inheritance and matrilocal living, or "female philopatry"—another way of saying they stayed with their families of origin in the place where they were born. It also meant men basically had to "audition" their way into a marriage and then live surrounded by a wife's kin, so that checks against power imbalances and male control of and violence toward women were built into the society at the most basic level. Rae Blumberg, chair of sociology at the University of Virginia, has written extensively on different types of agriculture and female fates. She tells us that in places where women's ancestors worked in rice paddies, including parts of Indonesia, Malaysia, Myanmar, Cambodia, Laos, and Thailand, they continue to have a meaningful measure of power and self-determination.

> [In these places] women are included...in the labor force, and women control at least some economic resources, such as income, credit, land, and/or other inheritance. Southeast Asian women long have been entrepreneurs and own-account market traders. This

gave them economic power over and above what they acquired through inheritance via the generally woman-friendly kinship/property system.

In contrast, where there was irrigated agriculture with *male* philopatry—that is, where men stayed with their families of origin and women moved to them—women did not fare so well. For example, in East Asia—including northern China, Japan, South Korea, and Taiwan—and in many areas of Pakistan, India, and Bangladesh in South Asia, with their male-dominated kinship and property systems, women tended and tend to toil as unpaid family labor. And since local markets in these places were male-dominated like inheritance, it was and still is difficult for women to earn by their own-account trade.

But nowhere, it seems, are conditions more dire for women than where *plough* agriculture prevails. Or prevailed. Wherever there was plough use for intensive agriculture, the fate of women took a turn for the disempowered, even abject. They became uniquely dependent, their autonomy comprehensively undermined, circumscribed, and in many cases even extinguished by a rudimentary piece of equipment and the host of social changes it ushered in.

LINKED FATES: WOMEN AND BEASTS OF BURDEN

Oxen-powered ploughs may have been used as early as the sixth millennium BC by Mesopotamians in the Fertile Crescent region. Use of smaller ploughs began as early as two thousand years before. Later, Egyptians and then the Romans and Greeks also used domesticated mules to pull heavier, larger ploughs. Unlike implements of what Danish economist Ester Boserup called "shifting cultivation"—digging sticks and hoes—the plough required significant grip strength, and enough upper and overall body strength to push/pull the plough, or to control the draft animal dragging it.

Anthropologist Agustín Fuentes tells us that one study of forty-six different meta-analyses shows that among the differences between the sexes that we tend to think of as "essential," there are only a very few that hold across cultures. !Kung boys focus on tasks as well as !Kung girls. Girls in three Middle Eastern countries—Jordan, Qatar, and the United Arab Emirates—outpace boys in math. But worldwide, men have greater grip strength, throwing velocity, and throwing strength than women. For these reasons men suddenly had and continue to have a physical advantage in plough-farming settings. In addition to requiring upper body strength, ploughing activity, which also introduced the unpredictability and relative danger of large animals, was incompatible with childcare. These two aspects of plough farming led to a new and rigidly gendered division of labor: men outside doing the farming; women specializing in secondary production, including childcare and food preparation inside the home. This distinction—outdoor/primary production versus indoor/domestic/secondary production—in turn gave rise to beliefs about the "natural role of women," including that they *should* be "inside the home," that mothers were "just naturally" primary parents, and that a woman's labor was less vital to subsistence and income than a man's.

In newly stratified settings where women were no longer primary producers, their fortunes were literally reversed. Now, instead of paying bride wealth—an amount exchanged for the privilege of marrying someone's daughter—men could demand dowries, and parents were obliged to pay others to take their daughters away and make them their wives. In some cultures, having girls became so "costly" that families began to practice female infanticide. In other places, parents gave their daughters away as concubines or secondary wives—the best they could hope for. A preoccupation with virginity also arose with use of the plough and the gendered division of labor that put women below men. Anthropologist Shere Ortner has observed that female chastity literally has a monetary value in some highly stratified societies where a low-ranking family's only strategy to move up may be a daughter's marriage into a higher-ranking family. And so "enforcement of virginity...becomes a family affair guarded violently by men and mythopoetically by women," Natalie Angier notes. If women were no longer primary producers, their secondary value had to be rigorously policed. And it was, in ways at once creative and comprehensive, by men and not infrequently by women themselves.

According to Stephanie Coontz, the work of the plough's gender hierarchy and stratification was soon abetted by female ornamentation. Initially in the Middle East and then worldwide in plough contexts, heavy jewelry, restrictive, elaborately decorative clothing, and long fingernails all communicated that a women did not work—it would be impossible to—and by extension, that her husband was wealthy and successful. And, not coincidentally, that women were not free. In this sense, the woman's decorativeness, ostensibly a "celebration" of this new version of femininity, also functioned as a figurative sequestering. In some areas, there was literal sequestering as well. Separation of the sexes, a widespread practice in the Middle East by 2000 BC, kept women out of public view and allowed high-ranking men to demonstrate to the world that they were so rich their wives and daughters not only didn't have to work; they didn't even need to leave the house. This, like their ornamentation, was an explicit demonstration of their surplus value and shored up the idea that they were property rather than people or producers, costly objects to maintain by men wealthy and powerful enough to do so. Conveniently and not coincidentally, literal containment and separation from men—as in a *zenana,* or "women's quarters," of a household, inner areas where no men were allowed—was also a way to ensure women could not stray sexually. *Beware,* everything from laws, moral beliefs, and literature now suggested to men, "lest the seeds of others be sown on your soil."

If that happened, if women were wayward, progeniture might be muddled in ways that mattered as never before: fathers might bequeath wealth, land, and power itself to sons not their own. Female monogamy—coerced, enforced, mythologized, celebrated, institutionalized, legislated—became the bedrock without which this new version of society, in which resources were passed down from patriarch to patriarch, would crumble.

Counting on women to be true became the highest-stakes gamble man has ever known.

JEZEBEL(S)

The story of Jezebel epitomizes how preoccupations with progeniture, female ambition, and female sexual autonomy were gradually mapped together in the tradition of Western thought and religion. As Lesley Hazleton has suggested in her masterful biography, Jezebel is a tissue of representations over time as much as she is an historical personage. Old Testament "editors" revisited that text repeatedly over centuries, and part of what emerged was the larger story of female fates, in the form of the story of one queen, the wife of Ahab and mortal enemy of Elijah.

A Phoenician princess who worshipped Baal, Jezebel is portrayed in the Old Testament's Book of Kings as a crafty, cunning, and power-hungry beauty. Her love of ornamentation—she is often represented looking coyly into a mirror, the original selfie-snapping Kim Kardashian—was only equaled, legend goes, by her craving for influence. Specifically, she wanted to convert her husband Ahab's people—northern Israelites and disciplines of Yahweh—to her own religion. She was allegedly ruthless in her pursuit of this goal, "destroying" as much of Yahwism as she could (the language, Hazleton points out, is vague, and even in the most negative rewritings, Jezebel is never accused of killing Yahweh's prophets or worshippers). Another critical detail of the Kings version of Jezebel: when Naboth, owner of an exquisitely beautiful vineyard, refused to sell it to Ahab, putting Jezebel's husband into a profound funk, she falsely accused the reluctant vintner of blasphemy out of spite. He was stoned to death. Having made so many enemies and earned the righteous wrath of Yahweh, once Ahab died and she was no longer under the protection of a powerful man, Jezebel's days were numbered. For a time, Jezebel ensured that her older son ruled, but he was pushed off a balcony in an "accident" that was convenient for Jezebel's enemies, to say the least. She quickly installed her younger son, but he was killed as well. According to legend, on the last day of her life, knowing she was to be killed, Jezebel applied full makeup, donned an elaborate wig, and dressed in her finest clothing. What may have been an attempt to appear queenly and noble was read by history as a ploy to seduce her murderer, Jehu.

> Now when Jehu had come…Jezebel heard of it; and she put paint on her eyes and adorned her head, and looked through a window…
>
> And he looked up at the window, and said, "Who is on my side? Who?" So two or three eunuchs looked out at him. Then he said, "Throw her down." So they threw her down, and some of her blood spattered on the wall and on the horses; and he trampled her underfoot. And when he had gone in, he ate and drank. Then he said, "Go now, see to this accursed woman, and bury her, for she was a king's daughter." So they went to bury her, but they found no more of her than the skull and the feet and the palms of her hands. Therefore they came back and told him. And he said, "This is the word of the Lord, which He spoke by His servant Elijah the Tishbite, saying, 'On the plot of ground at Jezreel dogs shall eat the flesh of Jezebel and the corpse of Jezebel shall be as refuse on the surface of the field, in the plot at Jezreel, so that they shall not say, "Here lies Jezebel."'"

Such a spectacularly humiliating fall, capped by the assertion that "they shall not say, 'Here lies Jezebel,'" was necessary in a text like the Old Testament, which was at pains to undo the legitimacy of previous religions and social arrangements. A certain amount of overkill was required to thoroughly void the authority of the prior world order, one embodied by a woman with power who attempted to backseat drive a patriline and who worshipped the old, established way. Baal was a god of the earth and of fertility, likely based at least in part on earlier fertility goddesses. And in Jezebel's native Phoenicia, royal women were commonly high priestesses with active roles in temple and palace relations. Jezebel represented not just the old ways but a pre-plough version of ultimate female power. Jezebel was also, by many accounts, a cosmopolitan and pragmatic polytheist, like many Phoenicians of her time and economic class, and believed that religious tolerance was important and efficacious. For the more fundamentalist prophets of Yahweh, in contrast, there was only one male God; he and his proselytizers would tolerate no others. As the story is written and rewritten in the age of the plough, there are repeated metaphors of adultery and out-of-control female desire to describe the worship of any other than the One God, who was represented as the rightful Husband of a wayward Bride Israel. When she "cheats" with other gods, she is denounced for adultery. In the words of Jeremiah, enraged about idol worship: "Have you seen what unfaithful Israel had done? She committed adultery with lumps of stone, and pieces of wood" (Jeremiah 3:2). Isaiah, Hosea, and Ezekiel similarly assert that Israelites have become "seed of an adulteress and a harlot." Israel is compared to a she camel running around in heat; Judea is "infatuated by profligates with penises as big as those of donkeys, ejaculating as violently as stallions." Yahweh is the jealous husband of a wife who is habitually untrue:

> *Let her rid her face of her whoring,*
> *And her breasts of her adultery*
> *Or else I will strip her naked*
> *expose her as on the day she was born...*
> *I mean to make her pay for all the days*
> *when she burnt offerings to the Baals*
> *and decked herself in rings and necklaces*

to court her lovers,
forgetting me...
She will call me "my husband"...
I will take the names of the Baals off her lips.
—Hosea 2:2–3, 2:13, 2:16–17

"Say my name," says this One God to the woman in his bed. And what if she will not? The price of infidelity is death. In the words of Ezekiel: "They will uncover you, take your jewels, and leave you completely naked...You will be stoned and run through with a sword...I will put an end to your whoring. No more paid lovers for you. I will exhaust my fury against you" (Ezekiel 16:39).

As against Jezebel.

Our contemporary use of the term "jezebel" to mean "an impudent, shameless, or morally unrestrained woman" demonstrates not just our indebtedness to the notion that monogamy is a sacred covenant that flourished in religious soils tilled by the plough. It also shows the fates of women who upset the order of things—religious, dynastic, political—in settings where agriculture was doing its earthly and conceptual work. Debased like Jezebel, women who do not toe the line will share her legacy: their grandest, most ambitious acts will be associated with and reduced to unseemly sexual appetites. It is telling that Jezebel's punishment for her assertion of power resulted not only in her death but in the defilement of her reputation and hence her authority: her very name came to be associated with prostitution (in which a woman is for sale) and false prophesy (in which a woman cannot be trusted). Her story dramatizes how, once anxieties about inheritance and paternity took hold in plough-centric contexts, authoritarian versions of possessive husbands were deified, and deities began to draw their conceptual power from what husbands felt compelled and emboldened by a newish world order to be. Female autonomy became ever more linked to cultural disorder and ever more perilous for its individual practitioners.

Jezebel's story and its subsequent rewritings are just one example of how female power was increasingly linked with sexuality and with deception. If women could trick men, men would expose their cheating and their supposed essential duplicity for all the world to see, sometimes literally. This prerogative was one harvested through the work of the plough. In ancient Greece, where the most widely cultivated crop was wheat—the most plough-positive of all crops—adultery was considered a serious crime, with repercussions at the level of couple, family, and the state. The man committing adultery with a married female citizen could be murdered on the spot, with a likely reprieve for his killer; the wife was immediately and automatically divorced. Interestingly, from 470 BC onward, the price for interfering with the transport of grain was also death. Just as meddling with the distribution of grain could lead to famine, a woman's adultery could result in illegitimate children, the thinking went, and only legitimate children were allowed to become Athenian citizens. Thus it was an offense with social consequences for married female citizens and men other than their husbands to have sex. This meant the transgression had to be "aired" in public, at once atoned for and displayed to the adulterers and the world at large as a matter of concern to all, and the site of rightful intervention. According to Aristotle, adulteresses in the Peloponnese were required to stand in a transparent tunic without a belt in the town's center for eleven days. This was an explicit assertion that what these women had tried to claim as their own—their naked bodies and sexuality—literally belonged to all who looked. In other areas, adulteresses were paraded around on a donkey with their lovers in a humiliating public display that made it clear that when it came to married women and sex, there was no zone of privacy, no act of self-determination that was not linked to the larger world and its power to determine her fate. As she sowed, so would she reap.

These fates were less terrifying than that of the adulterous, vengeful, and ambitiously unsympathetic Clytemnestra as told by

Aeschylus in *The Oresteia,* the 458 BC tragedy and cautionary tale. Clytemnestra repartnered over the course of her husband Agamemnon's long absence during the Trojan War, rendering her the polar opposite of the faithful, monogamous, and good wife of Odysseus, Penelope. Clytemnestra was enraged that Agamemnon had sacrificed their daughter Iphigenia to the gods on his battleship in a bid for favorable winds. During his long absence, the text implies, she took solace in her power to rule Argos, and in sex with her illegitimate "husband" Aegisthus. Again, she was no Penelope, who held her ardent suitors at bay by weaving and unweaving at her loom for years. Upon Agamemnon's return with his lover Cassandra, who crouched and lowed outside, knowing what was to come, Clytemnestra purred her welcome, drew a bath for her husband—and proceeded to ax or stab him to death. But rather than being protected by the ages-old rule of cyclical justice represented by the Furies, who sided with Clytemnestra because she was avenging the murder of her child, she was murdered by her own son, Orestes, at the urging of Apollo. Apollo then successfully argued his case against the Furies, absolving his client of the crime he had committed in Athenian court. There could be no more literal enactment of a new world order that did not tolerate women taking matters— whether sexual or legal—into their own hands. Female power and female privileges like those Clytemnestra represented were extinguished in a number of ways, including through the work of texts like *The Oresteia,* which flourished in the cultural soil tilled by plough use, enriching it in return. In this emerging new masculinist Order of Things, the death of a girl by her father's hand not only isn't a crime; it's a *right.*

Ancient Romans, notorious for their sexual excess, were more likely to consider adultery a basically private matter to be resolved within the home rather than the courts. It was a personal rather than a criminal offense. During the reign of Augustus, however, new moral codes were implemented, including one that permitted the paterfamilias to put both adulterous parties to death. It is no coincidence that during this period, Virgil composed his *Georgics,* a paean to agriculture and farming life, reciting it to Augustus around 30 BC. Nor is it insignificant that the Roman way of life was often symbolized by a loaf of bread—wheat was a plough crop and a household staple. Against this backdrop and Augustus's consolidation of power as he transitioned Rome from a republic to an empire with himself at the head, Augustus had his own daughter, Julia—vivacious, witty, and later the maternal grandmother of Caligula—exiled to a remote island of Campania for her many affairs, conducted openly while she was married to Tiberius. When asked why all her children resembled their father, she had famously quipped that she only took on new passengers when the boat was already loaded—that is, when she knew she was already pregnant by her husband. Noble though she may have been, in the reorganization of Rome under her father her own libido became a site of social control, and her deceptions and autonomy her undoing. Augustus called his intelligent daughter, beloved by the Romans for her generosity, "a disease in my flesh." Later, when Tiberius succeeded Julia's father as emperor, he withheld her allowance, and she died of malnutrition at age fifty-three in AD 14, the same year Augustus passed away, almost as if her fate, like Iphigenia's, could not be unlinked from her father's. In a context where female sexual autonomy was associated with lawlessness and potential chaos, even royal standing could not protect a woman from the consequences of alienating powerful men with her independent actions, now infidelities. Julia's exile was presumably a powerful lesson for other women: do not, in the words of Natalie Angier, behave in ways that risk "the investment and tolerance of men and the greater male coalition."

FARMERS' DAUGHTERS

What does any of this have to do with women today? Everything, it turns out. In a uniquely comprehensive analysis published in 2013, a group of Harvard and UCLA economists established that the plough has had as great an impact on our beliefs about men and women and about female self-determination as it did on the soil it tilled so efficiently. Where there is or has been plough agriculture, the effects are deep and wide-ranging: these societies have markedly lower levels of female participation in politics and the labor force, and they rank high on the embrace of markedly gender-biased attitudes. Perhaps most remarkably, the researchers discovered that even generations later and thousands of miles away, in utterly changed ecologies and regardless of religion, income, and intervening progress—medical improvements, economic development, technological change, and the production structure of an economy—we continue to reap attitudes sown by historical use of the plough.

The study's authors complied data from the Ethnographic Atlas, a worldwide database that contains information on 1,256 ethnic groups; the World Bank's World Development Indicators (2012) and Enterprise Surveys (2005–2011) for information on female labor force participation and female entrepreneurship; and the UN's Women's Indicators and Statistics Database (2000) for statistics on the proportion of women in seats in national governments. They also turned to the World Values Survey, a compilation of national surveys on attitudes, beliefs, and preferences, including beliefs about the role of women based on two statements: "When jobs are scarce, men should have more right to a job than women" and "On the whole, men make better political leaders than women do."

In areas where there were or had been ploughs and dependence on plough-positive crops—including barley, wheat, teff, and rye—respondents overwhelmingly agreed with the statements about men being more deserving of jobs and better suited to political leadership. And their agreement mattered. There were fewer female entrepreneurs, fewer women in politics, and fewer women with jobs. Remarkably, though, this wasn't just in places where the plough was currently or had recently been in use. Or places where it had been used at all. By studying the responses of the children of immigrants worldwide, the researchers were able to document the remarkable persistence of these beliefs and biases as well as their "spread." Even having a *heritage* of traditional plough agriculture predicts more comprehensive gender-biased attitudes and fewer women working outside the home. When the heritage is from both the mother's and the father's side, the impact is even stronger. If a woman's *husband's* ancestors were from a plough culture, that will also negatively impact her participation in politics and the workforce.

But how can the plough's influence still be felt in cities as modern as New York, Beijing, Tokyo, and London, places where farmers' markets are as close as we get to our (albeit recent) intensive agrarian roots? The study's authors point out that norms persist after the economy moves out of or beyond plough agriculture in part because these biases—"A woman's place is in the home" among them—are reinforced not only by individuals who learn from their parents and grandparents but also by a given society's policies, laws, and institutions. The authors also suggest that countries where people believe a woman belongs in the kitchen tend to have legislation and practices that uphold unequal property rights, asymmetrical voting rights, and scanty parental leave policies, even as attitudes about equality begin to change for the better. In that "lag," women continue to live their lives as second-class citizens in spite of surface ideologies of parity and equal opportunity. These societies may also create industrial structures that mirror their beliefs, specializing in the production of capital or brawn-intensive industries that shore up notions about gender inequality and reinforce the belief that women are fundamentally linked to the domestic sphere ("Women can't lift those heavy boxes or operate that machinery like men can!"). Finally, plough-culture beliefs about the role and "natural place" of women are inherently "sticky," the study authors observe—they persist because it's faster and easier to act on them than it is to evaluate every situation and decision based on, for example, an individual's personality, merit, or qualification. It's much more efficient to simply decide, informed by beliefs already in place, "Women aren't good at X."

The study controlled for dozens of other potentially determining factors: What if already-sexist cultures chose the plough? Does religion have as great an effect as the plough? And so on. But a thorough regression analysis led them to rule out these other potential factors and to conclude that, in fact, it was the plough itself that did women in, by *creating* conditions of female oppression. Further proof: the researchers found that anywhere in the world that was a better environment for growing plough-negative crops, such as maize, sorghum, tree crops, and root crops, today has more equality of gender roles and attitudes, as well as increased female social and labor force participation.

How free and enlightened are *we*? Not so much. It may not surprise us to learn that, during World War I, the British and US governments had a second war on their hands, on the domestic front, when they formed the Women's Land Army in an attempt to replace male farmworkers who had enlisted to fight overseas with women. There were angry denunciations in opinion columns and among farmers, economists, and everyday citizens. In spite of the desperate need for agriculture workers, crops that needed tending if the nations were to be fed, and thousands of women ready and able to do the job, public outrage was pronounced and difficult to turn. It seemed that, given the heritage of plough agrarianism, many would rather see food wither and spoil and risk starvation than see women crossing the line from home to field. A public education (read propaganda) campaign was quickly undertaken, based on the primary objection of farmers who turned eager female workers away: they were wearing pants. Thousands of US and

British government pamphlets and posters were put into production; they showed women *in skirts and dresses* ploughing fields, with messages beneath such as "God Speed the Plough and the Woman Who Drives It" and "Get Behind the Girl He Left Behind Him," with the ghostly outline of a soldier behind a woman standing in a field (she was wearing trousers, but perhaps as a concession to male outrage, she was yielding a "womanly" hoe, rather than "manning" a plough). After the world wars, a genre of jokes about "farmers' daughters" flourished. The farmer's daughter as a stock character was dumb and sexy. But she was less dumb than she looked when it came to sex; in fact, she was often "promiscuous," indulging with traveling salesmen and others who visited the farm. The conceptual punch line of the farmer's daughter joke as a category is always that when it comes to farm work, a woman's place is on her back. And that women are for reproduction and recreation, not production. They are also sexually bold and indiscriminate, and so in need of precisely the kind of controls that agriculture allowed men to exercise over women. Let them out of your sight, the jokes imply, and they will confound paternity faster than you can say "Daisy Dukes" or "Elly May Clampett." Gendered hierarchy and paranoid laughs courtesy of the plough.

We might tut-tut previous generations' deep and irrational investment in the cultural logic of the plough and presume that we are beyond such biases and jokes, but even now it continues to impact our day-to-day lives in remarkable ways. The US, though slightly above average, lags when it comes to gender parity. For example, as recently as 2000, we ranked 47th of the 181 countries for which information on female labor force participation was available. In the same year, women held a startlingly low 13 percent of political positions—ranking us a lackluster 50th out of 156 countries for which there was data. The Harvard and UCLA study authors note that these statistics "appear even less equal when we factor in the high per capita income of Western nations." *Plus ça change:* the International Labour Organization tells us that by

2017, the rank of US women in the workforce tumbled to 76th out of 180 countries; and for political participation, we earned an unimpressive rank of 100th out of 193 (though a record number of women registered to run for office in the 2018 midterms). In another study, this one compiled by Save the Children to commemorate International Day of the Girl in 2016, the US, the world's largest economy, ranked below Kazakhstan and Algeria for gender equality due to a low representation of women in political office, among other factors. (These included high teen pregnancy rates and a high rate of maternal deaths—14 per 100,000 in the US in 2015. Black women are three to four times as likely to die from pregnancy-related causes as white women.)

Such soil yields crops that are eerie, familiar repetitions. Slanderous mischaracterizations, remarkably vitriolic verbal attacks, and threats of physical harm against Hillary Clinton—all harkening to the spectacularly choreographed public containments and punishments of Jezebel—turned the tide against a woman reaching for the ultimate golden ring. She and all of us learned a lesson about incurring the wrath of the greater male coalition, including that masculine privilege is often mercilessly enforced by other women in settings where it is a better strategy to align oneself with those who have so long been victors. Fifty-two or -three percent of white female voters saw it thus in 2016.

As to sexual liberation per se, in spite of all the progress of second-wave feminism and the cultural inroads made by inspiring anthems by icons like Beyoncé and Janelle Monáe, and forthright sex-ed pieces on TeenVogue.com by Gigi Engle that make important information available to women while they make the Right cringe, and the current wave of women in sex tech led by amazons like Bryony Cole, and the trendy yet arguably subversive interest in polyamory among millennials who refuse to buy into mainstream gender binaries and roles, when it comes to sex, women remain, in some sense, fucked. As the authors of the Harvard-UCLA plough study put it succinctly, "Part of the importance of the plough arises through its impact on internal beliefs and values." We live the plough's unforgiving legacy every day, an inheritance that, for many of us, has come to feel logical or natural. It is not. Not only is the plough to thank or to blame for our monthly menstrual cycle; in our evolutionary prehistory, anthropologist Beverly Strassmann has found, our fat levels were lower from the constant effort of gathering, and so our cycle was more of a quarterly event. But our understanding that we "belong" to one man at a time if we are heterosexual women, or one person at a time if we are not, is something else we can pin on the plough. So are everyday realities like women being raised to sit with our legs crossed—what is between them is not ours to advertise or act upon, any more than outdoor space is our legacy or right to take up or even inhabit.

What looks like propriety is, from another angle, a culturally specific form of social censure, a lesson relentlessly and falsely imparted as "etiquette." "Some girls sit like this," other girls told me when I was an adolescent, placing their second and third fingers together tightly. "And some girls sit like this"—here they crossed their fingers. "But girls who sit like this"—they separated their second and third fingers wide—"get this"—their third finger held up in the air, obscene—"like this!"—here they snapped their fingers quickly. They were speaking the language of the plough. So are the guys who man-spread aggressively on the subway or public bus. This can feel like an assault against our personal space and our very right to be there, because it is. If we fail to remember that the legacy of the plough is that we stay inside, or minimize ourselves when out, there are always the containment strategies of street and workplace harassment, frotteurism on the subways and buses, and sexual assault. In 2012, the World Health Organization reported that among the main risk factors for a woman experiencing sexual violence, either by an intimate partner or a stranger, were living in a culture with attitudes of gender inequality and sexual purity; having or being suspected of having multiple partners; and the prevalence of ideologies of male sexual entitlement—that is, beliefs that men are "naturally" and by right more sexual than women, that they have more of a right to be out and about, and that women should stay home. If not, they will by rights be brought back into line. Beliefs of the plough.

When I was a young girl in Grand Rapids, Michigan, we played a game in our backyards and on the school playground as we sang a song called "The Farmer in the Dell." We stood, a whole big group of us, holding hands in a circle, with one boy in the middle. "The farmer in the dell, the farmer in the dell, hi-ho the derry-o the farmer in the dell," we sang at him. Then, as we sang, "The farmer takes a wife, the farmer takes a wife," the boy who had been transformed into the farmer in the dell chose a girl to stand in the middle of the circle with him. She was thus transformed into the wife. Next we sang, "The wife takes a child, the wife takes a child," and another of us was chosen. The child took a nurse. The nurse took a cow. The cow took a dog. The dog took a cat. The cat took a rat. And so on. Soon, several children stood within the diminished circle. The group inside might look like a collective, but it was clear that the farmer and his wife and the child were its conceptual center. We ourselves, the players, had been reorganized along the lines of a song, one about a farm, about agriculture. As we played this game, we rehearsed and repeated the social reorganization of our ancestors and the birth of the peculiar and novel family form that we lived in—pair-bonded, presumably monogamous parents and their offspring alone together. We reinforced for ourselves its naturalness, its righteousness, its normativity, every time we recited the words and acted them out. It was child's play, literally, and it was an education. It is a measure of the power of the plough that every single one of us longed to be chosen, to stand within the warmth of the circle. The boys wanted to be the farmer. The girls wanted to be the farmer's wife, the child, the pet, even the vermin, because we were all, in some deep sense, farmers' daughters.

VAGINAS: EVERYTHING OLD IS NEW AGAIN

Grown-ups also practice rituals that reveal truths about the culture we live in. In a number of privileged metropolitan niches, including the Upper East Side of Manhattan, where I lived, sent my children to school, and studied rites of femininity and motherhood for several years, there is a growing fixation on retrofitted virginity, the ultimate accessory in a culture that at once overtly objectifies women and romanticizes mothers. Self-described "medi spas" have opened to serve the well-turned-out inhabitants of New York City's richest zip code and its summer migratory setting, the Hamptons. These "spas" offer what they promise is a "quick, easy" procedure to "rejuvenate" a woman's vagina. Doctors use lasers with names like FemiLift, MonaLisa Touch, IntimaLase, and, my favorite, ThermiVa (why not just call it ThermiVag?) to allegedly "improve the laxity" of the vagina because so many women are worried that after kids "they are loose 'down there,'" in the words of one *soi-disant* vaginal rejuvenator MD. This procedure is distinct from labiaplasty, which promises—in the age of Brazilian bikini waxes, in which it is all out there for every lover to see—"prettier" exterior parts. Nor is it one of the surgeries that addresses medical conditions such as uterine prolapse or incontinence. No, "rejuvenation" is about "improved sensation" and "increased tightness," often after a woman has had several children. Well might we ask, Really? And, Improved sensation for whom? In 2017, the American Congress of Obstetricians and Gynecologists reaffirmed their dim view of such procedures, describing them as "not medically indicated." Further, they warned that "the safety and effectiveness of these procedures have not been documented." They also urge doctors to tell women who request the procedures about "potential complications, including infection, altered sensation, dyspareunia, adhesions, and scarring." Dyspareunia means "painful sexual intercourse." It is extraordinary to consider that this is a risk women under certain conditions are not only willing but eager to take in order to engineer what they hope, with no guarantee, will be even more pleasurable sexual intercourse not for themselves but for their men. In 2017, at an ACOG symposium, Cheryl Iglesia, MD, said there was not enough "formal evaluation for both efficacy and safety" of numerous vaginal enhancement procedures and surgeries.

Anthropologists might marvel to learn that in one corner of the peculiar economic and social ecology of the industrialized, post-plough West, women who are no longer virgins feel compelled to re-create that condition. They are supposed to pull off something along the lines of the miracle of the immaculate conception—to be multiparas, or women who have had more than one child, with the bodies and vaginal elasticity of nulliparas, women who have never given birth. They want not to surgically replace or fortify their hymens (as some women in the Middle East feel pressured to do before their wedding nights) but to "rejuvenate" their own eroded value in an environment where women may be conditionally respected for other things—beauty, motherhood, intelligence—but are arguably ultimately objects for enhanced male pleasure. Dr. Dennis Gross, a cosmetic dermatologist on Manhattan's Upper East Side, told me that he is getting more questions regarding vaginal rejuvenation. "Patients are asking for referrals, as well as my opinion regarding the effectiveness of the procedures," he says. Gross, who lasers and Botoxes some of Manhattan's richest, most powerful residents and has a popular skincare line, is at heart a skin-cancer nerd and a stickler for research. All this vajay business, which is potentially *big* business, strikes him as "currently more fad than science. As a scientist and laser specialist in dermatology, I very much doubt the validity of claims that lasers can permanently tighten the vagina and labia...or another common claim, that they can restore lubrication," he told me. He tells his patients as much. Some may go ahead and do it anyway: surgeons and ob-gyns continue performing the procedures, saying that their female patients *insist* on them. But mightn't we ask, "What do these doctors expect?" After all, these women's requests are in line with a culture that prioritizes male sexual pleasure and male sexual privilege. Are these doctors' allegiances firmly with their patients?

What if they, like the Wyandot, revered female sexual pleasure and autonomy so highly and viewed it as so important, so precious and vital to health, and even so powerfully healing to the larger community that their first instinct were to tell a female patient that when it came to that aspect of her being, there was no risk worth taking?

And what social circumstances might lead us from the examination room of a vaginal rejuvenation clinic—with its vapid reading materials and insipidly colored walls—to a place where female pleasure takes precedence, and men are so eager to provide it to women that they dutifully attend workshops and devour magazine articles and present their genitals to doctors for procedures for which there is a scarcity of data on safety and efficacy, all in a bid to please us? In this parallel universe, women run the world, have all the money, and birth the babies that propagate the species. And a plough has never been seen.

Our vaginas are not our own. And our very language speaks to our agrarian heritage and is inextricably entwined with our sexual selves, as if to suggest there is no escape. A woman who is having sex with a man is "getting ploughed" by him. And one who wants to be in charge of her own sexual destiny, who refuses to submit to the law of the plough—that she stay home, that she be monogamous, that she be dependent—is a ho (or is she a hoe?).

We are worn down by our culture's tendency to universalize and naturalize the gender divisions of the plough, the assertion that men everywhere just logically want and have always wanted women, lots of them, who are servile and nubile and fertile and good hearth attendants. And that women everywhere logically want men who are powerful and have resources, and that more than anything we want one of them, an alpha male, of our very own. "Men Want Beauty, Women Want Money: What We Want from the

Opposite Sex," one headline typical of these stories pronounces, summarizing a study of 27,600 straight Americans, published in the "peer-reviewed academic journal *Personality and Individual Differences*," the all too familiar "news" article quotes an evolutionary psychologist who says that when it comes to mate choice, men

> maximize their genetic contribution to further generations by partnering with women possessing cues of youth and fertility, and so have evolved to find such cues attractive and important, whereas women can do this by partnering with men with resources to maximize the survival and mating prospects of their children.

The expert in question says the alleged results of the study about gendered mate preferences are "unsurprising" and "demonstrated by numerous other such studies."

In fact, there is nothing universal or timeless or natural or scientific about these retroactive projections of our current-day conundrums. What these studies elide is perhaps the most important factor of all: context. Sociologist Rae Blumberg has pointed out that it is only in this *one* type of agrarian society, and for less than 3 percent of *Homo sapiens'* history, that women have been transformed from competent, self-sufficient primary producers who make their own decisions relatively autonomously into secondary producers and costly consumers who are, in some circumstances, fundamentally dependent on men. Female chimps and bonobos, our closest relatives, never stop foraging for themselves and their offspring. Female hunter-gatherers often continue to gather while pregnant; some even nurse and gather simultaneously. Mbuti women in the Ituri rainforest and Aka women of the Central African Republic are competent net hunters, working on their own and alongside their husbands to provision their families. All these practices give important clues about our evolutionary prehistory: dependence is new. It is human females of the Anthropocene—even and perhaps especially those living in the industrialized West post-plough—whose well-being and in some cases very lives are uniquely contingent on the support of males.

Might there be real change once plough-specific circumstances are comprehensively reversed? As women continue to make critical contributions to subsistence, as they have been doing since the 1970s; as we complete the transition from farming and industry and workplaces that value physical strength to workplaces that place a premium on thought, collaboration, and innovation; as we segue from the factory and the farm to contexts like developing apps and remote workplaces and flexible work schedules—in short, when ecological circumstances are right for women to flourish as men long have, when the advantages of upper body and grip strength and all the institutions that reinforced that advantage begin to fade—then the future starts to look a lot like the long ago, pre-plough past. And we see the outlines of the possibility of a world—like Oz on the far horizon—where attempts to control women's movements, bodies, and appetites seem at once audacious, misguided, and laughably futile.

CHAPTER FIVE

BEING HIMBA

In their ancestral lands in the far north of the Kunene River region of Namibia—a country bordered by Angola above, Botswana to the east, South Africa below, and first the Namib Desert and then the Atlantic Ocean along its western edge—live the Himba. They are the region's last seminomadic people, pastoralists who grow calabash, millet, and maize but also depend on the milk and meat of the goats, sheep, and cattle they raise. The Himba live in compounds of two dozen or so people, in huts of mud and cow dung, around which they build fences of mopane wood to contain their livestock. But they move often, setting out whenever grazing conditions decline. Only an estimated 30,000 to 50,000 Himba remain in Northern Namibia and across the border in Angola, after surviving near extermination by German colonizers in the early 1900s, intermittent years of devastating drought, and the bloody Namibian revolution of the 1980s.

Relatively isolated in the remote, mostly desert environment where they eventually settled after so much upheaval, protected by the Namibian government, and proudly attached to their ancestral traditions, the Himba have managed to preserve many of their long-standing cultural practices, even as they adapt to change by allowing themselves to be photographed (sometimes for money), journeying to shop at supermarkets, and sending their children to schools. Every morning Himba women cover their skin and long plaited hair in *otjize*, a vivid orangish-red mixture of fragrant herbs, butterfat, and ochre—a naturally occurring mineral from the region's soil—that has antimicrobial properties useful in an arid climate where bathing is rarely possible, and that the Himba believe makes them beautiful. Aside from this layer of *otjize*, women leave their breasts exposed. They wear fabric or cowhide skins around their waists, don leather headdresses that vary according to their age and social status, and carry their babies on their backs in slings made of wood and animal hide. Himba women wear heavy, decorative stacked bands of copper, iron, bone, and sometimes PVC or barbed wire around their wrists. They wear similar bands stacked from their ankles to their lower shins, too, which also serve to protect them from snakebites.

Himba women generally spend their days milking and tending to goats and cattle, gardening, collecting water and firewood, cooking, and repairing and building the structures around the encampment. They are almost always in close contact with their babies; older toddlers who have been weaned and children are also somewhat dependent upon one another, playing as a group, with the older kids informally teaching and tending to the younger ones. Livestock are in many ways the center of Himba life. In the twenty-three Himba compounds the UCLA anthropologist Brooke Scelza studied in the Omuhonga Basin area, about one hundred miles from the main district town of Opuwo, women often remain at the main camp while men make excursions to remote cattle posts, where they may stay for weeks and sometimes even months at a time.

Long-term physical separation of spouses is a fact of Himba life. So is infidelity, which Scelza, like many anthropologists and sex researchers, prefers to call "extra-pair partnership," "multiple mating," or "extra-dyadic sexuality." It is not uncommon for a married Himba man to take one of his several wives with him to the cattle stations or to have a girlfriend there (unmarried men spend time at the cattle stations as well). And many of the Himba wives who stay behind in the main camp take lovers while their husbands are away. This should come as no surprise given that infidelity is a cultural universal—anthropologist Helen Fisher, who began studying it in the 1980s, told the *New York Times* in 1998, "There exists no culture in which adultery is unknown, no cultural device or code that extinguishes philandering."

While they are not unusual in that they cheat, the Himba are remarkable in their relative openness about their extra-pair involvements. Married people discuss their "affairs" more freely among themselves than we do, certainly, and also speak about them with anthropologists like Scelza, probably because there is little reason not to: the Himba are one of the rare cultures where there is not the kind of taboo against adultery that we have and might expect to be "universal." Spouses expect a degree of consideration from each other, to be sure, and there is a code that governs how lovers are to behave—"I don't like it when her boyfriend is here in the morning when I come back from being away" is the gist of what one Himba man told Scelza. As Scelza explained to me, "There's a framework, and there has to be respect." But affairs are an open secret, or perhaps more accurately a non-secret. More extraordinary still, unlike many societies where only male infidelity is tolerated, *women* too are relatively open about having affairs. Among the Himba, female infidelity is widespread, openly acknowledged, and in many ways a boon to the women who practice it. In fact, Scelza discovered that through an unapologetic embrace of female "adultery"—a practice we Americans are so accustomed to thinking of as inherently risky and even perilous for women, or as a sign that something is undeniably "wrong"—Himba women actually improve their lot in life in ways that are scientifically verifiable and statistically significant. Their world appears to be a place apart, a universe where women who cheat, and especially *mothers* who cheat, come out on top.

A cattle-rich Himba man can have several wives—and often does. Young men typically get married for the first time at the age of nineteen or twenty. But they don't always choose their own brides. Arranged unions are common—young girls may be "married off" to strengthen a strategic alliance between families, pay back a favor, or otherwise serve the interests of a girl's mother and father. (These marriages are not consummated until a girl is older, and she may grow up and divorce her first husband in such a case, Scelza explained to me.) A man can have several wives simultaneously, but a girl or woman has one husband at a time. In this way, polygyny seems asymmetrically disadvantageous for girls and women, apparently limiting their options in a way that it does not for men.

But it turns out things are more complicated than they appear. Brooke Scelza discovered that, somewhat like Alicia Walker's interviewees, Himba women and girls have a "workaround" strategy. Dr. Scelza, a petite brunette and a mother who had two toddlers at the time I interviewed her, has observant, deep-set blue-green eyes and a calm, thoughtful demeanor. She began her career studying maternal and child health in Australia, and first came to the Himba's Namibia in 2009 in search of a natural fertility population—that is, one without birth control. She initially set out to analyze how Himba mothers and their adolescent daughters interact as the girls enter their reproductive years. True to her background in evolutionary biology, Scelza has described arranged marriages among the Himba as "a form of parent-offspring conflict that daughters often lose." Love matches, on the other hand, "reflect the young woman's own choices, with her preferences coinciding with or superseding those of her parents." Over lunch at the noisy, bustling UCLA faculty cafeteria where she had agreed to meet me, Scelza became animated as she explained that the crux of her work is an exploration of precisely how these different types of matches among the Himba—those made by parents with agendas versus those made by the lovers themselves—play out over each woman's life history, and over her children's. But she's interested in this issue in the broadest sense as well. What does it matter, Scelza wants to know, whether women choose or live out the choices of others? And when they are forced to do something they don't want to do, coerced into a situation that circumvents their options, what are their options then? To put it in the parlance of anthropology, what counterstrategies are available to these young Himba women in the face of constraints? Finally, Scelza wants to know not only how Himba women make the best of a situation not of their making but what their practices might reveal about our collective evolutionary past, present, and future, as well as the role that environment and ecology play in women's sexual and reproductive choices.

To understand the Himba, what their cheating ways mean, and the important implications for the rest of us, we need to take a long and somewhat complicated detour down the road of a scientific conundrum called "female choice." It is a path strewn with assumptions, agendas, biases, fruit flies, murderous male langurs, babies with more than one father...and hope.

SEXUAL SELECTION, CHOOSY FEMALES, AND FEMALE CHOICE

The notion of "female choice" looms large in Brooke Scelza's work, aligning her with a number of other scientists—many of them women—who have over the last decades challenged their field's fundamental beliefs about female and male reproductive strategies, as well as its emphasis on supposedly universal sex differences. "Female choice" in matters of sex and reproduction has, until relatively recently, been overwhelmingly portrayed as a passive affair. This characterization began with *The Descent of Man, and Selection in Relation to Sex* (1871), wherein Charles Darwin outlined his great, important, and original theory of sexual selection, a type of natural selection that arises when individuals of one sex prefer certain characteristics in the opposite sex. He believed that females of most species, including humans, essentially "auditioned" males, passively (in relative terms to male competition) turning some down in search of the one with the biggest horns or the most symmetrical features or the highest status, presumably because he had the best to offer: sperm quality, resources, protection. Darwin introduced this idea of selecting by auditioning, which was later dubbed "intersexual choice." He believed that males, on the other hand, actively fought one another to be noticed, to put their best qualities on display and to "win," either by *being* chosen or by excluding their male rivals so a female would have no choice but to mate with them. Cue two male bighorn sheep dramatically crashing their heads together, the startling noise of the impact echoing through the mountains. Now imagine a peacock displaying his extravagantly beautiful iridescent feather train. Darwin also noted the phenomenon of masculine striving and struggling and display, all this peacocking pageantry that is today called "intra-sexual competition." That is, competing with your *own* sex because you want to vanquish your rival either physically or by getting the *other* sex to notice you and choose you over him.

Because males were performing, displaying, and being chosen, the thinking went, it was *males* who were acted on by sexual selection, their traits passed along, or not, motored by female (comparatively) passive choice. It was just a heartbeat from this view that "active" males fought or competed or assertively displayed for "passive" females to the idea that females were not only discerning but also naturally *coy*, demure, and reticent in their mating strategy compared to males:

The female...with the rarest exception...is less eager than the male...she generally requires to be courted; she is coy, and may often be seen endeavoring for a long time to escape from the male...Man is more courageous, pugnacious, and energetic…Woman seems to differ from man in mental disposition, chiefly in her greater tenderness and less selfishness.

As primatologist Sarah Hrdy observed, "To Darwin, elusiveness was as integral to female sexual identity as ardor was to that of their male pursuers." And the stakes of this distinction between male and female, ardent and elusive, active and passive, coy and eager, selfish and tender, were high. Indeed, all of civilization, Darwin and his contemporaries suggested, hung in the balance. The English gynecologist William Acton, author of the ambitious and influential *The Functions and Disorders of the Reproductive Organs in Childhood, Youth, Adult Age, and Advanced Life, Considered in the Physiological, Social, and Moral Relations* (1857), may have influenced Darwin's thinking and was another voice contributing to the culture's discourse about "inherent" female sexual restraint and even aversion to sex. Women with sex drives, asserted this well-respected thought leader of his time (who also believed that masturbation depleted life energies and contributed to illness), were exceptional:

…the majority of women (happily for them) are not very much troubled with sexual feeling of any kind. What men are habitually, women are only exceptionally…There are many females who never feel any sexual excitement whatever. Others, again, immediately after each period do become, to a limited degree, capable of experiencing it; but this capacity is often temporary, and will cease entirely till the next menstrual period. The best mothers, wives, and managers of households know little or nothing of sexual indulgences. Love of home, children, and domestic duties are the only passions they feel.

In Acton's characterization, women are at once chaste, lauded, and sentimentalized supra-sexual beings; and creatures driven by biology (their menstrual periods). But in no instance do they exercise agency in matters of their sexuality, which, after all, they do not "have," their "passion" having been rerouted into "love" of the domestic sphere. In many ways, Darwin's view of sexual selection and Acton's take on female sexuality culminated in Krafft-Ebing's apocalyptic vision of what would happen if we undid such an order of things, which he offered up in 1886: "If a woman is normally developed mentally, and well-bred, her sexual desire is small. If this were not so, the whole world would become a brothel and marriage and family impossible."

Female passivity and sexlessness is the homeostasis that keeps the world in balance.

CONTRADICTIONS AND COUNTERSTRATEGIES

But were women of the era as sexually passive as Acton, Krafft-Ebing, and Darwin suggested they "naturally" should be? Female sexuality is both a biological and a socially scripted reality; it happens at the confluence of the clitoris and culture. Certainly these mansplainers could influence women's sexual behavior by engineering social expectations with their pronouncements. And we know that, worldwide and across species, the female libido morphs to the shape and size of its container. It can be as obvious and unapologetic as the estrus swellings of a female *Papio cynocephalus*, or as muted as the interior of a menstrual hut in Mali. It can be dutifully exclusive, or matter-of-factly polyandrous. Among not a few animal species, females appear to be monogamous—but are not. We call them "socially monogamous," but DNA tests show they may be far from it, genetically speaking. Some non-human female primates are so sexually assertive that they chase and slap males to get them to copulate (see chapter six), while female Muscovy ducks may be forcefully copulated against their wills by males with long, corkscrew-shaped penises (don't worry—in a protective counterstrategy, the females evolved vaginas every bit as complex as a secret passageway, complete with hairpin turns and dead ends, to make it harder for the sperm of males they haven't chosen to get the job done). Females, like males, are flexible sexual strategists, and even in an unforgiving container, many remain sexual. Lillie Langtry, the married mistress of Edward VII, was famously deploying her sexuality to great advantage between the time of Acton's and Krafft-Ebing's pronouncement. Less fortunate women of the era may have felt victimized by their sexual desires.

Consider the twenty-four-year-old middle-class Boston wife who threatened to destabilize the belief in inherent female sexual passivity and the entire social order by speaking, even privately to her physician, about wanting and needing sex. In 1856, an unfortunately honest patient the gynecologist Dr. Horatio R. Storer called "Mrs. B." told him of her vivid dreams of sexual intercourse with men other than her husband. These adulterous visions tormented her in her sleep. And even in her day-to-day life, she confessed, speaking to a man might trip off nearly overwhelming sexual feelings, fantasies, and urges about him. Mrs. B. further confided in the doctor that, while she had remained true to her husband, she feared she might not be able to hold off temptation forever. She attributed her problems to being childless, and also to her husband's trouble maintaining an erection and so his inability to have intercourse with her daily, as had until recently been their habit. In her book *Nymphomania,* Carol Groneman notes that given the prevailing beliefs about women being asexual, Mrs. B. must have been *extremely* worried about her adulterous thoughts and what we would today call her libido in order to override the fear of censure and discuss them at all. After a physical exam, Dr. Storer reported that "her clitoris was normal-sized, her vagina slightly overheated, and her uterus somewhat enlarged." He also reported that Mrs. B. complained her clitoris always itched. When Storer touched it, he wrote, she shrieked with excitement. The shaken doctor told her that if she did not immediately undergo treatment, she would probably need to be committed to an asylum. His prescription: that she abstain from intercourse with her husband, who moved out of their home temporarily, and that her sister move in to supervise her course of treatment. Mrs. B. was forbidden to eat meat or drink brandy and directed to avoid any stimulants that "might excite her animal desire."

> The patient was ordered to replace her feather mattress and pillows with ones made of hair to limit the sensual quality of her sleep. To cool her passions, she was to take a cold sponge bath morning and night, a cold enema once a day, swab her vagina with a borax solution... [and] give up working on the novel she was writing.

Agency was the issue. A married woman needing or desiring an orgasm from a lover or even her own husband was pathological. Thus merely speaking about it would bring down a vast array of sadistic containments masquerading as cures—everything from chemical torment of one's vagina to the quashing of artistic ambition.

Such hysterical reactions to the expression of female sexual desire worked to contain and constrain Mrs. B. And other women too. The paradigm that females are sexless and decorous protectors of the hearth prevailed for decades, even in the face of intervening generations of abolitionists, suffragettes, and crusaders from Ida Wells to Margaret Sanger critiquing it with their pointed activism. And while flappers—originally a derogatory English term for prostitute—made real strides by boisterously presuming the liberties and freedoms that suffragists and others attempted to engineer through lobbying, legislation, and political protest, with the onset of the Great Depression in 1929, historians of the era tell us, these pioneering young disruptors were bludgeoned back into propriety. In fact, even working outside the home was suspect for the next decade, and women who tried might well be subjected to public censure, "taking jobs from men." Making matters still more difficult for women of color, between 1932 and 1933, 68 percent of jobs posted by the Philadelphia Employment Bureau stipulated the jobs were "white only," doubling down on the discrimination.

Women arguably didn't have an opportunity to challenge rigid gender scripting that placed them in the domestic sphere and men in the world of action and agency, reasserting an overarching vision of female passivity consistent with Darwin's, Acton's, and Krafft-Ebing's, until men were off to Europe and the South Pacific for World War II in the early 1940s. Then, with holes in the industrial labor force, American women took jobs in factories and shipyards; others ran offices and their households. It was a world without men, a world of burgeoning female competence and confidence, even in traditionally male arenas like heavy manufacturing. Women wore jeans and made bombs in factories, with Rosie the Riveter exhorting them all along, "We Can Do It!" Female agency, aptitude, and autonomy were not merely tolerated; they were encouraged, nurtured, and publicly extolled as patriotic. Between 1940 and 1944, female labor force participation grew by nearly half. And with most men away, women weren't just working in factories, rising to the top in their office jobs, and generally running the show. Historians, cultural critics who study gender, and sex researchers have noted that "situational lesbianism" is common in contexts—from Saudi Arabia to all-girls schools to women's prisons to wartime—where there is a dearth of men. And with social scrutiny relaxed and men out of the picture, lesbians had unusual freedoms, notes historian Jessica Toops, while avowedly heterosexual women were more likely and able to pursue romantic and sexual relationships with other women, acting on what sex researcher Lisa Diamond calls "female sexual fluidity."

But such freedoms were contingent and relatively short-lived. The notion that females were naturally and should be sexually reticent, domestic, heterosexual, and a whole lot more got another shot in the arm in 1948. That year, an English botanist and geneticist named Angus Bateman, who had previously focused on the genetic properties of barley and rye and cross-pollination in seed crops, published a paper in the *Journal of Heredity* about *Drosophila melanogaster,* or fruit flies, and their mating strategies. What these flies allegedly did, and what it all supposedly proved, would have surprisingly vast implications for human women.

LAW AND ORDER, SCIENTIFICALLY SPEAKING

Bateman assembled and observed groups of equal numbers of male and female *Drosophila melanogaster,* held in bottles. They mated freely. Later, Bateman classified the offspring by genotype.

Bateman had undertaken this experiment because he was keen to emphasize that while Darwin had a theory of sexual selection based on observation, he had no *proof.* Bateman quickly made two claims based on his own study results. First, he asserted that males' reproductive success was more "variable" than females' reproductive success. That is, nearly 96 percent of the females reproduced, while only 79 percent of the males managed to. Bateman also observed that "male fertility increased in a linear manner as a function of the number of copulations achieved, whereas the fertility of females showed little increase as a function of the number of copulations beyond the first." That is to say, males benefited from copulating again and again, according to Bateman; for females, it made little difference.

Why should it be the case that males benefited from multiple mating, while females didn't? Why was what was good for the gander *not* good for the goose? Bateman and those who later embraced his findings believed that a female's reproductive success was limited by biology—the number of eggs she could produce—while for the male "fertility is seldom likely to be limited by sperm production, but rather by the number of inseminations or the number of females available to him." Like Darwin, Bateman was sure sexual selection acted more directly on males than on females, because of differences between the sexes when it came to the cost of producing gametes. Eggs were labor-intensive, relatively precious treasures; sperm, in contrast, were presumably much cheaper. There were so many of them! This incontrovertible biological difference not only drove but determined both sexual and *social* behavior:

> There is nearly always a combination of an undiscriminating eagerness in the males and discriminating passivity in the females. Even in a derived monogamous species (e.g. man) this sex difference might be expected to persist as a rule.

Bateman's paper and its assertions dropped at a moment—1948—when troops had returned home and were readjusting to a social world that had been radically reordered. How would men be reintegrated into a universe in which they had been, for a time, not only absent but irrelevant?

For starters, men needed their jobs in manufacturing and industry back. And so women would have to give them up. Society mobilized to get them to do just that—through shame, guilt, and a propaganda program about the social importance of stay-at-home wives and mothers. As historians have pointed out, the rise of 1950s suburban living in the US, with its dearly held belief that a woman's place was in the home and that to be female was to be fulfilled by the calling of intensive care for one's children, household, and mate was certainly aided and abetted by the GI Bill, television shows like *Leave It to Beaver* and *The Adventures of Ozzie and Harriet,* and even fashion (Christian Dior's lavish, wasp-waisted, and stilettoed "New Look" made it aggressively clear that it wasn't chic to dress for a factory line anymore). One government PSA from the period showed a female factory worker in court, imploring the judge for a light sentence for her son accused of vandalism. "The message to women was clear," writes historian Melissa E. Murray. "There was no need to [stay] in the labor force. Instead, women were needed back at the hearth in their traditional role as mothers responsible for the careful rearing of productive citizens."

Good mothers didn't work. They went to court to bail their kids out. They cooked and cleaned. Their work was the home. Bateman's conclusions participated in cajoling women out of the workforce in an admittedly indirect but hardly subtle way. Insights about *Drosophila melanogaster* helped reassert plough-informed gender roles by giving scientific credence to the idea that females are by nature sexually exclusive nesters who find satisfaction not in the world of action, competition, and earning but in monogamous heterosexual mating and intensive investment in their offspring.

Die, Rosie the Riveter.

Bateman's paper wasn't just efficacious in the short term, useful in the overarching social effort to guide women from the factories to the kitchen and reestablish the hierarchy between men and women that had been upset by the war's reorganization of who did what. Over the next decades, it became an urtext of sorts, indisputable evidence that sexual selection acts differentially on males than on females and that only males—reaffirmed to be "pugnacious, courageous, and assertive," just as Darwin had described them—benefit from multiple mating. "Intra-sexual Competition in *Drosophila*" has been cited directly more than three thousand times since its publication, according to Google Scholar; historian Donald Dewsbury notes it "became standard fare in textbooks" and lectures in the fields of biology, genetics, and anthropology. Just as important, Bateman's findings have been presumed universally relevant and generalized to females of other species, including, as Bateman suggested, to humans. In the 1970s, the dashing and controversial Harvard sociobiologist Robert Trivers popularized Bateman all over again, bringing his views to an even wider audience. Trivers refined Bateman's point by suggesting that a female invests more in offspring both before and after it is born, because fertilization and gestation—often of only one offspring at a time—take place in her body. And because if she is a mammal, she lactates. As a consequence, he argued in his theory of Parental Investment, her maximum reproductive output is limited compared to a male's. Males, on the other hand, could reproduce pretty much limitlessly, if they were sufficiently caddish. Which, it seemed, was in their best interest.

In this view of the "natural order of things," a female's one-shot monthly fecundity, energetically costly and risky gestation, and her consequent strategy of comprehensive investment in her young put her fundamentally at odds with males. She wanted *quality, not quantity*—one great guy with great genes and one or two young at a time to take care of intensively. But males, those comparatively footloose and fancy-free XY scoundrels with their boatloads of quick, inexpensive sperm, would naturally want to spread themselves around, siring as many offspring with as many females as possible. They wanted *quantity, not quality* in the mating and fathering game. The bottom line, yet again, was that monogamous social behavior and all the qualities presumed to go with it—being demure, choosy, reticent, and retiring—was essentially female behavior. Males, this line of thinking went, were naturally "eager."

Primatologist Sarah Hrdy points out that what has been called "the Bateman paradigm"—the linked notions that males have greater variation of reproductive success than females do; males gain from multiple matings and females do not; males are generally ardent and females retiring; and the implicit presumption that females are more logically and naturally monogamous than males—has influenced entire generations of thinkers. After Trivers put forth his gloss on Bateman, everyone from evolutionary psychologists to biologists to writers for *GQ* and *Maxim,* who produced pat article after pat article asserting that "men stray while women stay because of genes," perpetuated it.

If Bateman's conclusions about sex roles and sexual selection, and science and popular culture's embrace of it, read like a suspiciously wistful and retroactive justification narrative in which males are active doers, competing and winning and losing and striving and eager to spread their seed and then bolt, as passive, coy, choosy females rain on their collective parade and try to get them to be true while expecting never to pay for their own drinks, that's because it is. As real gains in equality put women in charge of their reproduction, their earnings, and their destinies more generally in the last decades of the twentieth century, Bateman's ideas would be periodically reactivated like a virus by anxiety about social change. Wherever and whenever women were independent and in little need of being protected and provided for, the notion that they should passively choose the one most powerful male to safeguard and provision them, and all that it implied about femaleness versus maleness, would be aggressively promulgated by a range of scientists, writers, and politicians whose interests it served. A simplified and essentialist version of sociobiology revved its engine and got remarkable traction throughout the 1970s (a 1977 cover of *Time* showed a man and woman hanging from marionette strings, arms intertwined, with the headline "Why You Do What You Do: Sociobiology") in part because, as had been the case in the *Drosophila* paper after World War II, it was a response to a home-front social and sexual revolution, including the dismantling of a rigid gender script and rejiggering of traditional gender roles. Thirty years later, as women in the US continued to make strides in the workplace, closing the pay gap and grappling with "having it all," Bateman's notion of universal, timeless biologically based differences of sexual strategy found expression in a bestselling memoir:

> In primitive times women clung to the strongest males for protection. They did not take any chances with a nobody, low-status male who did not have the means to house them, protect them, and feed them and their offspring. High-status males displayed their prowess through their kick-ass attitudes. They were not afraid to think for

themselves and make their own decisions. They did not give a crap about what other people in the tribe thought. That kind of attitude was and still is associated with the kind of men women find attractive. It may not be politically correct to say, but who cares. It is common sense and it is true and always will be.

The anthropologist Holly Dunsworth has written about all the ways Trump got evolution wrong here, from his misapprehension that it was competition rather than cooperation that helped us thrive to his fantasy that human females are "naturally" power-fixated gold diggers. This highly selective version of sexual selection's role in evolution is one that plays in Trump's America, and the version of masculinity it suggests—muscular, fearless, and dominant—arguably helped Trump win the election. It did not hurt that his opponent was an "unnaturally" ambitious woman who didn't know her place (or essence, apparently) and whom Trump suggested he might "lock up." ("Lock her up is right!" he enthused as supporters in Pennsylvania chanted the phrase.) Like Dr. Storer's patient Mrs. B. in 1856, women who slipped out of the bounds of the Trumpian Eden, where passive females seek the protection and sperm of active and assertive males, were a threat to be contained and then annihilated. Instead of recommending a borax vaginal wash, the man who is now our president used and continues to use verbal coercive tactics, including, famously—in a phrase that reasserted that essential differences were essential destiny while it echoed William Acton's preoccupation with menstruation—describing a woman who stepped over the line as having "blood coming out of her wherever."

But as for Bateman's science—popular, popularized, politicized, and sometimes populist—it wasn't merely biased by and influential upon its cultural moment. Over the intervening years a number of scientists, many of them women, began to suggest it was also highly questionable in light of how females of many species—including non-human female primates and women—actually behave. The presumptions built upon Bateman's findings ("Men have sports cars to get lots of women," "Women just naturally want to stay home with the kids and one man—that's how it was in caveman times," "All females need and want an alpha," "Males naturally want sex more than females do," and so on) began to fall like so many houses arrogantly, haphazardly erected on quicksand.

DEATH-DEALING MALES AND THE FEMALES WHO PLAY THEM

Primatologist Sarah Blaffer Hrdy was one of the first scientists to challenge Bateman's conclusions, though she told me she had no inkling that's where her work would lead at the time. "I just wanted to study langurs," she told me with a laugh as we sat in the living room of her home in Northern California and I asked her about being David to the Goliath that was her field's faith in the received notion of sexual selection, female choice, and "coy, choosy" females contrasted with "ardent" males. Hrdy's adventure started, as those of so many female primates do, with sex. For work on her doctoral dissertation while she was a graduate student at Harvard, Hrdy traveled to Mount Abu in Rajasthan, India, to observe Hanuman langurs (*Semnopithecus entellus*) there. She noted that the females sometimes left their troops to copulate with outside males, seeking them out for sex even when a more familiar male was in residence. Why would that be? And *how* could it be if, as Bateman asserted and everyone knew, "sexually adventurous females were not supposed to exist," in Hrdy's words? Hrdy had been inspired, even compelled, to trek to Mount Abu by what would turn out to be a life-altering undergraduate lecture in a course taught by Harvard anthropologist Irven DeVore. He mentioned that in a species of monkey she had never heard of before, Hanuman langurs, males sometimes attacked and killed infants. At the time, it was thought that this bizarre male behavior was due to overcrowding. At Abu, Hrdy did indeed witness males attacking infants but realized the attacks were almost always by males who had recently entered the troop from outside it. Stalking a female with an infant sometimes for days, these invading males acted with sharklike intent. When an opportunity presented itself, the male would attempt to seize the infant from its mother and sink his daggerlike canines into its skull or other body part. While females sometimes fought back, even forming coalitions with other females to fend off the attackers, the males usually won. Disconcertingly to us humans, and perhaps especially to us human mothers, the mothers of the dead infants would then mate with the killers of their offspring. Resident males, on the other hand, were extraordinarily tolerant of infants and never attacked them, suggesting that by itself population density was *not* the issue. What was going on?

For Hrdy, an idea soon began to take form. An infanticidal male "eliminated the offspring of the last choice a female had made," thereby causing the mother (who was no longer lactating) to resume cycling and to ovulate sooner than she would have had her infant survived, drastically "distorting her options." In order not to be outbred by competing females, she needed to mate with the male now available, the male who would presumably keep another potentially infanticidal invader at bay, even if that male was her baby's killer. "All this made sense in light of Darwin's ideas about sexual selection, that is, males competing with other males for access to matings with the outcome for the loser of not death, but few or no offspring," as Hrdy told me in an email recalling her fieldwork in Abu. But what about the females? What was motivating *them*? How might their behavior be adaptive? Once a male had killed her offspring and she cycled again, particularly if the murderous male was guarding her closely from other males, it was in a female's best interest to mate with him. But she wouldn't stop there. Once she realized that males were only attacking offspring born to females with whom they had never mated, offspring they could not possibly have sired, Hrdy hypothesized that females might seek to manipulate information available to males about paternity by preemptively mating with potential invaders. Confounding prevailing wisdom that female primates only mate at midcycle, when they are in estrus, Hrdy also realized that these females would solicit copulations from males at times other than midcycle, even when they were already pregnant. She wondered if such situation-dependent estrus behavior could be a preemptive female strategy to counter male infanticidal coercion. Might copulating with multiple males allow the female to "game" paternal certainty and plant a seed of confusion, so to speak? After all, by mating multiply, a female langur was engineering the possibility that these lethal males, potential killers of her infant, had actually sired it. And this, Hrdy realized, would make it less likely that a male would kill the infant that might be his. The only way to fool the males was to mate polyandrously, sometimes even in rapid sequence with numerous partners. Not only was this not "unnatural," it was beneficial, Hrdy asserted, suggesting that female langurs bred multiply as a form of insurance.

Later, Hrdy hypothesized that such mating behavior, which she reframed as "assiduously maternal"—behavior likely to keep her baby alive—and now widely reported for many species of primates, could under other circumstances actually increase the odds that males, even more than one "possible father," would protect, care for, and even provision her infant. All in all, given the right ecological and social circumstances, mating with multiple males might be very beneficial to females indeed.

Logical, reasoned, and grounded in solid science as her ideas were, Hrdy set off shockwaves with her suggestion that infanticide might be an adaptive reproductive strategy for males and, stranger still, that it might be adaptive for females to engage in multiple matings so as to confuse paternity. "Those monkeys are deranged," she recalls a prominent physical anthropologist saying dismissively of her work and her 1977 book on the topic, *The Langurs of Abu*. It was easier for that anthropologist, and anthropology in general, to pathologize an entire troop of langurs and dismiss Hrdy's many months of meticulous fieldwork than it was to concede that males might operate selfishly rather than for the "good of the species." Perhaps even more shockingly, Hrdy's insights challenged the Darwin-Bateman paradigm, which was so foundational to the thinking not only of scientists but of Americans, who were deeply invested in the generations-old belief that sexually passive, "coy" females who once mated with the "best" available male would have no incentive to stray.

In her 1981 book, *The Woman That Never Evolved,* Hrdy took aim even more directly at the passive, coy, monogamous female hypothesis, suggesting that observational data demonstrated it simply wasn't the case in many primates, including humans, and that Darwin's notion that retiring, disinterested, exclusivity-craving females drove sexual selection by seeking the one "best" male was more based in wishful thinking and social convention than in actual primate behavior. Moreover, she made the case that female primates, particularly mothers, were not exclusively tender, monogamous, and passive. Females might also be sexually assertive, selfish, shrewd, and, under some circumstances, not even necessarily nurturing.

In her later book *Mother Nature,* she would show that among primates where mothers need a lot of help from others in order to rear their young (as is the case in humans), the same mother who lavished her infant with attention under favorable ecological circumstances might, when short on social support, refuse to nurse it or even abandon an infant at birth. Rather than being unnatural, such a mother was balancing her own well-being against that of her current offspring and also potential offspring she might bear in the future. Such a mother might be devoted and doting—or indifferent. She might nurse diligently, long past the time when her conspecifics had given it up, or tirelessly allow her infant to ride ventrally, clinging to the fur rather than locomote on its own. And then that same indulgent and fastidious mother might set her infant down, casting it momentarily, or more permanently, aside. As with female mating behaviors, maternal behaviors were far more variable, flexible, and strategic than previously assumed.

Hrdy's assertion that female primates were sexually strategic and acted with agency left her open to criticism. One colleague writing in the *Quarterly Review of Biology* equated her hypothesis that female primates benefited from mating with multiple males with "parapsychology." Others made it more personal, accusing her of projecting. "So, Sarah, put another way, you're saying you're horny, right?" one colleague inquired. (Hrdy called this "one of the more mortifying moments of my life.") But her work also opened the floodgates for more research that challenged the status quo.

It was soon observed and eventually widely accepted that males of many mammal species committed infanticide to force females into estrus, and that females bred not passively but strategically, and often, and frequently with multiple males. From female macaques in captivity who craved sexual variety so much that they grew listless and depressed if keepers didn't cycle in new males every three years; to ostensibly "monogamous" female gibbons who copulated with other males when their partners were out of sight; to female chimps who risked their lives attempting to join new troops in order to copulate with novel males—there was good reason, primatologists including Meredith Small, Alison Jolly, Barbara Smuts, and Jeanne Altmann argued, to reexamine with a critical eye the presumed "universal" sex differences in sexual and reproductive strategy based on Bateman's principle. Females had a lot more agency than previously supposed. Under a variety of circumstances they *did* mate multiply and they *did* benefit from it.

How, exactly? Not only could "promiscuous" females decrease the likelihood of infanticide. They also could increase their chances of conceiving by upping their likelihood of getting high-quality sperm. They could hedge against male infertility. Multiply mating females improved their odds of heterozygosity—a good match between their egg and the sperm that fertilized it, resulting in a healthier baby. But there was more to it. It turned out there were *non-procreative* benefits of multiple mating for females as well. By copulating with a slew of males when she wasn't in estrus or fertile—basically by having sex recreationally—a female primate could deplete the sperm available to rival females. She could recruit males to her social group, thus having more potential caregivers and protectors and provisioners. She could trade sex for resources or "friendship." Of course Hrdy's female langurs didn't have some conscious endgame. They didn't mate multiply because they figured, "Hmmmm, better confuse the issue of paternity and line up multiple possible 'dads' to protect my baby" instead of attack it. Nor did other primate females think, "Boy, would I ever like to increase my odds of heterozygosity" or "get some really good genes," or—in species where male support is essential—get several males to care for or provision her offspring, thinking, "I need to line up several providers." Females solicited males because they were conditioned to additional matings that might feel good. And it felt good because of the way ancestral female primates were built. This was the "legacy" we human primates inherited from ancient ancestresses living under quite different conditions than women do today.

Sure, we have been portrayed not infrequently over the last centuries by science, medicine, and art as the passive, comparatively disinterested sex. But biology suggests a vastly different backstory, a tale of passionate, voluptuous pleasures and sometimes of tremendous risk-taking in the pursuit of sexual satisfaction. Our bodies are designed for sin; they are hedonists even when we're not.

WE'LL HAVE WHAT SHE'S HAVING: ORGASM AND THE CLITORIS

Women, along with female chimps, bonobos, and a number of other non-human primate species, evolved a forward-facing, richly innervated clitoris. Previously thought to be a mere button, now known to be a superhighway of decadent sensation-for-the-sake-of-it, including three- to four-inch-long paired legs, the human clitoris is truly, as suggests the ancient Greek word that denotes it, "the key" when it comes to understanding the anatomical and biological underpinnings of female sexuality. It is vast, the same size as a penis, but on the inside. Yet even just the part of the clit we can see, the glans—think of it as the tip of the iceberg, or perhaps better, the mouth of a simmering volcano—has more than eight thousand nerve endings, meaning it has fourteen times the density of nerve receptor cells as the most sensitive part of a man's penis, also called the glans. That makes the clitoris epically more responsive and excitable than the tip of the penis.

Terminology like "glans" aside, men—whose junk develops from the very same embryonic tissue women's does—are very different in one respect. Their penises are functional, for urinating as well as ejaculating, multitaskers for biology, sensation, and reproduction. Meanwhile, the little bud that stands at attention, the clit we thought we knew, is merely the ticket to the roller-coaster ride and serves no greater or lesser purpose than to make us feel good. The entirety of what is now known as the "female erectile network" (FEN) or "internal clitoris" snakes back nearly to our anus on either side; extends along our labia, which swell with pleasure; and includes our urethral sponge (previously called the G-spot) and something called the perineal sponge too.

And women, unlike men, can have orgasm after orgasm. "Women don't require a refractory period like men do, so we're able to stay aroused longer and have [subsequent orgasms] with little effort," says Rachel Carlton Abrams, MD, co-author of *The Multi-Orgasmic Woman*. Conventional wisdom has it that men come and are done.

But female orgasm is, in actual real-life conditions—in beds and showers and the backseats of cars, in dorm rooms and conference rooms and marriages and hookups and trysts—a moody bitch. She is notoriously reticent. And like the clitoris itself, which retracts under its hood when stimulated, female orgasm can be elusive. Her rewards take some know-how, and patience. According to Manhattan psychiatrist and sex therapist Elisabeth Gordon, MD, studies tell us the average time for a woman to orgasm from intercourse after stimulating foreplay ranges from ten to twenty minutes, while for men it is two and a half to eight minutes. "The only hard and fast facts regarding time to orgasm are that there is a range, and women take longer on average, and that it's faster from self-stimulation." And it's not uncommon for women to fear they are taking "too long," Gordon observes. There is no doubt that this latter fact is at least in part a symptom of a culture-wide failure to tell women that great sex is our right, and that we are entitled to "release" as we have been taught men are. Among heterosexuals, there is a significant "orgasm gap" as well as a sexual entitlement gap: one study found that when it comes to sex with a familiar partner, heterosexual men come a hefty 22 percent more often than women do. (Bisexual women fare no better than straight women, while lesbians come out on top, experiencing orgasm nearly 75 percent of the time during partnered sex.) Another study found that in first-time hookups, straight men have over three orgasms for every orgasm a straight woman has.

The *unpredictable* nature of orgasm—will we or won't we?—may drive us to constantly seek its fulfillment. We know that when it comes to playing slot machines, we become addicted not by getting what we want every time but by the happenstance nature of our win. Same with checking our iPhones. If we had the emails and texts we craved every time we looked, we would soon grow bored of and devalue the very rewards we sought. Consistent fulfillment doesn't stoke desire the way the hope and anticipation of unpredictable fulfillment does. It is intermittent reinforcement, with its non-pattern pattern of the occasional jackpot, researchers tell us, that keeps us coming back for more.

In addition, the fact that stimulation that leads to orgasm is *cumulative* is something that has long intrigued primatologists, including Hrdy. We experience a sense of "buildup" as we draw nearer to climax, and it takes time, particularly from intercourse. More time than it takes a man.

This specific cluster of characteristics defining female orgasm may well have helped make the human female, under certain conditions, a restless and relentless sexual adventuress. Our ancestors, like many non-human primates today, including our closest relatives, chimps and bonobos, may well have regularly consorted with several males in rapid succession, seeking, with each partner, to build up to the eventuality of an orgasm or multiple orgasm.

The proof is in the primates. By now it's well established that rather than being uniquely human, female orgasms occur in other primates as well, in chimpanzees and various species of macaques. Laboratory studies using implanted transmitters record physiological response to genital stimulation, including spasmodic contractions of uterine and vaginal muscles and changes in heart rates accompanied by distinctive vocalizations and facial expressions, such as "O faces," Hrdy told me as the sky clouded over and we contemplated the lunch of chicken potpie she planned that day. I sat with her for several hours. She demonstrated an O face, which is exactly what it sounds like, an open round-mouthed facial expression like the one female macaques, chimps, bonobos, and humans make at That Magical Moment. "This suggests that female orgasm is a legacy that predates hominins, making it not just very old but a retention from what was possibly also an essential adaptation for our prehuman ancestresses," she explained. (At this point Hrdy's husband, Dan, entered the room to discuss when we'd eat. "We're talking about the evolution of female orgasms!" Hrdy enthused. Dan turned and headed in the other direction, waving his hand and saying gamely over his shoulder, "I have heard a *lot* about that already.")

In an essay earlier in her career Hrdy observed, "Based on both clinical observations and interviews with women, there is a disconcerting mismatch between a female capable of multiple sequential orgasms and a male partner typically capable of one copulatory bout." And, she further suggested, since a relatively low percentage of women experience orgasm from intercourse alone, it's hard to warrant any claims (there have been some) that the female orgasm evolved specifically in humans as an adaptation for fostering heterosexual monogamous pair bonds. Au contraire. Given all the advantages of mating multiply, it makes sense that there might be this "variable reward system" in response to sustained, even cumulative, stimulation, unpredictable and delightful, that over millions of years has kept female primates soliciting successive copulations. It can be no coincidence, Hrdy observed, that so far female orgasm among non-human primates has been best documented in non-monogamous species. As she wrote to me, forget trying to explain the evolution of female orgasms or contemporary mismatches by studying women under current conditions. Rather, we need to ask how this ancient legacy, inherited from prehuman ancestresses, has changed over human evolution and human history.

Sex at Dawn authors Christopher Ryan and Cacilda Jethá suggest that the story of a woman's cervix makes Hrdy's version of females conditioned to seek orgasm with multiple partners in rapid succession for deep reasons even more likely. For the human female cervix, like that of a promiscuous macaque who may breed with ten males or more in rapid succession, actually serves not so much to block sperm, as was previously believed, as to busily filter and assess it, ideally several different types of it from several different males, simultaneously. It evolved not as a simple barrier but to sort the weak and bad and incompatible sperm from the good, suggesting by its very presence that there was a need to do such a thing—i.e., that females were mating multiply. Such a wondrous bit of equipment also partially buffers the female in possession of it against making a poor mate choice in the heat of the moment—our cervix is there to help us judge who's eligible when our eyes fail us.

Male equipment tells a similar story about the likelihood of a long history of females mating multiply. Consider the size of a human male's testicles. They are larger than those of gorillas, whose teeny-tiny balls relative to their body size suggest that only a small amount of sperm was needed to successfully inseminate a female, who is unlikely to have other potential mates (gorillas live in social formations some primatologists still call "harems"—a male and multiple females). A man's testicles, in contrast, are proportionally larger, arguably more like those of chimps and bonobos, whose females are notoriously promiscuous. Logically, when dealing with a female consorting with multiple males, you need a lot of sperm to compete with other sperm inside the vaginal canal. The more you can squirt, the better. As to sperm itself, it also tells a tale. Sperm plugs—just what they sound like: a mixture of ejaculate, mucous, and coagulating protein that gums up a female's vagina in an attempt to keep one's own sperm in and block a rival's from getting up there—are a thing among chimps and bonobos, with whom we share an estimated 98.7 percent of our genetic material, and numerous other primate species. When dealing with rival sperm, you don't just want to get yours in. If you weren't first to the party, you want to get the other guy's out. And the coronal ridge—the thing at the tip that makes the penis look like a shovel—is a remarkably effective remover of ejaculate. In one experiment, scientists found that a dildo with a coronal ridge removed nearly three times more of an ejaculate-like substance (made from a mixture of cornstarch and water) from a dummy vagina than ones without. And the final spurts of human male ejaculate contain a spermicide-like ingredient. "Take that!" it asserts to any rival who comes along in the subsequent hours (or minutes).

Still other researchers see our very cries of pleasure as proof that when it comes to being untrue, females were ever thus. Primatologist Zanna Clay actually studied chimp vocalizations during sex and learned it is a way females effectively signal to males, "Here I am, and I'm interested in you, other guys!" even during the act of copulation itself. Moaning and groaning may be an ancient script of sorts, by which we communicate to any other males in hearing range, "Receptive and ready just as soon as this is over!"

We are not chimps or langurs, of course. But Hrdy and the numerous scientists and thinkers she has influenced ask, Why would human females be designed as we are (and why would males have the penis shaped the way it is, and ejaculate with spermicide, and testicles the size they are) if women hadn't been able to seek out the rewards our bodies promised, presumably serially and without much trepidation or undue fear of serious reprisals or consequences? And if seeking sex with multiple partners had always been restricted and at times even as lethal as it is today, how could we be here, designed as we are now? To consider the clitoris and the nature of female orgasm and the cervix too, as well as male equipment and the way we have sex, is to confront not just the vague possibility but the likelihood that women are made for sexual gratification and for pursuing it, and for mating multiply, in ways that men—who come and are done—are not. Female biology suggests that women are built for sexual experimentation, for reckless days and heedless nights, putting us in conflict with our current cultural container, to put it mildly.

There is no one way of having sex we "evolved" for—we are flexible sexual and social strategists. But our essence, if we can be said to have one, is likely less matron and more macaque. Female infidelity is a behavior with one foot in the present day and the other in our ancient past, linked to anatomy, physiology, and reward seeking. And the best mother is the one who, when circumstances are right, does what it takes to line up allies who will be well disposed toward her offspring. She might do so on her back, or with her rump in the air.

In the field of primatology, from Hrdy's game-changing multiple-mating and infanticide hypothesis and insights about the nature of female orgasm to Barbara Smuts's unexpected observations about female olive baboons who choose mates from among numerous male "friends" to Meredith Small's assertion that the single most observable characteristic among female non-human primates is a preference for sexual novelty, presumptions that female monogamy is timeless and essential have taken a beating.

PROMISCUITY, THY NAME IS WOMAN

> —why, she would hang on him,
> As if increase of appetite had grown
> By what it fed on; and yet, within a month—
> Let me not think on't—Frailty, thy name is woman!
> —HAMLET, ACT 1, SCENE 2

Over the last several decades, as primatologists challenged the accuracy of the assertion that monogamy is our legacy, as well as the assumption that it was driven by females because of their biology, their insights pressured a shift of perspective about how, where, and why *human* females practice multiple mating. For example, on the Mosuo practice of *sese*, or "walking marriage," in southwestern China, wherein women live with their kin and sexual partners slip into their rooms at night. Mosuo men do not support their offspring financially or socially (it's a woman's brother who "fathers," so that Mosuo uncles are "dads"). And women are permitted to have multiple marriages. Rather than focus solely on how this arrangement benefited men, anthropologists began to see the benefits to women of raising their children in the context of an extended family without input or potential conflict from unrelated men. There are polyandrous arrangements in rural Tibet, where a woman may be married to several male siblings, a strategy that is thought to make it more efficient to farm the challenging mountainous terrain in order to provision kids and adults alike, and to prevent skirmishes over land inheritance. But it also benefits women, in an unstinting climate, to have several related "father figures" invested in her child's (and by extension her own) well-being. And there are many more societies with "non-classical polyandry" in which women have multiple partners simultaneously or over time, with very little or no social censure. Ethnographic evidence of such informal polyandry has been reported in a total of 53 societies (and primatologist and anthropologist Meredith Small, in a survey of 133 societies, said there was not a single one without female infidelity). By 2000, Sarah Hrdy asked, "Why is polyandry so rare in humans?" and immediately amended her question by posing another: *"Or is it?"* Hrdy observed that "informal polyandry"—women having multiple partners at the same time or in succession—is a reality, period.

The notion that there were universal differences of sexual and reproductive strategy based on the essential, inflexible biological fact of gamete production was being battered as Hrdy and other anthropologists documented that female polygamy or "promiscuity" was a flexible behavior, an adaptation to circumstances. Women were markedly more likely to partner up with more than one man under certain conditions:

- When men outnumber women. When sex ratios are skewed so that there are more men than women of reproductive age, women and men may be equally motivated for women to practice polygamy. In these circumstances, men might figure that half a wife is better than none. And that it is better to roll the dice and take the chance of having a child by a woman you share with another man than it is to have no children at all.

- When it is difficult for a single man to make adequate provisions for a family. When historic and economic change make it hard for men to, say, hunt and conditions are not right for farming, women may need more than one man to help them keep their kids alive and healthy. And in neighborhoods where there are high rates of male incarceration, women may, in addition to starting their reproductive careers early as a hedge against uncertainty, have children with more than one man, because monogamy is not an option. In all these instances, men may not be present, and if they are, they may have no choice but to look the other way if they too want healthy kids who survive to reproduce.

- When there is a custom of men sharing their wife or wives with potential allies. In these cases, women and not just men benefit from potential support.
- When women can rely on their kin to help them with child-rearing. In instances where a woman has her extended family available to her, they can help her bridge the gap when she is between partners, eliminate the need for her to have a partner at all, or buffer her and her child against possible consequences when she is experimenting with different partners.
- When women have a high level of autonomy. If she has her own resources, for example, or contributes meaningfully to the survival of the family or group with what she provides, or if she has financial autonomy, a woman is much more likely to have sexual autonomy as well. And the worldwide ethnographic data show she may well use it to have simultaneous or successive partners, rather than one.
- When there are few accumulated or heritable resources, as among foragers and horticulturalists. With no riches and no property to pass along, the issue of rightful inheritance—that is, the preoccupation of which child belongs to which man—may pale in importance relative to other concerns, such as the cohesion of the group. It also means there will be less perceived need to control whether a woman is monogamous or not.

In her work among the Pimbwe of Tanzania, where divorce is a matter of one partner moving physically out of the house, with no additional legal or formal proceedings, UC Davis human behavioral ecologist Monique Borgerhoff Mulder discovered yet another reality that challenged the Bateman paradigm. Through interviews and recording of reproductive histories, she documented that, directly contradicting Bateman's oft-cited assertions, multiple mating increased the reproductive success of Pimbwe women (meaning it increased the number of their children who survived to go on themselves to reproduce), but *not* of Pimbwe men. Borgerhoff Mulder further concluded that "polyandry is everywhere...but we think of it as polygyny." That is, when we view the world and female sexuality, social behavior, and reproduction through the lens of the Darwin-Bateman paradigm, we miss the very facts that challenge this view of demure females acquiescing to sexually assertive males, who supposedly benefit from multiple mating as women do not.

Indeed, at the outer extreme of multiple mating that benefits females, anthropologists discovered and documented that many indigenous peoples of the Amazonian lowland—at least eighteen tribes, including the Canela, the Mehinaku, and the Yanomami—subscribe to a belief called "partible paternity," which holds that a child can have more than one father. For example, when questioned by the anthropologist Kim Hill, who was attempting to learn about their kinship, 321 Aché—hunter-horticulturalists who live in eastern Paraguay—said they had a total of 632 fathers. They told Hill their different terms for their various fathers. *Miare* is "the father who put it in," while *peroare* is "the man who mixed it." *Momboare* means "the ones who spilled it out," while *bykuare* means "the father who provided the child's essence." Opaque as these descriptors might sound to us, they point to a mind-blowing and crystal-clear belief: intercourse with more than one man is the best way to make a baby, which "accumulates" like a snowball from successive applications of semen. Women in partible paternity cultures like the Aché and the Bari have sex with several men over the course of their pregnancy, and these men in turn support her and the baby when it is born. Anthropologist Stephen Beckerman discovered that among the Bari—rainforest horticulturalists of the southwest Maracaibo Basin, which spans the border between Colombia and Venezuela—kids with more than one father are more likely to survive to adulthood, thanks to improved nutrition and protection provided by their extra dads. Eighty percent of Bari kids with secondary fathers saw their fifteenth birthdays, while only sixty-four percent of those with a single father did. In these contexts, a woman who is monogamous may well be considered prudish, selfish, and deserving of condemnation. But a woman who lines up *too many* fathers will find that uncertain fathers are reluctant to help. The optimal number of fathers under the environmental and ecological conditions that prevail where the peoples who believe in partible paternity live appears to be two, Hrdy tells us. A notable exception: the Canela of central Brazil, where a woman may have ritual sex with twenty or more men during community ceremonies, leaving her with many "fathers" to choose from and rely upon.

In partible paternity societies, child-rearing, unsurprisingly, often becomes a collaborative endeavor, with many adults looking out for a child's well-being. Anthropologists call this collective raising of kids "cooperative breeding," and many believe it is both the "how" and "why" not only of female multiple mating but also of the survival and success of *Homo sapiens,* when other hominins bit the dust. It was not the monogamous heterosexual pair bond that made us who we are today and ensured that we would endure, they argue, but the shared raising of offspring by multi-member groups and females who mated multiply.

On the strength of this body of data, some scientists began to rethink the idea that men had the potential to reproduce without limit. They discovered that—guess what?—sperm is not so cheap after all. Since it takes millions of sperm to fertilize a single egg, the relevant comparison is not between a precious egg and a sperm that is cheap because males produce scads of them. The relevant measure is the difference between the cost of scads of sperm and the cost of a single egg. Measured that way, sperm is more expensive than we thought. And semen, it turns out, actually contains crucial bioactive compounds that are markedly energetically costly for males to produce. Moreover, males can and do run out of sperm—a phenomenon called sperm depletion. Between the actual cost and potential scarcity of sperm, it makes sense that males may themselves in certain circumstances be quite choosy and coy about which females they have sex with. (The study of male choice is increasingly popular in biology now.)

In addition to costly sperm and sperm depletion and the reality of male choosiness, anthropologists and zoologists now question the notion of male primates fathering dozens or even hundreds of offspring just by being sexually active. This idea simply does not line up with several realities on the ground. Namely: harems are rare in the primate world, conception is statistically rare as well, and rates of miscarriage are high. How likely is it that a male hits the timing of conception just right in a single copulation? Or in multiple copulations with multiple females? Not very. And since such a significant number of pregnancies across species end in miscarriage, stillbirth, and fatal breech births, the math gets even more unfavorable for the male who ejaculates and disappears. Mating and leaving means creating the possibility that the female will mate with another male, and also that his sperm failed to do the job, or that he will not be there to try again if the pregnancy does not result in a healthy offspring. Many scientists have recently come to believe that, given all these factors, *the range in male and female lifetime reproductive success actually tends to be equal.* This holds true for humans and a number of non-human primates as well. Finally, as many zoologists, biologists, and anthropologists have been able to demonstrate, offspring of many species are more likely to survive if there are high levels of not just maternal but *paternal* care.

For all these reasons—costly sperm, the difficulty of having and guarding multiple females, the difficulty of conception, the high likelihood that a gestation may fail, the fact that dependent offspring may do better with paternal care than without—inseminating and running was never such a great strategy. The idea of naturally polygamous males and naturally monogamous females (guys who favored multiple mating over care and gals who wanted the one "right" guy) was cast increasingly in doubt in the decades after Sarah Hrdy's insights about strategically promiscuous female langurs.

But perhaps the most fundamental blow to the belief that males benefited from multiple mating but females did not, making males "logically" more promiscuous than females, came from the laboratory of UCLA evolutionary biologist Patricia Adair Gowaty. After years of work on sexual selection, and in light of the growing body of evidence that females of many species did partake in and benefit from polyandrous or multiple mating, Gowaty put Bateman to the test in 2012, repeating his endlessly cited and vastly influential experiment, only modernized with DNA data. Gowaty discovered that Bateman's findings could not be replicated, even in the very *Drosophila* he had studied. Could Bateman's science, upon which he and a subsequent generation of thinkers had built their assumptions about female versus male nature, be wrong? At first, many experts were surprised. And surprised again—that until Gowaty, no one had ever thought to replicate Bateman's foundational work in more than six decades. It was a classic case of confirmation bias. Scientists and social scientists had sought out behaviors that confirmed Bateman's findings and simply didn't see the evidence— supplied by Hrdy, Small, Smuts, Jolly, Altmann, and others—that contradicted it as anything other than exceptional. Gowaty's lab work, combined with the burgeoning literature on populations where non-human female primates and women have sex and reproduce in ways that contradict the Bateman model, offered overwhelming proof that it was wrong to continue asserting universal difference in male and female reproductive strategies and sexual behavior based on the false dichotomy between "expensive eggs" and "cheap sperm" and between demure, monogamous females and naturally assertive, polygamous males. Males don't have meaningfully faster reproductive rates than females. These notions were so many castles in the air.

Now what?

OMOKA: THE MEANING OF A HIMBA WORD

Brooke Scelza had been influenced by both Gowaty and Hrdy, and inspired by each of their perspectives on females as anything but passive in the evolutionary and reproductive process. And while she had originally intended to study the relationship between Himba mothers and their adolescent daughters as the young women approached their childbearing years, she wound up stumbling on a word that set her on a different path, further contributing to the comprehensive upending of assumptions about female choice and coy, choosy, passive females.

When she first arrived at her Himba field site in Namibia in 2009, Scelza began a survey of the mothers she intended to interview, gathering their marital and reproductive histories. "Who's your husband? Is he your first husband? How many kids do you have?"—the basics every anthropologist asks of her subjects in the field in order to get an accurate demographic portrait of the population. But Scelza quickly found herself having an experience not unlike Kim Hill's with the Aché, many of whom told him, as he diligently worked on kinship charts, that they had more than one father. Early in the interview and data collection process, a woman informed Scelza, "This child is from my husband, and these two children are *omoka*."

Confused, Scelza asked her Himba translator what the word meant.

It meant "to go to the far place to get water," he explained.

Seeing the anthropologist's confusion, the translator elaborated that "going to the far place to get water" might be a way of creating cover, so to speak, when heading off to a tryst. *Omoka* child means a child "from the far place we go to get water"—a child a married woman conceives during an affair, or one born out of wedlock. The women knew whether they were having *omoka* children by counting back from the day of their last menstrual period and figuring out whom they'd had sex with and when.

Scelza had read about polygyny among the Himba, and that the women had lovers just like the men did. But this term was something new. She continued to press her translator, who insisted that, yes, the term was in common usage since, after all, *many* married women had children by men other than their husbands. And sure, he told her, go ahead and ask the Himba anything you want about these arrangements and practices. Married men and women alike will speak to you openly about their lovers and who fathered which child, he assured her.

Scelza told me that at first she suspected she might be misunderstanding the meaning of the word *omoka* and all it suggested. But as she continued asking women about their marital and reproductive histories, many of them repeated the term *omoka*, confirming that the practice was far from uncommon. A married Himba woman who is pregnant, in other words, is likely to have become so by a man other than the one she is married to. And a married woman with a child may well have had it by a man other than her husband. And nobody seems to think much of it.

Scelza suspected that the number of *omoka* kids a Himba woman had could unlock some secrets about female infidelity more generally. For starters, unlike many Western industrialized populations where women can "conceal" sexual infidelity by not bearing a child thanks to birth control, in a natural fertility population like the Himba there will be a much closer match between rates of infidelity and rates of extra-pair paternity—rates of kids born to women married to men not their fathers. In the US and the industrialized West, for example, rates of extra-pair paternity hover between 1 and 10 percent. That's very low, given that rates of female infidelity are thought to range anywhere from 13 to 50 percent in our world. From the Himba, for starters, Scelza could get a more unadulterated rate of female adultery to contribute to the worldwide ethnographic literature on women and extra-pair sex. And just as important, she might also be able to get information on *why* Himba women cheat.

First, though, Scelza had to figure out just how promiscuous Himba women were. The short answer was: very. She included 110 women in her analysis, recording 421 births. The women Scelza interviewed attributed each of their births to either her husband or an extramarital affair—an *omoka* birth. Scelza then classified each marriage as arranged or a love match. She felt confident of the women's paternity assertions when she saw that the women's calculations of when they became pregnant and by whom were supported by anthropologists' records that married Himba couples often spend "significant periods apart." In the end, Scelza determined that nearly 32 percent of the women in her sample had at least one *omoka* birth during her lifetime. Of the group of women who had at least one extra-pair birth, twenty had one, nine had two, and six had three or more *omoka* children with their lovers. Only 329 of the 421 births were from within wedlock. The long and short of it was that the Himba had the highest reported rate of extra-pair paternity of any small-scale society in the world: nearly 18 percent of all marital births were *omoka*. And just under one in three Himba women—nearly a third—had babies with their lovers while married.

But why? How can the Himba's beliefs and practices be so different from ours—and what factors, precisely, contribute to their radically accepting view of not only female "promiscuity" but the bearing of *omoka* children?

Scelza knew going into her analysis that biology, ecology, environment, and culture *all* play a role in human behavior. The Himba's comparatively relaxed attitude about extramarital sex was obviously a contributing factor in their tolerance of infidelity and *omoka* births. Himba women asked her repeatedly, "Brooke, why do you sleep alone all night in your tent?" When she replied that it was because she was married, they laughed or shrugged and teased her. "That doesn't mean you can't have a lover," they insisted. "Aren't you lonely in your tent by yourself, Brooke?"

But this belief that a "lonely" woman can and should take a

lover regardless of whether she's married didn't emerge from thin air. Certain ecological and environmental factors create a context where the conviction that it's normal for a married woman to have sex with a man who is not her husband can take root. "The Himba have few heritable resources," Scelza told me, "and fathers do not invest heavily in kids." These realities mean that men are at less risk of misdirecting energy and investment to children not their own. In addition, Himba children help out around the compound, becoming net contributors to the group at a relatively young age compared to kids in other contexts, like the industrialized West, where kids are costly and burdensome to their parents. These differences mean that Himba men are motivated to tolerate paternity uncertainty—basically because it costs them very little, and even benefits them in some ways. Kids do chores, herd, and generally offset the cost of their keep and then some. And a Himba man's wife's lover often drops off food for the *omoka* child, further lowering the "cost" to the husband.

In addition, Himba men do not pay a high bride-price for their wives; and their cows are not passed down patrilineally, a practice that would create the possibility that a father might bequeath his cows to another man's child. For all these reasons, a Himba man has very little to lose if his wife has a lover or even a child by another man. Moreover, if a married man is at a remote cattle station with his girlfriend, the benefits of guarding his wife at home in order to prevent her from taking a lover of her own become prohibitive. It's impossible to be in two places at once and extremely difficult to watch over an autonomous woman from a distance. It's also pretty unpleasant to obsess over it. It is better and less "expensive" in every sense for a man to develop a tolerant attitude, and enjoy a girlfriend at the cattle station or in town who may, after all, bear him a child of his own. It also might serve him to have someone else watching out for his wife in his absence.

As for Himba women, specific social circumstances work in their favor as well when it comes to affairs and *omoka* children. While a Himba woman moves to her husband's compound upon marriage, she usually maintains very strong ties to her own parents and siblings and other relatives, visiting their compound often. If she has co-wives, as many Himba women do, owing to more or less formal arrangements, they can watch her children and keep her husband happy while she visits with her family for days at a time, or while she gives birth and then recovers among her own kin. Where women have strong ties and access to their own kin in marriage, they have increased autonomy, including sexual autonomy. Among the Himba, the reality of the *omoka* child proves this is the case. And, Scelza told me, there are plenty of benefits for the Himba woman with a lover. If her husband is away and there is a drought and she needs to pay for supplementary food, or she needs to take a child or herself to the clinic, she has a larger circle of helpers. "Unlike the Upper East Side of Manhattan, where cheating is an incredibly risky strategy if you're married to someone with high status and high wealth, for Himba women it makes complete sense and insulates against risk," Scelza explained, making the importance of context dramatically clear and personal for me.

So why doesn't *every* Himba woman of childbearing age have an *omoka* child?

In her research, Scelza discovered something else. Reviewing her data, she realized there were no *omoka* children born to women in love matches. Of the seventy-nine women she interviewed who had chosen their own husbands, not a single one had an *omoka* child. Meanwhile, there were *omoka* children in nearly a quarter of arranged marriages.

Far from the choosy, coy female that Darwin and Bateman imagined, or the specter of the more heavily invested mother who would naturally want quality over quantity, some Himba women assertively and actively exercise choice after their options have been circumscribed, Scelza concluded, going for both quantity and quality. In the face of coercion—being compelled to marry a man they have not themselves selected—their counterstrategy is to do what they are asked to do but also to do what they want. They have affairs. And then they have babies with their lovers. *Omoka* children and the high rate of extra-pair paternity among the Himba prove that Himba women are what Hrdy wants us to understand all primate females, including women, to be: not essentially retiring and naturally monogamous because of our biology but creatures who live at the intersection of biology and culture and ecology, making us "flexible and opportunistic individuals who confront recurring reproductive dilemmas and trade-offs within a world of shifting options."

We might well think that if exerting their choice to have an extramarital relationship helps Himba women in arranged marriages achieve emotional and sexual satisfaction, it is reward enough. But there's more to it, Scelza discovered. Himba women who have arranged marriages and then take a lover or lovers and bear their children actually improve their reproductive success. (Even when a young woman divorces her first husband, Scelza explained, he remains responsible for any children she bore during her marriage to him. Even if they are not his own. This makes an early arranged marriage a better deal than it may appear on the face of it.) Scelza documented that women in arranged marriages with lovers have more children who survive to age five than do the Himba women who marry the men they choose themselves. Clearly, mating multiply is beneficial to these women's reproductive success.

Scelza, studying the Himba and when and why they "go to the far place to get water," has served up a version of female choice that is strategic and far from sexually reticent, and presented us with a population where having "affairs" benefits women in terms of the number of helpers they have and the number of children they have. It is a glorious rebuttal to the Darwin-Bateman paradigm and a blow to the insistence that men and women are naturally one way or another socially and sexually because of who they are biologically. But one of the most important things about Scelza's work with the Himba may be that it throws us a fascinating, unexpected, and richly suggestive curveball that forces us to continue thinking through female choice. Himba woman who exercise unconstrained choice, marrying the men they pick themselves and then choosing to stay true to them, have *lower* reproductive success. They may do what they want and stick with that independent, personal decision—and in so doing, they may potentially disadvantage themselves in the most basic and fundamental way, by having fewer children who survive to adulthood. Scelza was cautious about this detail when I asked about it. She pointed out that lower reproductive success and being monogamous might not be a simple equation, and there might be an implied causality in this instance "that we're not sure of." It's possible, for example, that these monogamous women simply have lower fertility, or their partners do. But the possibility that monogamy may be straight up disadvantageous in particular contexts, including among the Himba, is a distinct, compelling, and game-changing notion.

Is monogamy a privilege or a prison for women? Is it a choice, or does it subvert choice? Is it a luxury or a deprivation? The lesson of the Himba and the *omoka* child is: it depends. On context. The interlocking, impossible-to-disentangle factors of biology, culture, and environmental circumstances mean sexual and social behaviors will be malleable; gamete production cannot explain or account for much beyond itself. For the Himba, cheating women who have had their hands forced by the choices of others come out on top in the game of reproductive success, while monogamy potentially disadvantages those women who are privileged enough to choose it, along with choosing their own husbands. This may be why, when I asked Brooke Scelza whether doing fieldwork among the Himba and speaking to those women about sex had changed her personal view on monogamy, she nodded. She joked about having two children under the age of four, and her work, and her marriage, and said that in addition to not wanting to hurt her husband, who, like her, lives in a culture that expects monogamy even as it winks about its improbability, she could not imagine adding an affair to the mix. Then she laughed and told me she loved her husband very much and wasn't implying that were it not for being busy with kids and work, she would be having extra-pair dalliances—she didn't mean that at all. "It's more that in our society it's hard to imagine having the bandwidth for that." Then she said, with utmost care, "Well, it *was*. I used to think it was very straightforward. It was hard to understand women who felt differently than I did. Now I see that all of this is very, very complicated."

Scelza's remarkable achievement, among others, is helping us understand that "going to the far place to get water" or not going there, even in a context where there is comparatively little social censure or judgment about which you choose, is nevertheless a choice with surprising and profound consequences.

CHAPTER SIX

BONOBOS IN PARADISE

Darwin, with his tremendously influential assertion that the female is reluctant and reticent, sexually speaking, never saw some of the sexual behaviors that a number of female primatologists have brought into the spotlight over the last several decades. In many species of non-human primates, these scientists discovered, a female will initiate copulations much more frequently than a male does—often by presenting her posterior. But that is only the beginning of her assertiveness. Sitting next to a male she has chosen and giving him a "Let's get this party started" grimace may be followed, if he is insufficiently ardent, by grooming him. A female macaque, Linda Wolfe and Meredith Small tell us, may then leap on this favored male, rubbing her genital area back and forth over his torso. And Darwin would have blushed at the antics of the lion-tailed macaque female, who will pester a male over and over if he is unresponsive, pulling his hair, screeching, and jumping up and down in front of him. When that doesn't work, female lion tails have been observed vocalizing and literally writhing on the ground in sexual frustration and impatience, waiting for the male to get a clue and get busy with her already. Female ruffed lemurs, meanwhile, approach and slap males to get their sexual services, while female capuchins will chase males, emitting high-pitched whistling, whining vocalizations and smacking them, once they catch up, to prompt them to mount and copulate. A capuchin female may be so busy soliciting males that she does not eat during her days-long sexual peak. Mating replaces food as the greatest necessity and highest priority in her life. This is the "demure" and "reticent" sex.

As for "weaker" libidos—guess again. For most female primates, a single copulation with one male is just the warm-up. When they are sexually receptive and sometimes even when not, they may seek out copulation after copulation with numerous males, one after the other, often in rapid sequence. Female chimps in one group averaged 3.6 daily copulations while in estrus, and never with just one male; an Indian female rhesus was observed soliciting four different males in less than two hours. A female chacma baboon would be unimpressed by her rhesus cousin's appetite; chacmas have been observed to mate with three males in three minutes. Unconstrained, woolly spider monkey and Barbary macaque females will copulate with just about every male they encounter. While these behaviors may seem undiscriminating, they are anything but: what really gets our non-human primate female cousins going is a fellow who hasn't been around long, or even better, a total stranger. Female chimps leave their natal groups to have sex with "stranger" males and then return home. Female patas monkeys "roam the savannah looking for males other than their harem leader." Squirrel monkey females look for action outside their troop all the time. As mentioned previously, Kim Wallen and his colleagues at Emory University's Yerkes National Primate Research Center know it's important to introduce new males into their macaque population; otherwise the females lose interest in sex entirely. Even supposedly "monogamous" gibbon females hook up with new males when their mates are out of sight. Small summarizes that a thirst for novelty is the single most observable trait among all the sexual behaviors, preferences, and drivers of female primates. In fact, female primates couldn't be further from reluctant breeders or seekers of "intimacy" with a single "best" mate, or dead set on doing it with "the alpha." Indeed, Small suggests that it is difficult for us humans to wrap our minds around "just how little importance nonhuman female primates attach to knowing a male before they mate with him." Au contraire, our primate sisters are sexual adventuresses, driven by the thrill of the unknown and unfamiliar.

And not a few of them like to get busy with other females. Linda Wolfe discovered that roughly 75 percent of the two troops of female macaques she studied regularly mounted or were mounted by other females. Female langurs also have sexual encounters with other female langurs; in three thousand hours of observation of a troop in India, researchers found that there were no females who *didn't*. Could a penchant for sexual variety—homosexual as well as heterosexual acts—be an extension of the female primate's craving for novelty? Could the sex of one's partner be less important to a female primate than the excitement of the new and the unexpected, and the pleasures they confer? And what's the relationship between the social and the sexual for female primates of the human and non-human varieties?

These questions and the issue of pleasure bring us to one of our very closest primate relatives, the bonobo, with whom we share nearly 99 percent of our DNA. Bonobos (*Pan paniscus*), formerly known as "pygmy chimps," do in fact look like taller, slimmer versions of their other close relatives, chimps (*Pan troglodytes*). They live in only one place in the wild: the Congo Basin of the Democratic Republic of Congo, formerly Zaire. Bonobos also live under human care in seven zoos in the United States, and in several European countries. My questions about female sexuality, female pleasure, female sociality, and female "infidelity" brought me to San Diego for several days to speak with Dr. Amy Parish, a primatologist who trained with both Sarah Hrdy and Frans de Waal. Parish, who had been inspired and mentored by the same woman who sparked my own interest in primatology at the University of

Michigan, Barbara Smuts, had created a considerable commotion in her field very early in her career by reporting what she observed in her work with bonobos. Since then, she has periodically lobbed insights based on her research at the San Diego, Stuttgart, and Frankfurt zoos that blew up the prevailing view of primate social behavior—that humans, like chimps, are inherently prone to (mostly male) conflict and violence, and that male dominance, including infanticide and sexual coercion of females, is deeply woven into our evolutionary legacy. Through careful study and many hours of observation and data collection, Parish brought forward groundbreaking insights about bonobos, insights that reveal an important, surprising, and untold aspect of our hominin prehistory.

At the San Diego Zoo, the bonobos are tucked away, hard to find, even, relative to their primate brethren. To get to the gorillas, for example, you just amble up Treetops Way, one of the more heavily trafficked routes through the beloved SoCal institution, until you come across the signs leading you to their enclosure, often lined four or five rows deep with spectators. But getting to the bonobos requires a trek through the Treetops Café at one of the highest points of the zoo and then a meander down around a longish, winding staircase. After that, you hope you're headed the right way, as there is minimal bonobo signage. When I finally arrived at their enclosure at 9:30 a.m. for my first day observing them, it was already hot and sunny, and I could hear a chorus of screeches and squawks from the nearby aviary. I was as impressed by the bonobos' setup as I was perplexed by their far-flung location: there are several different sets of massive windows through which to watch the nine bonobos doing their thing in a one acre or so enclosure complete with tire swings, a waterfall and stream, an elaborate and extensive jungle gym made of ropes, plenty of greenery growing up from the ground, and lots of boulders and grassy patches on which to sun and socialize. Bonobos are slimmer than chimps; they have longer necks and smaller heads and often somewhat longish hair that is parted down the middle, giving them an uncannily human—and more specifically, late Beatles—aspect. At the opposite end of the enclosure from where I stood, I saw an adult bonobo who reminded me of Ringo taking the measure of me.

Bonobos are harder still to find in their native habitat and even harder to study. Because they live in an area with a long history of political unrest and violence, for decades it was impossible for primatologists to observe them in any sustained way. It's only within the last quarter century or so, thanks to fieldworkers in Congo and others, including Parish, who study them under human care in zoos, that anyone got a handle on who and what they are. There was no bonobo gene sequencing until 2012, at which point we learned that bonobos are more closely related to humans than they are to gorillas and at least as closely related to us as are chimps. A 2017 studying comparing human, chimp, and bonobo muscles confirmed what previous molecular research had suggested: "Bonobo muscles have changed the least [from our common ancestor], which means they are the closest we can get to having a 'living' ancestor," according to the research head of the George Washington University Center for the Advanced Study of Human Paleobiology. Some paleontologists believe that bonobos look a great deal like our pre-hominin ancestor *Australopithecus afarensis*. Female bonobos have more pronounced breasts than other female primates (though a bit less pronounced than ours), and posturally, bonobos resemble humans quite a bit, especially with their tendency to walk bipedally. Like us, they have sex ventrally, or face-to-face, something very rare in other primates. And bonobos are known to both spontaneously console victims of harassment and revel in being consoled. Researchers say that in doing so, bonobos follow the same "empathic gradient" that humans do, offering support to kin, friends, and acquaintances. Except for a difference in frequency, human and bonobo babies have extraordinarily similar laughs when they are tickled.

But perhaps the most remarkable thing about bonobos, and

without question the most remarked upon thing about them, is their sexual practices. Basically, they seem to have sex constantly throughout the day, with just about anybody. Meredith Small reports being in a room of three hundred or so primatologists and journalists for a screening of some early footage of bonobos in 1991, before much was known about them. Moments after the film began, the room fell utterly silent as the assembled took in the spectacle of these primates having sex more times and in more positions and combinations than most humans in any culture could even imagine. Their creativity, apparent appetite, and lack of inhibition were stunning. Small describes watching bonobo sex as "like watching humans at their most extreme and perverse." The film footage was Parish's. She was twenty-five years old that day when she shared it, diminutive and blonde. When she used a projector to show a close-up of a female bonobo's anogenital swelling covered in ejaculate from several different males, a male primatologist in the audience turned to her mentor, Frans de Waal, and demanded (I like to imagine in an outraged, hoarse whisper), "How can such a delicate young lady speak about such things?"

Bonobos do in fact have lots of sex. Lots and lots of it. In one study, Parish and her colleagues documented that they did so sixty-five times as frequently as capuchins, who are no slouches when it comes to getting it on. Bonobos are also what we might consider indiscriminate about the sex of their partners. Adult male bonobos copulate with any number of females every day but are just as happy to massage the penises of other adult males in their troop or another troop, or stand rump to rump and rub their scrotal sacs together. Younger bonobos, both male and female, are fond of French kissing and fellatio. Adult female bonobos, for their part, enjoy being mounted by males and not infrequently mount them as well. Females equally or even more eagerly practice what primatologists term (rather uninspiredly) "G-to-G contact," which is just an easier way of saying "genito-genital contact." Lying on top of each other, or facing each other while lying on their sides, the females press and grind their vulvas together in pursuit of pleasure. Which they find. Their clitorides—which are larger than a human female's and more externalized—become engorged, and they often shriek as they rub against each other. It feels good enough that they do it roughly every two hours on average. In fact, field scientists have documented many instances when female bonobos ignored the overtures of males in order to indulge in this type of girl-on-girl action. In a research study spanning several months, primatologist Zanna Clay and colleagues noted that "females engaged in significantly more sexual interactions with other females than with males." And why not? As Parish has observed, the bonobo female's clitoris is large enough that it is easily stimulated. It can even be used for intromission. That is, a female bonobo can penetrate another female bonobo's vagina with her excited, engorged, and not tiny clitoris. This is not a frequent occurrence, but it happens. Leave it to female bonobos to invent a dildo that's always there for you.

As I stood at the large window of the enclosure at the zoo, a bonobo knuckle-walked over to me, clearly curious. I surmised from the chart of photos I had been studying that her name was Lisa. She seated herself at the window and stared at me. I stared back. A family with a toddler and a baby in a stroller stood next to me. Lisa stuck her finger up her anus, pulled out a greenish-yellow dollop of feces, and considered it. Then she popped it into her mouth and chewed with gusto. The woman near me shouted, "Did you see that?!" She exclaimed loudly, over and over, "That monkey is disgusting!" The couple grabbed their toddler's hand, pivoted their stroller, and rushed away, the mother announcing repeatedly that she simply couldn't believe what she had witnessed. Eventually I couldn't hear her anymore. I was alone, staring at Lisa, who stared at me and picked at her teeth. It occurred to me that the bonobos might be tucked away because, with all their screwing and sucking and scissoring and shit eating, they are not exactly rated-G great apes. Our very closest relatives are far from family friendly.

* * *

Bonobos are highly affiliative and altruistic, meaning they love hanging out together and will put themselves out for other bonobos, Amy Parish was telling me. We were standing at the windows of the bonobo enclosure. Parish, who is from Saint Joseph, Michigan, but has embraced the ethos of Southern California, where she moved in 1990, wore sunglasses with heart-shaped lenses and spoke with a singsongy, SoCal inflection. She told me who was who in the troop. When the bonobos caught sight of her, a few of them made a beeline toward us and then reached up to the glass, as if to touch her hand through it. Parish did the same. She told me about experiments she had recently begun with the bonobos in Stuttgart, playing video of them and humans doing various things to figure out which videos and activities they preferred watching (in a follow-up interview, she told me they had loved videos of humans doing modern dance and hated videos of leopards, humans dancing like snakes, and the zoo's vet, which moved them to kick and slap the video monitor). I was surprised that bonobos liked watching bonobo videos. Laughing, Parish put her camera up to the window and played back some video she had just taken of a juvenile bonobo who was particularly interested in us. It was immediately transfixed, face pressed against the glass, staring at the movie. "Yes. It's *you*," Parish said, speaking directly to the bonobo, laughing again. Parish has an initially disconcerting way of "chatting with" the apes so that, in spite of knowing of her reputation, when I first saw her do it I had a flash of anxiety that I had possibly flown across the country to hang out with someone slightly nuts. What I quickly realized, however, is that her feelings of connection to the bonobos come from her science, and vice versa. Empathy and to a certain extent identification with these primates, along with rigorous training, a passion for data, and extensive knowledge, are what have made it possible for Parish to generate the remarkable insights she has about their behavior, and in the process upend some of our fundamental understanding of ourselves. At one point, as the bonobos were being fed, a high-ranking female named Loretta caught sight of Parish and became visibly excited. She charged to the edge of a large outcropping she was standing on to be as close to us as possible and then repeatedly lifted her chin in a head-bob gesture remarkably like a teenager saying, "What's up?" Parish did it back, and they repeated this back and forth for a good minute. Then Loretta clapped her hands together and touched her head. Parish did the same thing. Loretta repeated the gesture but touched her mouth after, and so did Parish. When I asked what she was doing, Parish explained, "Basically, she's saying, 'What's up?' And when I do the gestures back, it's a way of greeting and reestablishing a rapport." Loretta, whom Parish told me is one of her favorite bonobos, was clearly sweet on Parish too.

About a year after Parish first started studying the bonobos in 1990 (they were at the San Diego Zoo Safari Park then), something extraordinary happened, something that made things click for the primatologist. She had been spending entire days observing them and collecting data on their behavior, often arriving early in the morning and then eating lunch while watching them, not wanting to miss anything. One day, Parish was trying to get a good photo of the troop's highest-ranking female. The bonobos had just been provisioned, and this particular bonobo, Louise, sat with a giant bunch of celery in her hands, twenty or thirty feet away from Parish. Parish called the bonobo's name repeatedly (they respond to the names their human caregivers give them), but no dice. Louise was not going to help Parish get a better angle for her camera shot. In fact, Parish sensed that Louise was intentionally ignoring her. Parish called out her name yet again. This time, Louise turned toward her human interlocutress, looking at her directly and, according to Parish, with what seemed like exasperation. She stood up, deliberately tore her celery bunch in half, and tossed part of it at Parish. It landed at the scientist's feet with a plop. The great ape figured the other great ape was trying to mooch some food and decided to oblige her. In essence, she was saying, "Yes, all right, you're one of us. One of the girls."

"All those days of observation, all those hours, I sat there eating my lunch in front of her, never sharing," Parish told me as we stood surrounded by zoo-goers oohing and ahhing at the bonobos through the glass. "And yet here she was, sharing her lunch with me." This remarkably socially gregarious and altruistic act was an Aha moment for Parish. From her first days working with them, Parish had noted that bonobos were female affiliative and very sexual. The celery-throwing incident, an act of bonding generosity across the line of species, was all the more extraordinary and telling because of bonobo social structure. They are a male philopatric species. That is, males stay in their natal groups, within a network of kin, while females disperse at sexual maturity to ensure there is no inbreeding. While it's good for the species and individuals alike to have unrelated breeding partners, this arrangement generally means a life of misery for females who are, after all, interlopers of sorts, arrivistes in their social settings relative to males. The implications are hard to ignore: among other non-human primates, female dispersal/male philopatry means that females are at the bottom of the totem pole relative to the males who've stayed in place and the females who've been there awhile. It also means males are in charge in obvious ways—they eat first, get groomed more often, and can commit infanticide and physical violence against females, not to mention coerce females sexually without consequence. After all, what recourse do unaffiliated females have?

This formula—that male philopatry equals male dominance—seems to hold across *all* non-human primate species and was certainly true among bonobos' closest relatives, chimps. Those males often "patrol" and have been known to kill solitary, roaming male chimps. And within their troops, chimp males and females alike kill infants and are violent toward low-ranking individuals. A female chimp, particularly a low-ranking one, can ill afford altruism of the kind Louise showed, or any form of risk-taking.

But not so bonobos. Female bonobos leave their natal groups at sexual maturity, but they also eat before the males do, Parish noted early on. And the females get groomed so often that some were nearly bald (bonobos in captivity behave almost exactly as bonobos in the wild do, according to De Waal, Parish, and others, except that the ones under human care, with more time on their hands, groom one another more often and more zealously). The males, in contrast, wait their turn to eat after the females, have lots of hair, and rarely receive grooming from the females they themselves are eager to groom. These two factors—eating first and being groomed more often—strongly suggested to Parish that females might have sway in other ways.

In the popular imagination, bonobos have a somewhat hippie-ish reputation. They're portrayed as the "free love" primates but are also supposedly a more likable, peaceable version of their stressed-out, lashing-out chimp cousins. Several articles even refer to bonobos as pacific, "Make love not war" "swingers." It has long been believed that bonobos have sex to diffuse potential tension—when they come upon a cache of food, for example, or a new bonobo troop, having sex is a way to bond and take the stress level down. Parish pointed out that this was happening as we observed them being fed. Once the food was flung down to them, at least one pair of bonobos began to "consort" immediately. Only then did they get down to the business of eating.

But in addition to seeing that bonobos were female affiliative, socially gregarious, and very sexual, Parish quickly realized there was a clear pattern of female-on-male violence. Females swatted, chased, smacked, gouged, and bit males, who mostly seemed to know better than to annoy them. Parish had seen a male in Frankfurt with only eight digits intact, and she knew of another male who had had his penis nearly severed from his body (the vet was able to reattach it, and the male went on to have erections and successfully reproduce, though you have to wonder how good he felt about the females from then on). Parish asked her mentor, De Waal, about it. He had worked with the San Diego population in the 1980s, when they were younger, and had in fact recorded a list of injuries but didn't recall the males being injured more often or more seriously than the females. Still, Parish asked to see records—both De Waal's and the logs zoo veterinarians had kept of bonobo injuries over the years. Sure enough, of a total of twenty-five serious injuries, twenty-four were inflicted on males. By females.

That clinched it for Parish. She realized that in spite of male philopatry, bonobos were female affiliative, female bonded, and, most extraordinarily of all, female *dominant,* sufficiently so that females eat first, are groomed more often, and have the authority to attack males. All this in spite of the males being physically larger and ensconced within a kin network of automatic allies. About fifteen years ago, according to news reports, a senior keeper at the San Diego Zoo, Mike Bates, experienced female-bonobo dominance and violence literally firsthand. As he signaled a pregnant female to approach for a medical assessment, she managed to reach through the bars of that section of the enclosure and catch his sleeve, pulling his hand close enough to her mouth to bite. Which she did, severing the tip of his index finger and spitting it out on the ground. Another female approached. She picked up Bates's fingertip and held it in her own hand. As Bates headed to the hospital, his colleagues used treats to barter for the return of the digit. The price was five raisins. The fingertip was reattached, and Bates's hand looks normal today. But if you peer closely, you see the scar that tells the story of female aggression.

Parish told me there was another, even darker side to female dominance among bonobos. Male bonobos are often reluctant in the face of female pursuit. So reluctant, in fact, that Parish says without reservation, "The situation of male-female sex sometimes looks coercive to me." That is, the females force males to have sex with them. This might seem impossible, but males get erections from anxiety, so it is easy enough, mechanically speaking, for females to force the males to mate with them. A female bonobo tends to be the initiator of sex. She does so by putting her arm around a male as if to say, "How about it?" The males who appear coerced will try to shake the female off repeatedly. During sex, they may give distress vocalizations and try to escape. As Mike Bates told me, "It's in your face. You can't not notice it. They will pick out a male and just stay on him. A female will be all over a male so that he can't get away from her solicitations. She'll keep walking around with her arm around him, again and again. It's well documented."

Female bonobos manage to dominate males because they form coalitions of two or more whenever they perceive a male is challenging them. It doesn't take males long to stop trying and to realize who's in charge. But how are these females, who are unrelated and who disperse from their kin, able to form coalitions? Why is the species the only exception to the trend of male philopatry leading to male dominance in the first place? It's the sex, Parish told me. "They choose what feels good, and what feels especially good is having sex with other females, probably because of the front-facing, relatively exposed, innervated clitoris." In fact, Parish told me, when a female bonobo is solicited simultaneously by a female and a male, she will nearly always pick the female (other primatologists have observed this preference as well). On my second day observing the bonobos with Parish, then-three-year-old Belle sat directly in front of us, right up against the glass. She had a long piece of grass looped around her torso, like a necklace. Her legs were splayed, and she poked between them with one finger. She was playing with her clitoris, which was about the size of a large pencil eraser. Clearly, she was enjoying herself. Another day, Parish and I watched Belle mount her big sister Maddie, who was lying on her back; they indulged in some G-to-G swishing back and forth. Bonobos don't just reduce tension with sex. Females are grinding and G-to-G-ing their way to establishing goodwill and connectedness, or reinforcing goodwill and connectedness already in place, using sex to build a sisterhood of sorts. And bonobo sisterhood is powerful. "We don't see infanticide or females being sexually coerced, and we don't see males being aggressive to females in any way," Parish explained. "But we cannot ignore female bonobo violence toward males and female dominance among bonobos." Parish observes that for a long time there was resistance to her discoveries. Not everyone was as sanguine and open-minded as her mentor, De Waal, who quickly agreed with Parish. Other primatologists insisted that bonobos didn't have a dominance hierarchy at all or that bonobos were "egalitarian" or, my favorite, that bonobo males "allowed" females to *think* they were dominant. Why the refusal to see what Parish saw? After all, other researchers have documented females using G-to-G contact for reconciliation, tension regulation, and other forms of bonding. "Females showing males aggression is written off as exceptional because of our powerful narrative of what's natural," Parish told me when I asked her over dinner one night in downtown San Diego. She had never expected her findings to be controversial, she said. A careful scientist and self-described "Darwinian feminist," Parish is patient in the face of resistance and bias, focusing on the data and the big picture that primatology, like primates, has evolved over time.

"There's an implicit bias against matriarchy. A lot of people, including scientists, seem to resist the idea that what bonobos do—that females are sexually assertive and strategic, that they build female-female coalitions through sex, and that they are a female-dominant species, period—is part of our evolutionary lineage. Bonobos are part of the narrative arc of humanness," Parish said, making her point as if it were precisely what it is: a fact.

I was momentarily stunned by the simplicity and profundity of what Parish was asserting. Our closest non-human primate relatives are non-monogamous. Females have baroque anogenital swellings, the better to attract the interest of multiple males, not one "best" alpha guy. In fact, there are no alpha guys, because they are a society of alpha gals. And this is so mostly thanks to gals preferring sex with one another. Which they do because of how wonderful it feels to rub their front-facing, exposed, and richly innervated clitorides together.

It all begged a number of questions about our world and the bonobo world, which we might think of as the original hookup culture. If human females lived under these conditions—a world that was female bonded, female affiliative, and female dominant, and where females had the freedom to be blatantly pleasure focused—then sex on college campuses would look very different indeed. It certainly wouldn't be about women serving men's needs at the expense of having their own fulfilled, as Peggy Orenstein discusses in her book *Girls and Sex*. Affirmative consent, analyzed so thoroughly by Vanessa Grigoriadis in *Blurred Lines* and familiar to millions of teens in the US thanks to a video comparing it to offering someone tea, would not be an issue—men would not dream of assaulting women in a world where sex happens publicly, women are there to watch it all happen, and "Girl Power" is the actual order of things, not some abstract motto about how things might be. More generally, Parish's work is richly suggestive of other possibilities: What if human sexuality is more like bonobo sexuality than chimp sexuality? Specifically, what if human *female* sexuality is as much informed by our bonobo sisters as it is by comparatively abject chimp females (who risk violence when they themselves have multiple, rapidly sequential consorts during and also outside of estrus)? What if all our presumptions of alpha males being dominant adventurers in sexual conquest, and women as passive recipients seeking a single dominant male's attention, come from the long shadow cast by the plough, not from how we evolved? What if women are in fact "wired" at some level to be sexually dominant and promiscuous, and to use sex for pleasure and building social bonds with other women—and it is primarily environment that has resulted in our behaving otherwise? In short, what if bonobo-ness is one of the drivers of women's deepest longings: the powerful, polymorphous, perverse fantasies on display in Meredith Chivers's lab; the sexual ennui of the long-partnered, low-desiring women who participate in Marta Meana's research and the unexpected sexual autonomy of those who told Meana that, hell yes, they'd have sex with themselves; and the wide and unambiguous swerves from the script of sexual reticence and longing for partnered security seen in Alicia Walker's study participants?

I revisited my conversations and emails with Parish in my mind for many, many weeks. Her insights and perspective seemed relevant to every interview I had done, every question I had about my own marriage and libido, every conversation I had with women who confessed that they were "unfaithful," or told me they were sexually bored in their marriages or partnerships, or that they stepped out not in search of companionship but for sex. Unexpectedly, Parish's point of view also left me better prepared for an event I attended after my trip to San Diego, giving me a unique lens through which to view the behavior of a group of female *Homo sapiens* who use "promiscuous sex" to build bonds with one another. They do so for pleasure, and without apparent guilt or regret. They do not live in Namibia or Botswana, where women have also used non-dyadic sex to their benefit. This tribe gathered in a soaring townhouse in the modern metropole of Manhattan, and in a luxurious loft in downtown Los Angeles.

I had first heard about Skirt Club in a 2016 *New York Post* article by Mackenzie Dawson. The headline was "This Sex Club Gives Men Major FOMO." The article chronicled the adventures of the founder of a roving, underground women's "play party." She went by the pseudonym Geneviève LeJeune and told Dawson that she was married to a man. She had founded Skirt Club after being groped at grotty sex parties in London that left her thinking, *I could do this better. It could be more luxurious. And for women only.* LeJeune explained that far too often she found herself in contexts where her attraction to and yearning for adventures with other women was "leveraged" or interfered with by men who wanted in on it for their own gratification. What might a *women-only* gratification gathering for women like LeJeune— women who identify as "bi but in a committed straight relationship" or simply "curious"—look like?

She set about creating it. Today there are Skirt Club parties in Shanghai, Vienna, Los Angeles, San Francisco, Ibiza, Miami, London, Berlin, Sydney, Tokyo, Shanghai, and Washington, DC, with themes like "All Tied Up" (with a bondage tutorial), "Retro Pin-Up Girls" (with a burlesque performance by a comely Dita Von Teese type), and "Strict" (a BDSM-themed event). They are billed as exclusive, high-end, femme-y affairs, free of the yucky plastic mattresses and grabby guys that LeJeune sought to replace with well-dressed, well-groomed, successful women in chic, sexy lingerie and heels and little else.

But what really riveted me was the photo that accompanied Dawson's piece. Two women with dark tousled hair that tumbled to their shoulders and obscured their faces sat close together; one was leaning in and clearly kissing the other on the neck. Her hand was on the bare thigh of the object of her desire, grasping, suggestive. Both women wore black bustiers that showed off their toned arms and legs, and bunny ears on their heads, giving it all an ironic twist. But the heat between them felt real, and I could not drag my eyes away, wondering what it would be like to be in the midst of a group of women this attractive and this uninhibited (of course the photo was staged, but it worked, on me and apparently not a few other men and women who became fascinated by Skirt Club). A little Googling revealed that the parties were "members only" and that there was an application process. This was after the Ashley Madison hack, and while I dreamed of attending as research for this book, I didn't relish the possibility, however remote, that I might share information online that could someday, somehow, be used against me. Plus the application process was intimidating. What if my request were rejected? I let the delicious and enticing idea of attending Skirt Club go.

But Bryony Cole, the tall, blonde host of the *Future of Sex* podcast who stands close to six feet in heels, wasn't having it. When I interviewed her at a café in downtown Manhattan for her perspectives on the present and future of female sexuality and female infidelity, she spoke about virtual-reality sex. Was it cheating when the other person was basically a hologram? What about the kind of sex in which you merely shared a screen with another person? She wondered whether sex robots, mostly designed for men, could actually liberate women who craved variety and novelty, allowing them to remain true in long-term, committed partnerships while experiencing a version of the thrill of being with another. And she had great hope for platforms like OMGYes, an online sex-education program for women with an interactive touch screen that walks you through a dozen techniques to reach orgasm; and Dame, a line of female-MIT-grad-developed vibrators, dildos, and sex toys, all designed with comprehensive research about female pleasure and user focus in mind. Tech held so much promise for women that Cole declared we had entered a new era of "vaginomics." But she also mused aloud about an in-real-life ecology where women could have a measure of release from constraint: "Have you ever been to Skirt Club?" she asked me. I exclaimed that I had been reading quite a bit about Skirt Club and LeJeune, and Cole insisted that I come as her guest to the next play party. She was a friend of LeJeune, she explained, and this was something I simply had to experience.

I received the address and details about the party the day before. The instructions specified the address—it was downtown, of course. I wasn't to mention Skirt Club but rather to say simply that I was invited to C.'s party should a doorman or anyone else ask me. It shouldn't be an issue, though, as I would be greeted in the lobby by hostesses from Skirt Club. The theme was "All Tied Up," and there would be a performance at 8:30 sharp of shibari, the ancient and elaborate Japanese art of bondage. The party ended at 2:30 a.m. At least I was pretty sure that's what "Carriages at 2:30 a.m." meant.

My husband, who was amused and not a little intrigued by my Skirt Club invitation, had encouraged me to go, even though I was at the tail end of a cold and wanted to spend the day and the evening in bed. But the night of, at his urging, I dragged myself to an upright position and dressed in a long-sleeved, extremely form-fitting, knee-length black leather dress. He observed, "You look appropriate for either a funeral or an all-women sex party," and then he laughed like a hyena, which I was quick to remind him was a female-dominant species with hypertrophied clitorides. He told me I had permission to do whatever I wanted. I told him crankily that I didn't need permission, and he looked taken aback. "Oh, *really*," he teased, recovering. My research was getting under my skin, and I was very nervous on the trip downtown.

At the door, two beautiful, willowy, dark-haired women in kimonos and high heels greeted me, walking me through the lobby to the apartment door. They were, I learned later, hostesses, and in exchange for welcoming guests and helping everyone feel comfortable, they attended the parties for free. Inside the dark entryway of the apartment, a beautiful redhead named Isobel held a clipboard and checked me in. She tied a silky black string with an old-fashioned miniature key around my wrist. This, she told me, was the bracelet for first timers. Two more hostesses in kimonos and heels whisked me back to a bar, where a dozen or so women were getting their cocktail on. I noticed the owner of the cavernous and elegant apartment standing in the middle of the room with its double-height ceiling and fireplace, because how could I not? Tall and blonde, she wore her hair in a ponytail...and little else. A G-string revealed butterfly tattoos on her bottom, and on top she sported a harness that exposed her nipples. She seemed perfectly comfortable that way and also clearly inspired the guests, who soon peeled the tops of their cocktail dresses down to their waists, or disposed of them entirely. I scanned the room and took in the variety of body types and diverse group of women, ranging in age from their early twenties to their fifties. But this was Manhattan, after all, and most of the bodies were remarkably toned.

I tried hard not to ogle the scantily clad women all around me—there were fifty guests that evening, I later learned. One woman had stripped down to a black bra and panties and many lengths of bright yellow rope around her waist like a belt. Even this early in the festivities the room buzzed with excitement. We might have been at a ladies' luncheon or a bridal shower as we sipped champagne and chatted but for the fact that everyone was standing around in lingerie, flirting. A tall and beautiful Chinese woman with a chic choppy haircut approached me. She was an interior designer, fashionably dressed in black leather leggings and an exquisite red push-up bra. When I told her I was writing about the party—no names, I promised—she exclaimed, "I like this party because no one has to wonder what's going to happen. We're all here for sex!" I felt my throat constrict as we sat down on a couch together, our knees touching.

LeJeune, who is petite and delicate looking, with pale skin and dark hair and mesmerizing hazel eyes, came over to where we sat chatting. She patiently answered a number of my questions about the attendees, telling me that tonight they were a mix of students, doctors, lawyers, mental health professionals, podcasters, artists, and more, all while also giving instructions to her assistant about adjusting the lighting. "Lighting's the most important thing at a party, whether it's a dinner party or a sex party. Except maybe alcohol." She laughed.

An effervescent blonde standing near us told me she was from a ritzy town in Florida and that this was not her first Skirt Club party. It was her fifth, and it had worked perfectly with her schedule, since she was in town for Gala Season. This was a socialite with a difference. Her breasts strained against the plunging neckline of her tight nude pleather dress. She asked me, sotto voce, why all the women were wearing stockings and garter belts. Was that a New York thing? Like her, I was bare legged, and didn't have an answer.

Soon, a special guest with the Instagram handle "Kissmedead-lyDoll" was giving us tips on shibari—Japanese bondage—using a willing, appealing blonde in a red velvet dress as her "victim." "If you are going to use the rope on someone's neck, be sure to either go high or go low. Never across the Adam's apple area," the raven-haired expert instructed. She stretched the rope across the blonde, bound twentysomething's crotch. Then she attached a vibrator to the rope high on her victim's back and turned it on, sending her into a paroxysm of pleasure as the sensation vibrated all the way down. At this point in the proceedings, I thought of myself as part of a slightly surreal Tupperware party. The fact that so many attractive women were sitting around nearly naked did very little to offset the sense that we were a group of women participating in the tradition of politely watching a demonstration of a household accoutrement (albeit a kinky one) in someone's living room.

Until the body shots. The lights went even lower, the music got even louder. One woman after another lay on her back on a white leather sofa, giggling as her legs were sprinkled with salt. A lime was stuffed into her mouth. Shot glasses of tequila rested near her face, and the game was on. "Victims" were licked, literally from head to toe (well, toe to head). Then the disinhibited partygoers headed for the large hot tub on the terrace, an impromptu make-out session in a cozy den, and the bedrooms. By 11 p.m., a group of eight naked women were on a bed upstairs, having sex in every imaginable configuration. They were grinding and giving and receiving oral sex. One woman used a dildo on another woman, who writhed and groaned on her back in the middle of the bed. Like stockings, inhibitions were shed. "I've been married for almost twenty years, and I just had sex with another married woman. This party helped me find myself," a remarkably fit and entirely naked woman enthusiastically told me as we watched the goings-on from what I deemed a safe distance. As she pulled her thong and spike-heeled boots back on and a woman on the bed behind her climaxed noisily, I did not doubt her. An attractive woman in a bustier and thong, her heels long cast aside, reached out and asked me if I wanted to join her on the bed. I demurred and headed downstairs. Fascinating and hot as I found my first Skirt Club party, I couldn't cross the line. At the door, the beautiful young blonde woman who had been tied up approached me. She said she was sorry I was leaving and that she hoped we could see each other again soon. I offered my phone so she could give me her contact information and then I headed out. In the lobby, I could still hear laughter and pumping music. The bonobo bacchanal would continue for hours.

Several weeks later I found myself at another Skirt Club party, this one in L.A. The theme was "BDSM," and the venue was a loft downtown tricked out like a dungeon. Walking down the long, dark hallway lined with candles, I quickly realized I wasn't in Kansas, or Manhattan, anymore. The main room was jammed with women, many of them in their twenties, a number of them already naked. In the middle of the room was a large cage. A suspension machine hung from the ceiling. The bar was so crowded I couldn't get near it. "These girls in L.A. drink a lot more, and they waste no time getting down to it," LeJeune told me with a wink when I found her. No one seemed to need icebreakers or getting-to-know-you chitchat—they were already making out and grinding on sofas. Others were dancing and groping under a black chandelier. A woman in nothing but a black thong and black electrical tape over her nipples stood in the cage, beckoning me over. To reach her I had to walk past a tall blonde with Brigitte Bardot hair and a black leather miniskirt who was in a lip-lock with an equally statuesque brunette in black lace panties and a black lace bra. But I also walked by women talking about work, women exchanging business cards, women who appeared to be networking. They did so brandishing riding crops and handcuffs and cat-o'-nine-tails. I was relieved when it was time for the performance and I could sit down next to a wel-

Since the days of Plymouth Colony, a double standard about infidelity has prevailed in the United States. Married women who stepped out were guilty of adultery, while married men who had sex with unmarried women were prosecuted for the lesser crime of fornication. In 1639, Mary Mendame of Plymouth Colony was convicted of adultery and "whipped at the cart's tail" while walking through the streets. (*Army Stock Photo*)

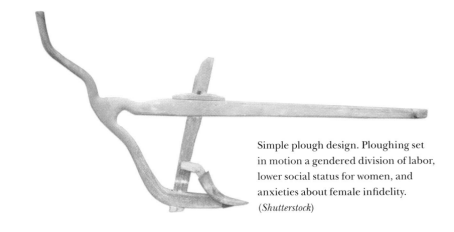

Simple plough design. Ploughing set in motion a gendered division of labor, lower social status for women, and anxieties about female infidelity. (*Shutterstock*)

Christian missionaries and other Europeans were often scandalized by the high status and sexual autonomy of Wyandot and other Native American women. As these women were primary producers and often lived matrilocally, they had equal say in social and political matters, and their sexualities were relatively unconstrained. This illustration depicts Jesuit missionary Jean de Brébeuf ministering to a Wyandot tribe. (*Getty Images*)

Public outrage ensued when the US and British governments encouraged farms to hire female farmhands during World War I and World War II. To appease angry male farmers, the women were encouraged to wear dresses and skirts.

"Farmer's daughter" jokes, now dated, have an overarching "punch line": that women are inherently promiscuous, thereby justifying all the constraints and containments to which they have been subjected in plough agriculture settings. (*Illustration by Pat Dorian*)

In this nineteenth-century painting by John Byam Liston Shaw, Jezebel's supposed "high self-regard" is literalized as she gazes into a mirror. Jezebel came from Phoenicia, where women were often high priestesses in the Baal religion. This put her on a collision course with the prophets of Yahweh, who believed in one male God and often used tropes of female infidelity to denounce worship of other gods. (Jezebel, *1896, Shaw, John Byam Liston [1872–1919] / Russell-Cotes Art Gallery and Museum, Bournemouth, UK / Bridgeman Images*)

Without Jezebel, there could be no Kim Kardashian. This wax version of Kim at Madame Tussauds in London borrows heavily from the iconography of the Jezebel painting, just as Kim's reputation—a wealthy, powerful woman who is allegedly shallow, hungry for renown, and sexually appetitive—mirrors Jezebel's. The differences are slight: Kim's attendants are her social-media followers and fans—and in this instance the museumgoers. Her phone is her mirror. (*Shutterstock*)

In this contemporary representation, Jezebel has the unrealistic waist-hip ratio that is a preference specific to plough-based or formerly plough-based ecologies. Note the serpents, barely disguised vagina dentata, at Jezebel's feet. Jezebel's name came to be associated not with political power and religious pluralism but with false prophecy, prostitution, and, later, a brazen woman who enjoyed sex and was in every sense "untrue." (*Saúl Shavanas*)

The Himba, seminomadic pastoralists who live in Namibia and Angola, have the highest rate of extra-pair paternity ever reported in a small-scale human population. Anthropologist Brooke Scelza, pictured here taking notes while sitting with a Himba woman and her baby, has written about how female "infidelity," a fact of life among the Himba, benefits women and children. (*Peter Hauser*)

Primatologist Amy Parish explains that Loretta the bonobo's "Shrek-like bald-ness" is proof of her dominance: everyone wants to groom her, and grooming removes hair. Parish, who studied female-on-male violence among bonobos, told the world that they are a female-dominant species. (*Amy Parish*)

Billed as a "play party" that "empowers women from the bedroom to the board-room" by founder Geneviève LeJeune, Skirt Club is a constraint-free environ-ment where mostly "heteroflexible" women gather. Not unlike female bonobos who prefer having sex with one another, these women use sex to cement social bonds, build coalitions, and find pleasure. (*Victoria Dawe; photo courtesy of Skirt Club*)

Beyoncé's ballads of self-determination literally interrogate asymmetrical male sexual privilege, as in *Lemonade,* which is framed by the central question "Are you cheating on me?" Against a backdrop of enduring cultural hypocrisy about female desire, Beyoncé asserts that some of us experience nearly unquenchable bacchanalian lust, as in "Drunk in Love." Performing at the 2017 Grammys as a pregnant queen, she invoked various goddesses—Oshun, the Black Madonna, and the Virgin Mary among them—who derived their awesome power from sex and reproduction. (*Getty Images*)

Issa Rae's series *Insecure*, with its rich plotline about a "nice girl" cheating on her boyfriend, set social media aflame. (*Shutterstock*)

June Dobbs Butts, a hidden figure of American sex research, was the first African American trained at the Masters and Johnson Institute. Her articles on sexuality for *Ebony* and *Essence* reached thousands of black readers. (*Louie Favorite,* Atlanta Journal-Constitution)

Dr. Gail E. Wyatt, a clinical psychologist and sex therapist, was the first African American woman to be licensed as a psychologist in the state of California and the first African American woman PhD to reach full professor in a school of medicine. Wyatt published an ambitious update to Alfred Kinsey's work in 1988. (*UCLA*)

When married Hollywood superstar Ingrid Bergman had an affair with Roberto Rossellini and became pregnant in 1950, she was savaged by the press and even denounced on the floor of the US Senate as a "powerful influence for evil." (*Gordon Parks, The LIFE Picture Collection / Getty Images*)

Kristen Stewart experienced comparable blowback in 2012 when she had an affair with a married director while in a relationship with Robert Pattinson. Stewart here wears an updated version of Bergman's all-white ensemble. She also mirrors Bergman's sidelong gaze, a photographic framing that gives them both a haunted look while also seeming to suggest that women who step outside monogamy are "shifty," indirect, or dishonest. (*Backgrid USA*)

Bucking the script of masculine possession, the man married to a "hotwife" embraces her infidelities, often encouraging her by setting up her dates and paying witness to and otherwise reveling in her being untrue.

coming male-to-female transsexual with enviable breasts and two women who had traveled to the party from Vancouver.

The sex-positive performer was a dark-haired dominatrix in all black. Her sub (or submissive) was like a blonde rag doll in the hands of her mistress, who capably attached the leather cuffs she wore on her wrists to the suspension machine overhead. Then the domme—I thought of her as the alpha female—started whipping her, gently at first, with a cat-o'-nine. Gradually, she started bringing the leather fringes down harder and harder on the woman's bottom. Occasionally she stopped to walk around in front of her and give her a long, lingering kiss. The room was crammed as sixty women, many of them tipsy, strained to see and to hear over the loud music. The dominatrix unhooked her sub and came over to the couch where I sat with the transsexual and the Canadians, who seemed to evaporate. Alpha-domme leaned down and asked me something I didn't understand. "Can you move over a little so I can give her a spanking here?" she repeated. I did. She sat near me on the couch. The submissive stretched out across her mistress's lap and rested her head on mine. The domme reached her arm up and cracked it down hard on her sub's bottom. The woman gave a little cry and smiled, clearly enjoying herself. After a few more minutes of this, the dominatrix asked whether I'd like to try. She was being generous and affiliative, doing a little coalition building, perhaps, by offering to share her partner with me, and I considered for a long moment how much it was like Louise tossing half her celery stalk to Parish. I thought of how my husband had granted me permission—it grated me still to think of the term he had used—and encouraged me to participate rather than just observe. I wondered whether etiquette required me to accept her offer. Then I thanked her and said no. The sub writhed under her mistress's hand for several minutes more until the spanking was over. The party seemed to thin out, and I wondered whether it was ending early. Then I realized that lots of women, excited by the performance and the evening, had headed for the bedrooms.

When I got up to explore, I learned there was less group sex than there had been in New York; in a room piled high with pillows, five couples were using vibrators, going down on one another, and enjoying what I now couldn't help but think of as G-to-G contact. In another bedroom, three women were attending to each other in the dim light with such singular focus, precision, and stillness that they looked like a statue. I sat down on a sofa with a beautiful brunette, who turned out to be a mom of several kids; at her husband's urging, she had come hundreds of miles for the party. Like me, she was a writer, and we traded stories about our work as we walked, with a real estate developer, out to the sidewalk to our respective Ubers. It had been an evening of sororal pleasures in every sense, and I wished Parish had been there to witness it with me.

Dr. Lisa Diamond is a University of Utah professor of psychology and gender studies. She coined the term "female sexual fluidity" and spoke at a New York Psychoanalytic Psychotherapy Study Center workshop the same week as the Manhattan Skirt Club party I had attended. In a room filled to capacity, Diamond—who has spiky black hair and wore glasses with bright red frames—discussed the term "homopossibility" and the underlying idea that while we may be born gay or straight, our environment plays a role in what we do and what we "become," sexually speaking. And that this suggests, in turn, that our sexualities can sometimes morph. Indeed, over the course of a two-decade longitudinal study that began with nearly one hundred women who had had involvements with women, Diamond discovered that the fairer sex is also change-able, or "fluid," with desires that are sometimes contingent on circumstances, opportunities, and context as they are on our sexual orientation and the gender of the other person. For example, an intense female-female friendship may render a woman more likely to consider being with another woman. So might being in an environment where being with someone of the same sex is destigmatized—a city or a clique free of homophobia, for example, or an all-girls school, or a summer community like the Hamptons, where women stay out for the whole season while their husbands remain in the city, showing up only on the weekends. Or a woman might find her desires changing with her life stages. I interviewed someone who told me about a friend's daughter, who went to college straight, had a boyfriend her freshman year, a girlfriend her sophomore year, and then two more boyfriends. She ended up marrying a woman. Diamond's work suggests that we have to rethink our deepest assumptions about same-sex desires being fixed and our sexual identities necessarily being forever.

I reached out to Diamond via Skype for an update on her work and to get her thoughts on Skirt Club. "We all have an orientation—that's a real thing," she explained as she sat in her office with its piles of books and articles. " 'Fluid' is a term I came up with to describe something I was seeing in my work—variation. You have an orientation but that orientation is not as deterministic as we think. Our orientation is a fact, but it doesn't always provide the last word on whom we're attracted to." Diamond began her work at a time when not a lot of research was being done on female sexuality, let alone lesbians and bisexual and "fluid" women. The initial group of women who participated in her study ranged in age from sixteen to twenty-three, and all had had or currently had same-sex attractions. Diamond was a graduate student at Cornell at the time, and she interviewed the women all over Upstate New York—"Syracuse, Rochester, Binghamton, Ithaca, Elmira, wherever I could get in my Toyota Corolla." It was a brave move—many of her fellow graduate students were studying more mainstream phenomena, like infant cognition. "Here I was studying lesbians. I'd wonder, *Am I ever going to be able to find a job?!* Sometimes it felt like me and my mentor against the world," she recalled. But Diamond was driven to keep on. "As a feminist and a lesbian, I was unhappy about how little was being written from a developmental perspective about female sexual identity," she told me. Diamond had skin in the game. She herself had come out while in college at the University of Chicago. She told me that as an undergraduate, she would often read the gay newspaper in her apartment and then go outside and walk two blocks to throw it away so her roommates wouldn't "know." Like Parish, Diamond is a scientist's scientist, with an open mind and love of data. But she also brought something unique to her work—an intimate understanding of what was at stake in getting at the truths of female sexual preferences and practices. And an investment in it that was fired by personal experience.

After her initial interviews, Diamond did follow-ups by phone every two years. When I spoke to her, she was in the middle of her twenty-year follow-up interviews with the women. "They keep saying, 'Oh my god, we're so old!'" Diamond told me with a laugh. She wasn't initially looking for sexual fluidity all those years ago, she told me, "but it just bubbled up" in the conversations with her participants. Even though women who identified as exclusively lesbian pretty much stayed that way, there was undeniable variation in whom they were involved with and whom they were attracted to. Very few were "gold star lesbians"—women who only sleep with other women. One woman who had in fact only been with women for the entire twenty-year period told Diamond during their most recent interview that she and her wife had broken up. This woman, newly single and devastated, had then become involved with a man. She told Diamond, "I think I'll end up with a woman again, but maybe I just needed a change."

Choice and change are not the same thing, Diamond explained to me. "These women tell me, 'I wasn't expecting to be attracted to a guy, but it just happened!' They're not choosing it. It's surprising to them." For a long time, Diamond says, what was called women's "passing bisexuality" or "malleability"—she's straight, she's gay, she's straight again!—was looked at as "noise in the data," a problem that got in the way of answers. Diamond has flipped that understanding around. Such findings about changeable, changed-up female sexuality don't cloud or pollute the data, she says—they *are* the data. Fluidity is the thing.

Diamond initially thought that women were more fluid than men across the board. But a recent study of 179 men in the Salt Lake City area who identified as straight, bisexual, or gay changed her mind. "When I asked the straight men whether they [masturbated] to [porn] images and videos of other men, they said they did. Gay men told me that, yes, sometimes they did masturbate while thinking about women or watching videos of women. I wasn't expecting that to happen, but when you think to ask the questions, you get the answers. Unfortunately it doesn't always occur to us to ask the questions."

Diamond told me that these men were mostly in their twenties and thirties. She believes "this new generation of men appears more open to relationships that go outside their orientation" and that men have the capacity for sexual fluidity as well. "Society has tended to be more restrictive of men. There's something about women where people are able to say, 'Well, sure, they're affectionate and friendly and so blah, blah, blah.' But men get shut down right away. It's very stigmatized for them to be curious or experiment. So it's possible that the initial thinking that women were more fluid was due to social control of male heterosexuality. And that as the social control loosens among certain groups, we'll continue to see more male sexual fluidity."

Fluidity among men and women alike is simply the capacity to develop attractions not determined by your orientation or the other person's gender, attractions that might not stick around, Diamond explained. And as she points out, we're currently more likely to see it in women, due at least in part to constraint. When a friend tells me that her widowed mother, married to her father for forty years, is now married to a woman; when Elizabeth Gilbert leaves her companion of over a decade, the one she fell in love with in *Eat, Pray, Love,* for her terminally ill female best friend, the writer Rayya Elias; when avowedly heterosexual women have dalliances with the female trainers they call "pussy whisperers"; when Piper, engaged to a man, reignites a passionate affair with a former girlfriend in prison on *Orange Is the New Black;* or when women are mostly in relationships with men but go to an all-women sex party, we are seeing female sexual fluidity. In fact, of the women who attend Skirt Club, the majority identify as a two on the Kinsey scale—mostly heterosexual but more than incidentally homosexual. Assumed straight women getting with other women is a common enough trope in the cultural imagination that there was a recent *Saturday Night Live* skit about it that spoofed a 1950s sitcom. The title: "Whoops! I Married a Lesbian."

"One of the things that strikes me is that heterosexually identified women who have had sex with women at some point often say the experience made them feel more entitled to communicate about what they wanted," Diamond observed after I told her about Skirt Club. "They'll say, 'Pumping at my vagina isn't really doing it for me. There are other things you can do to my body that will thrill me.' This group of women seems to be less willing to tolerate bad sex." Diamond said she hoped that women who went to Skirt Club might communicate with their husbands and boyfriends what they liked about it, and what they had learned about their own bodies, and what they wanted. "What we know now," Diamond mused, "is that fluidity is real. And that our notion that it's men who always necessarily want variety and women who necessarily want stability is not consistent with what actually happens."

I wanted to get Diamond's expert, informed thoughts on monogamy while I could. She told me that she concurred with Meana that long-term relationships could be especially tough on female desire. She mentioned that an attraction to novelty is part of our legacy and that we habituate to sexual stimuli over time. That is, the more we have it with someone, the less thrilling it becomes. *Oh, that again. You again.* The mistake, Diamond told me, is to think that habituation and boredom mean there is something wrong with you or your partner, or with your partnership. Or that there is nothing to be done. A strong predictor of desire in long-term relationships, she told me, is when couples make an effort to do something new together. "I'm not talking about just sex. It could be skydiving," or taking a dance class, or going on a zip line. "When couples participate in new and thrilling activities together, they often report a resurgence of puppy love from seeing their partner from a new angle. And the simple fact is that our partners don't stay the same over time," Diamond says. If we want to be monogamous, we can look for and find novelty in that same person. She concedes that it isn't easy—"We wouldn't have all these self-help books if we could just snap our fingers and make it as novel as it used to be!" But it can be done. One way, I considered, might be going to an all-women sex party and then telling your partner about it afterward. You're not "participating in a thrilling and new activity together" for the party itself, obviously, but being with each other afterward could certainly be novel and exciting.

Straight men in our culture have relatively easy access to massages with happy endings, strip clubs, prostitutes, and pornography without much shame if they're seeking these services from women (because, after all, "Men like to look" and "It's what guys do"). Skirt Club is the rare tensional outlet for *female* "infidelity" that maybe isn't, a pretty extraordinary niche where women can show up, have sex, and then matter-of-factly go home to their heterosexual marriages or partnerships. Granted, they are having sex with women, which men might find less threatening and more titillating and "safe" than their female partners having sex with other men. But it still struck me as meaningful that LeJeune was in some sense evening the score thus. And that there was an outcry about her daring to do so. While her project was at once embraced by women who wanted a piece of the action—Skirt Club now has seven thousand members worldwide, she told me—it has also been derided from all sides. The article I wrote about Skirt Club L.A. garnered dozens of comments, many of them from apparently enraged men who demeaned and devalued the parties in terms that showed their hand: many wrote that they were sure the pictures were doctored and that the women were unattractive, for example. "You can't exclude me because I wouldn't want to be there anyway," they assert. And any woman who would want to do such a thing must, perforce, be undesirable. Meanwhile, other more progressively minded critics have called Skirt Club exclusionary, looks-ist, expensive, a habitus for newbie femmes. It is frequently dismissed as soft-core, male-fantasy-inflected "Victoria's Secret lesbianism," a somehow suspect compromise formation for women who are merely toying with same-sex sex rather than really committing to it (a *Rolling Stone* article called it "a sex party where straight women are gay for a night" as if such a practice is suspect and inauthentic). There is, perhaps, plenty to criticize. But the assertion that it is somehow watered-down lesbianism-lite or "fake" doesn't mesh with or describe the complexity of what I witnessed—including assumed straight women going at it (with other women) like I'd never seen before within a space designed for them to do so in comfort and privacy from the rest of the world. Their pleasure and orgasms seemed very real.

Diamond and Parish have helped articulate a new language for something not so new (if we take the long evolutionary view of things), something confounding to our established and comforting categories. The phenomena of female sexual fluidity and coalition building through sex is not limited to bonobos, or to women in L.A. and Manhattan. It does not only happen in glamorous cities like Berlin and Vienna, or "enlightened" places like San Francisco. In Lesotho, a small country surrounded by South Africa, it is not uncommon for married women with children to have a *motsoalle*—basically a special female friend and sexual partner. Often these *motsoalles* are taken by women whose husbands are off doing manual labor for days at a time, but not always. Among the !Kung, it is common for adolescent girls to experiment with one another sexually before marriage. And the *mati* is a widespread institution among

Creole working-class women in the city of Paramaribo, Suriname. *Mati* are women who have sexual relationships with men and with women, either at the same time or one at a time. While some *mati*, especially older women who have borne and raised their children, do not have sex with men anymore, younger *mati* have a variety of arrangements with men, such as marriage, concubinage, or a "visiting" relationship. Women's relationships with women mostly take the form of visiting relationships, though some female couples and their children live together in one household.

In our backyards and far away, female sexual fluidity may seem to suggest that women are uniquely designed for sexual receptivity and sexual pleasure, allowing us to find it, even if only in our minds, with a nearly infinite variety of sexual partners. While we have no hard and fast figures, it's clear that there are any number of women whose sexual behaviors might contradict their avowed sexual orientation. As for women's sexual fantasies, daydreams, preferences for pornography, and imaginations, when we consider this whole category of non-behaviors that nonetheless tell us a story about female sexual desire, the numbers of women who think about being with a woman would no doubt shock us—unless we are couples therapists or sex researchers, who tend to take these things in stride, publish academic papers about it, and wait for the rest of the world to catch up. A Boise State University study of 333 women who identified as heterosexual found that 43 percent had "made out with" another woman. In a *Glamour* survey of more than 1,000 women aged eighteen to forty-four, 47 percent of respondents said they'd been attracted to another woman, and 31 percent had had a sexual experience with another woman. And it's not limited to women being "gay until graduation." As Lisa Diamond commented on the study, "We consider it a sign of maturity to figure out who you are sexually...We have this idea that sexuality gets clearer and more defined as time goes on. I've seen it's really the opposite."

Proof that female sexual fluidity and infidelity are more

widespread than we might imagine, and happen in the most unexpected places and at every life stage, also presented itself in a
conversation with my friend and colleague Deesha Philyaw, a writer
and activist. She told me about a short-story collection she was
working on, about sex and church ladies.

CHAPTER SEVEN

SIGNIFICANT OTHERNESS

Deesha Philyaw's "Eula" is a short story full of beauty, surprise, tenderness, and disappointment. Set in the last hours of 1999 and early 2000, but ranging further back in time into the lives and relationship of its two main characters, Caroletta and Eula, it brings you in fast with its deft alternation between suggestive minimalism à la Joan Didion and the intimate mingling of recipes and sex that made you love *Heartburn* by Nora Ephron. But only if those artists were refracted through the sensibility of Zora Neale Hurston, a participant-observer of cultures of blackness, a storyteller with skin in the game. From the first sentences, you feel the immediacy of these characters and their connection:

Eula books the suite in Clarksville, two towns over. I bring the food. This year, it's sushi for me and cold cuts and potato salad for her. Nothing heavy. Just enough to sustain us. And I bring the champagne. This year, which like every year could be our last, I bring three bottles of André Spumante...and year 2000 glasses to wear. The lenses are the two zeroes in the middle. For all we know, the Y2K bug will have us sitting in the dark one second after Dick Clark counts down in Times Square. But that's alright with me. Because that André sips just as well in the dark.

After we get settled in, Eula digs into the potato salad...She's real particular about what she eats. About most things really. She likes things just so...But she can't tell that I bought the potato salad from Publix, added some chopped boiled egg, mustard, pickle relish, and paprika, then put it in my Tupperware bowl. She eats seconds, pats her belly, and tells me that I outdid myself.

Eula and Caroletta are both schoolteachers, and "best friends for half our lives." They met in tenth grade, we learn, "the only black girls in our Honors English class." They were both diligent but also daydreamers, planning their double Hawaiian wedding in the margins of their math notebooks, connected and complicit. "Our husbands would be railroad men like our fathers. We'd teach at the high school, join the ladies auxiliary at church, and be next-door neighbors. Our kids would play together," the narrator explains of the plans they nurtured as girls.

But things turn out differently. Like Caroletta with her doctored store-bought salad, life performs a sleight of hand, we are told, so that Eula's thirtieth birthday finds them both single, teaching in the very high school where they had carefully plotted out such a different future for themselves. Caroletta has done plenty of sexual experimenting, seeking out "what too-rough boys had to offer" when she was younger, and "short-lived flings with men whose names weren't worth remembering" as she matured. Eula, on the other hand, is chaste, like the biblical Ruth "waiting for her Boaz," a supplicant in a powerful man's field of grain tilled by a plough, where she picks off scraps until Boaz takes notice and they marry.

Eula only appears to be like Ruth. As the two friends celebrated her thirtieth with too many wine coolers, Caroletta tells us, Eula ended up on her friend's lap, "her skirt bunched up around her waist. I saw the white cotton panties between her thick brown thighs. She smelled like vanilla. 'Do you ever feel like you could just bust?' she asked me, her breath fruity and hot in my face."

That night, the narrator says, "she slid my fingers inside those white cotton panties and forgot all about Boaz. We stayed up until we were slick with sweat…A month or so later it was New Year's Eve, and Eula called to say she'd booked a suite." Thus their annual tradition began.

So as we meet them, on the precipice of a potential disaster, the moment of transition not just one year but from one millennium to another (about which our anxieties seem so quaint and unwarranted in retrospect), Eula and Caroletta are in a well-worn groove of mostly once-a-year, caution-to-the-wind drunk sex that they afterward pretend never happened. Splitting oneself in two cannot be easy, and Eula struggles.

> After we're finished eating and polishing off a bottle of André, I start the shower. We like it boiling hot. The heat relaxes me, but I feel like it does something else for Eula. She stays in there long after I get out. Through the steamy shower door, I see her pink shower cap. Her head is bowed, and I wonder if she's asking God's forgiveness for stepping outside of His favor as she continues to wait on His provision.

Their decade-long affair that isn't has not been simple for Caroletta either. Once, stirring the roux for a gumbo she knew Eula craved ("my Grandma Pauline's gumbo, but without the okra"), she endured Eula's breathless excitement about an upcoming date with a man she thought might propose to her. The date ended in disaster as the man's estranged wife stormed onto the scene. Caroletta, meanwhile, spent the night sitting up in bed eating gumbo, "another woman's husband snoring lightly beside me." She wonders, of Eula's men who never pan out, "if Eula finds fault with all these men because secretly she doesn't want any of them, and is just doing what's expected of her…these are the kinds of things Eula and I don't talk about."

Caroletta's resentment about their arrangement still simmers under the surface like the ingredients of the roux she remembers making. And when Eula shares her New Year's resolution that she won't be "alone"—without a man is what she means—for another Valentine's Day, it nearly boils over. They have an argument about religion that is also, in a roundabout way, an argument about what they are up to in the hotel room year after year. Eula is devastated to learn that Caroletta is not a "virgin," that she has slept with any number of men over the decade of their intermittent intimacies. Caroletta is mystified and hurt that Eula considers *herself* a virgin—haven't the two of them been having sex together?

As the countdown to the next thousand years begins, Eula prays.

CONTROLLING IMAGES

Women's rights advocate and author of *Drop the Ball* Tiffany Dufu has spent her career advancing women and girls. As former chief leadership officer of Levo and former president of the White House Project, she has mentored hundreds of young women, encouraging them to reach higher, dream bigger, even run for political office. In her book, Dufu recalls a formative moment: volunteering to lead her Sunday School class in a prayer, she was told by her teacher, "Boys are the leaders." As the daughter of a pastor and the apple of his eye, Dufu was taken aback and momentarily ashamed of herself. The lesson stayed with her a long time. "The black church is an institution that dramatically shapes the African American experience, whether you're in the church or not. For so long it was and in some communities remains the core social infrastructure. So black identity becomes synonymous with and defined by the church," she observed. Her lesson in leadership as a young girl was revealing and significant not just personally but socially. "Because black men are in the pulpit and control the narrative that prioritizes race over gender, that is the priority. To be a respectable black woman is to support and protect black men," she told me. And to be seen as failing to do so, whether by being too eager to lead, or being sexual, or not being heterosexual, is often perceived as a threat to black masculinity. Dufu, one of the most upbeat and energetic people I know, told me of the exhaustion of being "expected to participate in a tradition of black women sacrificing themselves to uphold black men as respectable," and of managing the expectations of both the dominant culture and the black community simultaneously, of "performing for these different audiences." Sexism in the black community complicates black women's identity, thinkers from Florynce "Flo" Kennedy to Audre Lorde to Dufu have shown us. From the church, Dufu learned about community and leadership. It was, in a profound sense, home. But it was also where she got schooled, where one day she was taught that it was unfeminine and even selfish—a violation of a race and gender script about what it was to be a "good black woman"—to have too much ambition.

Like Dufu, Philyaw has long been fascinated by the black church; all its contradictions and rules spoken and unspoken have provided fertile ground for her storytelling, though I was unaware of this for the first years of our acquaintanceship. I got to know her initially through our mutual work supporting and writing about women with stepchildren and adult stepkids—she was for many years the co-host with her ex-husband of an online radio show on co-parenting after divorce. We kept in touch as our work focus shifted, mine into writing about motherhood and sex, Philyaw's as she increasingly concentrated on writing essays and fiction, much of it about relationships, parenting, race, feminism, pop culture, and female sexuality. When I wrote an article on assumed heterosexual women on the Upper East Side having affairs with their female trainers on the down-low during the summer months in the Hamptons, Philyaw reached out to tell me about her interest in and writing about the unexpected sex lives of women in her world, her contemporaries and women she remembered from childhood. She sent me some of her writings. In addition to "Eula," I devoured her essay in *Brevity* titled "Milk for Free." In it, she movingly, impressionistically chronicles what she learned about sex as a child—from the Jackie Collins novels she read on the floor of the children's section of the local public library, from older lady neighbors who urged her not to give away the "milk for free," from her first real boyfriend the summer after sixth grade, from the neighborhood drunk from whom her mother and the police could not protect her, and from the long-repressed memory of the time, when she was two or three, that a white lady detective showed up at their home because Philyaw's mother had been raped.

Like Tamara Winfrey Harris, the cultural critic and author of *The Sisters Are Alright*, Philyaw unflinchingly looks at the particular burdens and dangers black women face in expressing and even experiencing their sexuality—constraints created by history and economics and ideology. Also like Winfrey Harris, she refuses to capitulate to the notion that being an African American woman means being "broken" and works assertively against that pervasive portrayal. Philyaw writes about women with strong libidos and big brains for whom sex is complicated, joyous, illicit, rote, thrilling, or end-of-the-line boring. The predicaments of her protagonists, including herself in her first-person essays, feel raw and real, deliciously complex.

"I grew up in a predominantly black neighborhood," Philyaw told me when we spoke by phone one afternoon and later when we spoke in person in New York City. "And being part of the church shaped me growing up, even though my mom and grandmother didn't go. They'd say, 'When I get myself together I'll go to church.'" Philyaw laughed when I said I had never heard of this belief, that you had to work hard on and improve yourself before you could even show up at church. Wasn't church for everyone? Philyaw patiently explained that it might have been not wanting to be judged for their behavior, including their sexuality, that kept some of the women she grew up with from going, and that in this way "the church was like a mirror." She herself would attend with neighborhood friends or her half sister as a kid but was "off and on about it once I was in my preteen years. I fell into that dichotomy of good/bad and struggled mightily to be good. There was definitely a strong current of 'Keep your legs closed.'" Sex, she told me, "was not something that sounded pleasurable. Boys and men took it from you, was the basic message." She faded away from the church as a preteen, but by her junior and senior years of high school, she was going again.

With a young woman's sensibility this time around, Philyaw tried to make sense of it all. "Every once in a while there was a story—the choir director or youth minister of one church or another would run off with somebody's daughter." The contradictions she saw, like the Madonna/whore dichotomy messaging she heard, were "all very confusing and very confining," she told me with a sigh.

But there were wonderful things about church as well, namely the women she saw there, models of what she calls "attainable black womanhood." Some were well-dressed, proper ladies in proper hats. They were married and matronly. Then there were the unmarried women of her church, carefully turned out, at once authentically and performatively devout. Philyaw fondly likened them to "peacocks preening and displaying, waiting for the Lord to send them a man in a place where women outnumbered men four to one." These women, she realized, "wanted to be wifed up and chose, validated by the institution of marriage." All these women—the peacocks and the matrons, the church ladies who were stern and the ones who wiggled their hips—set Philyaw's imagination on fire. They were different from the women she knew who "danced and wore tight jeans and cussed and played spades and slept with men they weren't married to." But how different, after all? And how similar, in the end? "I wanted to know if the proper ladies in my church—the peacocks and the matrons— were like the rest of us. Did they have urges? Did they masturbate? Were they lonely? Did they secretly invite men and women to their beds?" Years later, when she heard through the grapevine about two women in another town—upstanding members of a church who met yearly for sex in a hotel—Philyaw was riveted by the idea, and the seeds of "Eula" were planted.

Meanwhile, her novel *Good Girl Anonymous* centers on Rebecca, a vividly intelligent woman in a monogamous marriage who is, in Philyaw's phrase, "living bored." With her husband's prominence in their church a force that at once lifts her up and keeps her down, Rebecca fulfills all her longings by writing a secret, sexually explicit blog. One day she is outed, all her most private fantasies about the UPS guy revealed for the world to see, and there's a big blowup with her righteous spouse. "The question is, will she stay in this marriage that doesn't serve her but lends that respectability, or will she walk? Will she [obey], make repairs, walk a fine line with her husband forever after, or will she change and realize this isn't what she really wants, and decide that she can leave?" Philyaw, who has been close to several women who were involved with married men, knows how to mine a rich vein. "From the age of five on, I saw women living two lives," she explains with a laugh when I ask her where the finely wrought characters and dilemmas come from.

In writing about Eulas and Carolettas and Rebeccas, Philyaw risks censure and criticism of a sort not all female writers encounter. "Respectability" casts a shadow over her and a long line of black female artists—from Josephine Baker to Alice Walker, from Beyoncé to Kara Walker to Issa Rae and more—who strive to produce challenging, honest work about female sexuality as it's actually lived by African American women. Sometimes when they attempt to do so, these creators find themselves accused of dragging down their race by not portraying all black women in an unrelentingly positive light. Or they sense, based on experience, that they might be so accused. As Winfrey Harris explains, this sense of obligation to represent themselves and their characters and their art as ever upstanding and "respectable" springs from a deep well of misrepresentation and racism. In the eras of imperialism and slavery, she notes, "[s]tereotypes of black women as asexual and servile, angry and bestial, or oversexed and lascivious were key to maintaining the subordination of black women. They also provided a counterbalance to the identities of middle-class and wealthy white women, who had been placed on a pedestal as perfect illustrations of femininity—beautiful, pious, pure, submissive, domestic, and in need of protection." Stereotypes including the mammy, the ho, and the angry/strong black woman, rooted in the history of using women as domestic slaves, breeding machines, and field slaves, respectively, continue to dog "other" African American women to this day. Winfrey Harris points out that these "controlling images," as cultural critic Patricia Hill Collins calls them, including the idea that black women are hypersexed and dangerously carnal, are all too obviously alive and well when Don Imus calls the black women who play basketball for Rutgers "nappy-headed hos" and Bill O'Reilly goes after Beyoncé, who has been married to the same man for over a decade and celebrates sex with her husband in several of her songs, as behaving like a "thug," blaming her for what he fantasizes is an epidemic of teen pregnancy (which is actually at an historic low). The breadth of these controlling images—hoochie, freak, matriarch, mammy, bitch, welfare queen—all serve to distort social reality, "portraying injustices against black women as simply consequences of the natural order," in the words of sociologist of gender and sexuality Victor P. Corona.

And portraying them as hypersexual feeds into the deeply ingrained, deeply dangerous idea that they are less in need of and less deserving of protection from sexual assault. According to experts, including UCLA sexual behavior researcher Gail Wyatt and lawyer, political scientist, and Rutgers associate professor of gender studies Nikol G. Alexander-Floyd, African American women are more vulnerable to these types of attacks and yet are less likely to report the attack for a number of reasons, many of them linked to the specific historical experiences of and pressures on black women. "The sisters don't want to report the brothers because we know what's going on in penal institutions," one counselor at a National Sexual Violence Prevention Conference told *Los Angeles Times* reporter Gayle Pollard-Terry. Pollard-Terry also notes that black women may be reluctant to report sexual assault because they are unable to trust police or find "people who look like [me]" among detectives and sexual assault counselors; because black ministers have historically rallied around black men accused of sexual assault; and because of a more general fear of not being believed. Chillingly, one study found that white female college students felt less intent to intervene and less personal responsibility to intervene, and imputed greater victim pleasure, when the hypothetical victim of sexual assault was a black woman.

Modeling "respectability" is one response to dangerously dehumanizing, controlling images, caricatures that justify the oppression of black women in the US or portray them as "too sexual." In her article "No Disrespect" for *Bitch* magazine, Winfrey Harris explores the history of what she calls "respectability politics" in the black community. She notes that such politics "work to counter negative views of blackness by aggressively adopting the manners and morality that the dominant culture deems 'respectable.'" Black civil rights protestors wore suits and ties, jackets and heels, to marches, using their Sunday best to project a message: "Your stereotypes are untrue; we deserve equality; we, too, are respectable." But such a powerful reframing is not without its problems, Winfrey Harris notes. She traces the ways respectability politics as a liberation strategy "has the potential to harm more than uplift," for example when it held newly freed black women to the standards of white womanhood, which positioned real women deserving of protection as inherently childlike and submissive. Respectability politics is the force that can hold Beyoncé to a standard of acting like a nice girl or else (be seen as out-of-control licentious), while a performer like Madonna was not only free to be graphically sexual but viewed as in control of her image and sexuality as she did so (thankfully, Beyoncé gave her middle fingers up, hands high to all of that).

Philyaw knows this double-standard respectability dilemma intimately. "I had a lot of fears in the beginning," she told me in our first conversation about her work. "Even when I *thought* about sitting down to write, I felt this pressure. Like the stories had to end with people becoming better, strengthening their faith, being in strong marriages. The teaching I had was that everything had to glorify God. And that everything you create has to show black women as *respectable*." This obligation can seep into every aspect of lived experience. As one interviewee told Winfrey Harris, "I recognize as a black woman that I don't have the luxury of having a wide range of emotions for fear of being called angry. I'm careful about how I present myself, especially with non-black people. Whenever you have a conversation with someone, you feel like you're carrying all of black womanhood on your shoulders." That deeply felt mandate, the pressure to always uplift and present oneself as perfect and pleasing, didn't exactly square with Philyaw's mission to tell stories about complicated and authentic-feeling female characters with flaws, emotional ranges, and agency. And in "Eula," by presenting us with a version of female sexual fluidity and lesbianism within ground zero of respectability, the church, Philyaw took further risks still. But for her, the characters needed to be themselves honestly, genuinely. Writing against the headwinds of bias and respectability politics and figuring out how to tell the stories she wanted to tell the way she wanted to tell them was a gradual process, she says. It happened word by word, paragraph by paragraph, page by page, as she dared herself daily to create the characters she felt and wanted to know better—characters like her, who dared.

HO POLITICS

George Clooney just got married…nobody's
calling *him* a ho!
—ISSA RAE

Like Philyaw, Mireille Miller-Young has been standing tall while navigating racial and gender bias and respectability politics for much

of her career. For starters, the associate professor of feminist studies at the University of California, Santa Barbara, who earned her
master's and doctorate in American history and the history of the
African diaspora, is a scholar of pornography. She describes her
book *A Taste for Brown Sugar* as an examination of African American women's representation and labor in porn media, meaning she
seeks to understand the black women who act in porn as both images and image makers. In the course of this work, she has looked
at thousands of photos and videos of black adult entertainment actresses, and has met with and interviewed dozens of performers to
uncover their varied motivations, concerns, and strategies. Miller-
Young is one of the first scholars in the US to undertake such a
study, and in doing so, she discovered and documented that porn
videos with black actors had lower production values than those
with white performers, and that black women who worked as porn
actresses earned on average only half to three-quarters what white
women did. She explores the lamentable reality that in porn, black
men tend to be represented as animalistic in their desires and appearance, and black women as "ready for anything." Indeed, black
women's images in porn particularly, she writes, "show that the
titillation of pornography is inseparable from the racial stories it
tells." Black female characters in porn storylines are often represented as both desirable and undesirable. They're seen and shown
as sexually potent, exotic, and different. But all these same qualities, Miller-Young says, threaten prevailing ideas about femininity,
heterosexuality, and racial hierarchy. This pull in two directions is
evident, she notes, in the many porn video plotlines where black
actresses elicit ambivalence from white male actors, who want and
don't want them. A recurring storyline is of a white male character who is "scared" of a sexually assertive black female character.
In a 1977 movie called *Sex World*, the actress Desiree West plays
Jill, a guest at a therapeutic sex fantasy hotel who is paired with a
pompous and racist white male guest called Roger. After he mis-
takes her for a maid and then protests that he's "not prejudiced,"

he just happens not to like "you people," Jill sets to setting this bigot straight—with sex. His face transforms from disgust to curiosity to lust as she unveils and narrates her body parts one after the other, singing their praises and celebrating her sexual power unabashedly, in rhyme ("Between my *thighs* is where my rhythm *lies*"). Miller-Young's work helps us understand Roger's ambivalence as one that mirrors our culture's. And she also guides us to see how Desiree West's "animated and transgressive performance of her scripted lines—the way she infuses them with 'spoken soul'"—is one of many ways black women found and find ways to work within and against powerful, limiting roles in the porn industry.

Miller-Young is particularly interested in the adult entertainment actresses who perform in bondage and use racial stereotypes to market their bodies. Of sex educator/writer/performance artist Mollena Lee Williams-Haas, who starts her show in chains, unshackles herself, and then chooses to get into bindings again, Miller-Young observes the performance's subtext "about slavery...it's actually a continuing legacy that shapes our lives. It shapes our opportunities in a society and how we're treated and how we see ourselves...and so she uses that representation to display that she now has power but that that power she has is connected to that history." Miller-Young is fascinated by the way porn "takes up the challenge of subverting norms, even as it catalyzes and perpetuates them."

Black women who work in porn face a lot of misconceptions. Misunderstanding comes from two directions, Miller-Young explains. "One is from people of color... [who believe] you're selling out—that you're...signing on to exploitation and racism and making racism worse for everybody else...by participating in what they feel are stereotypical images or understandings, because largely people of color have been exoticized and hypersexualized and seen as having a deviant sexuality... The feeling of people of color in a lot of communities is that you're...making the community look bad...you're an embarrassment, and you're...creating shame for the community—a really powerful shame." At the same time, there are misperceptions "from white people who…predominantly have had this…: knowledge passed on to them that people of color are hypersexual. And so they may think that they're just naturally that way instead of performing a character…or performing in a film that has a script, that those…people of color sex workers really are just representations of how all black men have big dicks and…how women of color really are just more kinky and want sex more than everyone else."

Like the actresses in the films themselves, Miller-Young has been accused of making the community look bad. Or she has simply seen the value of her work questioned. During an interview with Miller-Young and sex researcher Dr. Herb Samuels on NPR, the host Farai Chideya acknowledged this dilemma, saying, "A lot of my relatives probably right now are saying, 'Why is Farai even covering this?'" Overtly hostile critics have suggested that Miller-Young demeans herself and people of color with her work; still others have "said that by showing these images of porn stars, I [am] re-exploiting them. But I'm fascinated by the 'ho,'" Miller-Young observes, refusing to back away from the powerful trope that causes discomfort, shame, excitement, and ire. "She is a figure that all black women have to contend with, whether you are sex workers or professors." The real problem with the ho image for adult entertainment actresses, Miller-Young learned from talking to them, is that it devalues their labor. By deploying the ho, by not giving African American female actors the opportunity to play other roles, the porn industry maintains a segregated, niche market for black sexuality where actors are paid less, and kept there.

This dilemma has larger implications and is not limited to the actresses Miller-Young studies. In the new and unregulated world of online dating, more than one African American woman in her late twenties or early thirties told me, swipe right on a white guy and you may well live the same issue of being devalued by the trope of the ho he holds in mind and perpetuates as he taps on his phone or laptop. "You cannot believe the stuff a white guy might presume and say to a black woman who's on a dating app," a graduate student at an Ivy League school told me with a shake of her head. "First of all, we need data on how often a white guy will even swipe right on a black woman. Not that often, in my experience and that of my friends. And when he does? There is a good chance it is because he assumes she is a 'freak' or 'kinky'— that she'll do stuff a white woman wouldn't." Hiding behind their online anonymity, these men feel emboldened to let down any veneer of respect or civility, giving free rein to their bias. This young woman reported that she and her peers experienced that not a few white men in the online dating world presume they are into BDSM before asking ("It's not that I think BDSM is 'wrong'; I don't!" she told me. "But the fact that so many white guys presume black women are necessarily into it says something"), ask if they're into anal sex in a first text exchange, and frequently demand, "Is it true that you like to [fill-in-the-blank]?!" assuming her to be a stand-in for her supposedly sexually "wild" race. In the world of online dating, several young black women told me, white guys treat them as if they're hypersexual, ever ready, unfeeling, and basically subhuman. This is the special penalty these women are subjected to for daring to want sex and connection and for pursuing it like everyone else does.

For Miller-Young, controlling images of black womanhood are something black adult entertainment actresses confront, are subjected to, and exploit in turn. She discourages us from viewing black women in the sex industries as victims and nothing else. They're social actors as well as performers, she says, working within and against constraints, making a living in a culture and a niche that has devalued their sexuality, and leaving their mark. And counterintuitively, they may sometimes have a degree of agency that African American women on dating apps do not.

Miller-Young is not alone in her meditation on the ho and her articulation of what she calls "Ho Theory." In her viral *New York Times* op-ed, "How We Make Black Girls Grow Up Too Fast," sociologist and author Tressie McMillan Cottom writes that when she was fifteen years old, she got a lesson during a family dinner at her aunt's house. Mike Tyson, the most famous boxer in the world at the time, had recently been found guilty of raping eighteen-year-old Desiree Washington in a hotel room. McMillan Cottom's male cousin defended Tyson, saying of Washington, "Y'all act like she's a woman. She is—excuse me, Auntie—a ho." When her cousin demanded, "What was she doing in that hotel room?" McMillan Cottom pushed back and insisted that "she could have been butt naked in that room and it shouldn't matter." But the lesson had been imparted: "I learned that being a woman is about what men are allowed to do to you...I learned black girls like me can never truly be victims of sexual predators." Part of the legacy of the hypersexualization of black women, she observes, is that "if one is ready for what a man wants from her, then by merely existing she has consented to his treatment of her. Puberty becomes permission." All women and girls in our culture are vulnerable to this kind of violation and violence, McMillan Cottom observes. "But for black women and girls that treatment is refracted through history and today's context." In fact, according to research in Monique W. Morris's book *Pushout,* people of every race and gender see black girls as more "adultlike" than white girls their own age. And thus the grown-ups upon whom they depend—teachers, principals, administrators—don't give these girls the attention and protection they need. "Left to navigate school by themselves because they are 'grown,' these girls are easily manipulated by men."

You can see unsupported girls' stories unfold again and again as McMillan Cottom lays bare the compromised and frayed social infrastructure that leaves them exposed. The ensuing "cycle of neglect and abuse" is unlikely to end as long as we continue to view black girls as at once uniquely capable and strong, inappropriately "grown," and disposable. McMillan Cottom says watching men she loved—her cousin, men at a house party who wanted to watch a video of R. Kelly having sex with a girl who was apparently underage—"turn a girl into a woman and a woman into a ho" never left her.

A few years earlier, on the Crunk Feminist Collective website, a lively debate about the 2011 Toronto SlutWalk contributed to bringing awareness of "the ho" and all its racialized and gendered underpinnings into mainstream consciousness. A group of mostly white women in Toronto, who were outraged by a police officer saying that if young women wanted to be safe they shouldn't dress like "sluts," gathered to march in protest, wearing "slutty" attire. In short order, other SlutWalks were organized around the world to "take slut back." Calling the response "creative, appropriate, and powerful," Crunktastic, co-founder of the Crunk Feminist Collective, wrote that she also felt some ambivalence when she read the mission statement of SlutWalk, with what she described as its righteous indignation over being called a slut. Warranted, yes, but where, Crunktastic wondered, was the empathy and advocacy for women regularly called "bitch" and "ho" on the street and in hip-hop directed at black women? The "How dare you" quality of the SlutWalk manifesto struck Crunktastic as the manifestation of privilege from white girls who have a baseline expectation that the world will extend them respect and value their worth, but not much awareness or insistence that women of color deserve that too. After all, they are more likely to be subjected to the kinds of harassment and demeaning treatment the SlutWalkers were protesting. If white women could recognize SlutWalk as being rooted in white female experience, wouldn't that make it easier to build coalitions and solidarity with other movements that are more inclusive of women of color? Until then, Crunktastic wrote, until there was a reckoning of this sort about what *kind* of womanhood was being defended in SlutWalk, she affirmed the value of the protest but didn't think it was likely there would be many "Ho Strolls." The piece incited a discussion that pushed feminists everywhere to keep their movement relevant and intersectional. In

A Taste for Brown Sugar, Miller-Young circles back to the article and the issue of the different versions of personhood and womanhood being protected, suggesting that "perhaps we should line up on the Ho Stroll—that is if we feminists take seriously the perspectives and lessons black sex workers have to teach us about sexual rights."

INSECURE

Issa Rae, creator, co-writer, and star of the hit HBO series *Insecure*, celebrates the fact that protagonist Issa—whose life and adventures are based loosely on her own—has what she calls a "ho phase" and leverages female infidelity as a rich plotline and irresistible narrative device. Rae, who previously created the hit web series *The Misadventures of Awkward Black Girl* and wrote the *New York Times* bestselling memoir by the same name, has blended her storytelling with irreverence from the very beginning. And like Philyaw, she got creative traction from the black church early on. In an interview with Larry Wilmore, on his *Black on the Air* podcast, she recalls that the very first play she wrote was for church, noting that most of the congregation was socially conservative and elderly. The performance, written by Rae and directed by her mother, was called "The Old and the Rusted." It was satirical, poking fun at church politics and dynamics and the older, traditionalist people and ways of the congregation. They laughed and seemed to enjoy being made fun of. The response thrilled her, and set her on a course. In college at Stanford, she created a mockumentary called *Dorm Diaries* and connected with the future co-star and co-producer of her web show *Awkward Black Girl*. In voice-overs and dream sequences, the show's protagonist, J—played by Rae—narrates the often-mortifying situations she finds herself in with coworkers, friends, and love interests. Rae has said that she created the show because she was tired of Hollywood stereotypes of African American women. "I've always had an issue with the [assumption] that people of color—

and black people especially—aren't relatable. I know we are." The show, whose first season she funded in part on Kickstarter.com, garnered more than twenty million views and nearly 350,000 subscribers on YouTube as of this writing, winning a Shorty Award for best web series in 2012.

Much like *Awkward Black Girl, Insecure* is motored by the sensibility of main character Issa, who, when we meet her in the beginning of season one, is in a listing relationship with her long unemployed live-in boyfriend Lawrence and working at a nonprofit for underserved kids called We Got Y'all, run by a woman whose white sanctimony is as brightly assertive as the ethnic caftans she wears. Issa often drifts off into rap reveries that tell us how she *really* feels about her coworkers, boyfriend, and life predicaments. Early in the season, she reconnects via Facebook with her handsome former flame Daniel, her "'what if' guy," the one she'd always wanted to pursue something with. She is soon wondering what it might be like to have sex with him. And once the two of them begin texting, she longs to know. The more Lawrence flounders, the more Issa pulls away, pining for hot sex and excitement with Daniel.

"Maybe I'm not satisfied. Maybe I wanna be dicked down properly. Face down, ass up, surrounded...," she complains to her single friend Molly.

"Lawrence hasn't put it down in a very long time," Issa tells Molly, a successful lawyer, noting she's curious about what it would be like to have sex with someone new after five years with the same man. Issa wants excitement. She wants variety and novelty. She wants Daniel, or just someone who isn't Lawrence. "Maybe I need to get on one of those apps like you...I just wanna see what's out there!" Rae is unapologetic about her protagonist's curiosity, the pull she feels to be with and do somebody new. At first the show might seem to be playing into a timeworn trope: Lawrence is down, unmotivated, and basically not being a great boyfriend. They've grown increasingly alienated from each other. But then she and Lawrence reconnect emotionally. He finds an interim job. They recommit to each other, feeling happy and connected. Lawrence and Issa seem to be back on track.

But Issa goes to Daniel's recording studio anyway, and has incredibly hot, fun sex with *him*. In her interview with Wilmore, Rae explained her choice to write it the way she did. In part, she felt it was authentic to show that women don't just "fall into" infidelities and dalliances. Like Alicia Walker's study subjects, they often seek them out, because they want them: "She had already opened this door at the first episode, and once the woman decides, like, 'I'm opening this door,' she's gonna walk through it," Rae mused to Wilmore. This decision wasn't about being angry at Lawrence or being disconnected from him. In fact, in a fundamental sense it wasn't about Lawrence at all. It was about Issa and what she wanted, and about Issa acting on what she wanted. It wasn't about her lackluster boyfriend, who was trying to get his life together, Rae told Wilmore. "It was about *her* and fulfilling this fantasy and being this person that she had set out to be, this active person who made different decisions." Rae is talking about agency, something Issa struggles with and sometimes fumbles. But Rae wants her to have it. Like 50 percent of the women who admitted they were unfaithful in a comprehensive 2011 survey of more than 100,000 US adults, Issa stepped out because she wanted to, because sex with a new person was an exciting idea and then an exciting reality.

But Issa feels horribly guilty after her liaison with Daniel. She regrets what she's done and avoids him, then tells him it was a one-time thing. She recommits to Lawrence, feeling at once renewed in her connection to him and tremendously remorseful. It wasn't enough for viewers. The backlash was astonishing. Social media lit up, with thousands of commenters identifying as #TeamLawrence or #TeamIssa. Many were infuriated at Issa.

Rae didn't back down. Men were a new audience, she observed, and men (and a few women too, but nowhere near as many) were mad. Lawrence was their stand-in. But as Rae says, *It wasn't about him. It was about her.* In this she echoes the thinking of Esther Perel, the therapist and author of *Mating in Captivity* and *The State of Affairs,* who challenges us to move beyond our paradigm of personal betrayal in thinking about infidelity. Perel wants us to consider that the affair may not be an indictment of the person being cheated upon. Nor a sign that he or she—the person who has been "betrayed"—has failed. Or that the relationship necessarily has big problems. Maybe, but maybe not. Not infrequently, Perel has found, infidelity has nothing to do with him or her or the relationship at all. Hard as it is to imagine that something that causes so much pain, something a partner does that devastates us so thoroughly, might be somewhat unrelated to us, it is sometimes the case. This idea may feel terrifying, because it shows how little control we have over what a spouse or partner does. Even if we're "perfect" they might step out. People have affairs or extra-pair involvements because they want to. Not necessarily because they don't love us or don't want us or because they can't commit to us or because they are afraid of how much they love us. Not because something is wrong with the relationship. They might do it because they were attracted to someone else and went for it. Rae says it was so for Issa. Lawrence wasn't being such a great boyfriend. Then he was. It didn't matter.

Eventually Lawrence discovers Issa's secret, her one-time indiscretion—as is so often the case, her cell phone is her initial betrayer—and leaves her. He quickly finds a gorgeous new girlfriend, and then another, while Issa is utterly miserable. She cries. She loses her focus at work and nearly loses her job. She fantasizes about getting back together with Lawrence. She goes on a series of awful dates. On one of them, she breaks into one of her rhyming reveries, faux cheerfully, desperately denouncing herself, calling herself a liar and a cheat, and advising her date, *"Run away!"*

When Issa finally began to recover and reemerge into the world for a little fun, the Twitterverse had a lot to say. Much of it along the lines of: Issa hasn't been punished enough yet for stepping out.

Thus, anyone "siding with Issa" was a target by proxy. Anyone on #TeamIssa was trash AF; Issa was a toxic person. There were tweets about how anyone on #TeamIssa was a ho. The gender war was ratcheting up. But why, some wondered. As Damon Young wrote on VerySmartBrothas.com, "Lawrence, essentially, is a proxy for all the men…who enjoy seeing women experience some sort of comeuppance. Team Lawrence exists to shame Issa."

Rae's response as an artist was to tilt into the wind. In this post-breakup period, she decided, her main character would go through a "ho phase." She explained it this way: "A ho phase is…it could be a rite of passage that women go through, but it's basically the sexual liberation of exploring your options… 'I just want to get my number up. And see what's out there.' It's really just about, like, pleasure at the end of the day. Pleasure and exploration." Turning the dark mark of ho-dom on its head, Rae reclaims the term and reframes it as nothing more and nothing less than an adventure women are entitled to if they want it. That doesn't mean double standards melt away and dangers don't exist, of course. The internet buzzed with outrage that Issa the character had betrayed a "good black man." And when Wilmore observes that "a guy's ho phase is called his life," Rae concurs. "I feel like [for] guys, it's not a phase—it's just ho…It's just ho-ery and that's it. And that's accepted. Even that language, like women have to have a phase…you can't be a ho for the rest of your life, and men…that's expected of them…George Clooney just got married…nobody's calling *him* a ho!"

PIONEERS AND PROVOCATEUSES

Sexologist and sexuality educator Frenchie Davis, a master of education in human sexuality candidate, lives to discuss and dissect precisely these types of contradictions. Being a black woman who is openly, professionally, and personally interested in sex, she told me when we talked—first on the phone and later over lunch when she was visiting New York from Washington, DC—is a high-wire act. All her life, Davis says, she received messages—from family, friends, and her religion—about who and how to be as a black woman. Eventually, she realized she wasn't going to be that woman. "I wasn't going to be a mother, I might never be a wife. And I won't be a 'good girl.'" Davis, who studied at Howard University and is pursuing her MEd at Widener University, founded Libido Talk, a sex education media events company, in order to push her sex-positive message out online, at conferences, at intimate talks in people's homes, even in bars. She hosts a monthly event called Sip.n.Sketch in DC, where men and women come together to drink cocktails, chat, and sketch nude models. "Why are we able to simply appreciate the model's body in this context," she asks the men who attend the event to wonder, "when we might objectify her in short shorts on the street?" These are just some of the "hypocrisies of the world," as Davis described them when we spoke, that drive her to engage again and again with her community on the topic of sex, and female sexuality in particular.

One of her most popular events is a night of sex trivia (What's the most common sexual fetish? A fixation on shoes and feet! Which US president was supposedly gay and went to events with his partner? James Buchanan!). "There's no place I don't go—libraries, coffee shops." Davis laughed when I asked her about venues. But she particularly wants to serve black communities, and for her that often means getting out the message in the spaces they come together: churches. "I try to work with churches as much as possible, to help people see that, yes, you *can* put these two aspects of your life together," she says, "and I figured, 'Hell, they do bingo in those basements. We can do sex bingo!'"

Davis, one of the country's few African American sexologists, is a fan of humor. On her Instagram account, she wears a red T-shirt emblazoned with the words SEX GEEK and posts messages like "it's not premarital sex if you never get married!" and "I gently slid her panties to the side...so I could fit the rest of her socks in the drawer." She believes in confounding expectations and biases about what it means to be black, female, and sexual. But Davis's motivations are deep and serious. When she was younger and living in Detroit, Davis told me, she lost several close friends within a span of a few weeks to what she describes as "sexually related violence." Two of these friends were shot and killed when relationships went awry, one by a boyfriend who didn't want her to go to college. "I had a lot of questions about black love. And the lack thereof. And the link between black love and violence. What are the origins? How did these things happen? There had to be reasons. I have quested to find out."

Writing about the intersection of love, sex, and race was part of her search. In 2003, Davis made her first major television appearance on HBO's *Def Poetry Jam* series, performing her spoken-word erotica. Since then, she has performed and lectured at more than fifty colleges and universities across the country and internationally, frequently sharing the stage with the likes of Mos Def, Sonia Sanchez, and Jill Scott. Davis was the first African American to write a book of poetry sold at New York City's Museum of Sex, *Not from Between My Thighs,* which pastors throughout the country have purchased and used for sex-positive discussions at their churches. "I have to keep bridging this gap," she explains. "Bringing my activism and writing and academic training together is the way to do that."

Frenchie Davis is in many ways continuing the work of two trailblazing African American female sex researchers, June Dobbs Butts and Gail E. Wyatt. Wyatt was the first licensed black female psychologist in California. After earning her doctorate from UCLA, she published the nation's first study on African American female sexuality in 1988, using a 478-item structured interview she developed and called the Wyatt Sex History Questionnaire. Wyatt wanted to follow up on the famed Kinsey study, *Sexual Behavior in the Human Female,* published in 1953. Noting that Kinsey's interviewers were mostly white males who asked women about taboo sexual practices and desires, Wyatt decided the interviewers of African American women for her study would be "clinically trained black females who developed rapport with subjects prior to the interview and monitored the subject's reaction to affect-laden topics in order to adjust the pace of the interview." In other words, Wyatt was introducing a sorely needed awareness about the realities of race, gender, and controlling images to the interview process. Because of this, Wyatt and her interviewers were able to collect comprehensive sexual histories, beginning from childhood, of the sixty-four African American women in her own sample. The study suggested some new findings: since Kinsey's original studies, "[black] women have broadened their sexual repertoires to include a variety of behaviors besides vaginal intercourse" (Wyatt believed this was likely in the context of primary relationships). Wyatt and her colleagues concluded that "only 26 percent of the Kinsey women reported six or more sexual partners as compared to 60 percent of the new subjects." And Wyatt uncovered interesting facts about black women and infidelity: "Among ever-married women, there was only a slight difference between samples on extramarital sexual activity. The proportion of women who had engaged in extramarital sex was 31 percent in the Kinsey sample as compared to 40 percent in ours."

Wyatt, a minister's granddaughter who had studied deportment, traveled to Europe, and had every privilege as an upper-middle-class girl growing up in Los Angeles's newly integrated Leimert Park, may have seemed an unlikely candidate for a career in groundbreaking sex research. And she encountered plenty of obstacles in the form of respectability politics once she decided to devote her career to the study of sex—everything from HIV transmission to sexual abuse and intimate partner sexual coercion to the legacy of US slavery and rape, which she analyzes in her book *Stolen Women*. "Can't we just tell people you're a teacher?" her mother once asked. Wyatt is indeed today a professor of psychiatry and biobehavioral sciences at UCLA's school of medicine. But she cannot forget, she told a reporter several years ago, the time she sat in a hotel lobby in Cleveland, dressed in an emerald green dress with a Peter Pan collar, wedding band on her finger, waiting for her husband so they could set out for a wedding. Two white men walked out of the hotel bar, looked her over, and said, "She must cost at least a hundred dollars." Controlling images that black women cannot escape did not stop Wyatt; they set her ambition and her work ablaze, igniting a prolific career of insight, resistance, and accomplishment. But we might wonder how much more she and other women could do if they could reclaim their time and all the energy sapped from them by pushing back against bias.

June Dobbs Butts, another African American sex researcher, took a different path to change the way we think about women and sex. Dobbs Butts was the daughter of one of Atlanta's most respected black political influencers, and she was eventually the aunt of Atlanta's first black mayor. Her family lived in the same neighborhood as Martin Luther King Jr., who was a friend of Dobbs when they were in high school and college. All six Dobbs sisters attended Spelman College—most eventually pursued advanced degrees. But their father still frequently expressed disappointment that he didn't have a son. It stuck with her, and in one interview she recounted the way when his grandson was born, the whole family made a trek at her father's behest as if to visit the baby Jesus. In contrast, the birth of a girl was considered ho-hum. It was a lesson about being female that Dobbs Butts never forgot.

She grew up to train as a sex therapist and counselor, eventually earning her EdD in family life education from Columbia. After serving on the board of Planned Parenthood, where she met William Masters and Virginia Johnson, Dobbs Butts became the first African American to be trained at the Masters and Johnson Institute. But she brought her very own thinking to the field. Dobbs Butts viewed sexuality through the lens of all the shifts happening in American culture in the late 1960s and early 1970s—the civil rights movement, America's reckoning with its racist past, and our country's worship of power and dominance—and committed herself to the project of crossing important and relevant research over into popular culture. Specifically, she wanted black men and women, whose sexualities had so long been mired in stereotypes and misrepresentations, to have access to facts. In 1977, she wrote *Ebony* magazine's first feature article on sexuality, "Sex Education: Who Needs It?" and penned other sensationally popular pieces like "Sex and the Modern Black Couple" for that magazine. She went on to contribute to *Jet* and *Essence,* where she wrote their most popular monthly column, Sexual Health, from 1980 to 1982. She repeatedly took on the massive and frequently controversial task of confronting the same sexual hypocrisies Frenchie Davis calls out today. As Dobbs Butts observed, "Americans snicker at sexual references in polite society, yet are embarrassed to talk about their sexual lives, especially if they are experiencing inadequacies or discomfort." Her work went a far distance to disentangle black sexuality from the death grip of controlling images, and in many ways she, like Wyatt, paved the way for today's most important, provocative African American female storytellers and image makers.

READY FOR IT?

The popularity of Davis's workshops, and of both *Awkward Black Girl* and *Insecure,* are just a few examples that suggest a considerable share of us are ready to be challenged and delighted and surprised about sex, double standards, relationships, and what it means for an African American woman to be in charge of her libido. Even when that means letting her libido be in charge of her. Might our culture also be ready for women to write and produce and present women who aren't stereotypes, and aren't constrained by constraint? Like Roxane Gay, whose short story collection *Difficult Women* gives us female protagonists who are unapologetically "untrue," sexual, and complicated, and not infrequently angry about being shunted aside for it; like Shonda Rhimes, who had the audacity and storytelling genius to present us with characters and storylines we couldn't have imagined being permitted to see on TV only a few decades ago—Rae, Philyaw, Miller-Young, and Davis are paving the way forward. Meanwhile, the rage at Issa the character, the persistent shadow cast by controlling images, suggests that when it comes to who gets to represent the future of sex and gender, of men and women and beyond, who gets to talk about it, who gets to write and direct and produce the story of what black women want and how it will be, the stakes are very real, and very high.

CHAPTER EIGHT

LOVING THE WOMAN WHO'S UNTRUE

I had deliberately chosen a nondescript restaurant, one nobody I knew ever went to, for my meet-up with a married man. He had texted, "Let's go somewhere private."

I wasn't wearing my wedding ring—I hadn't since that day of the workshop on consensual non-monogamy. The man I was meeting was attractive—dark-haired and fit—and always attentive. He was smart and handsome and he made me laugh and sometimes I wondered what it would be like to be with someone like him. Or to be with him. Catching sight of him across the room, I smiled, knowing that in seconds I would be able to embrace him. If this sounds like a setup for a story about an affair, it isn't. It's far more salacious and interesting than that, because the man I was meeting had a story to tell.

Tim and I had been introduced several years earlier by a mutual friend. A life coach of sorts, though he doesn't use that label, he had been a trusted confidant at a difficult moment in my life. My husband and I had hired Tim to act as something between a midwife and a therapist as we rearranged our relationship and household along more equitable lines once I decided I needed to work full-time again post-kids. It was a challenging process, even for my easygoing husband, because I wasn't sure what I wanted, and because the changes we were trying to bring about felt like an inconvenience in the best instance and a terrifying upending of the order of things, albeit an imperfect order of things, in the worst.

As is often the case with relationships forged in times of distress, mine with Tim felt comfortable, almost intimate, very quickly. He is several years older than I am, telegenic, calm, and positive—he once had a high-pressure, fast-paced media job—and by the time we were meeting that day, he knew a *lot* about me. He knew how I reacted to stress, what triggered my temper, how I worried about my children, what I am afraid of. Soon after our initial phase of working together, Tim moved. I had been nervous, but he assured me we could be in touch electronically. By now, we were no longer working together, but I considered him a good advisor and friend and often texted him for his opinion when I began to write an article or confront a knotty issue in my professional or personal life. Tim would usually respond to me within the hour, modeling composure and humor that invariably set me at ease while showing me how to be a better person. "Now send her a nice email and then move right along, for the sake of your health and your career. No reason to cut off a possible path to more success," he advised once when I confessed I had told a producer who cut me out of a news segment of my annoyance. Ever pragmatic and optimistic, he said "It's what writers do" whenever I brooded, then recommended that the second I felt negative, I tell myself, "Right. My brain's doing *that* again." I saw him whenever he was in town, which was every few months or so.

Tim was so generous and centered that it made me curious about how he got that way—seemingly impossible to ruffle, steady, happy. I began to ask him about his work and life and childhood, pressing for details about what he liked to do in his free time, his marriage, and his grown children. He was gracious and answered my questions but let me know that he felt most comfortable when focusing on other people. "People are never boring," he said with a laugh more than once. I respected Tim's clear sense of what he did and didn't want to share with me.

But at this particular meeting, it would turn out, Tim wanted to let me know more about himself. As we sat across from each other with the clatter and noise of people all around, he asked me for some additional details about my book project, which I had described to him briefly several months before. Tim asked a few more questions about my recent work. Then he looked at me intently, leaning forward to close the gap between us over the table, and said, "So here's something kind of interesting. My wife has two husbands."

Tim first caught sight of Lily at work when he was in his late twenties. They were both in the news business and in the process of adjusting to the hectic, do-or-die ethos of a daily publication, the need to understand, edit, and communicate a story of consequence in minutes and under pressure of breaking it before other news outlets did. "Lily just had this way of knowing what to lead with, no matter how confusing the news item was. She was so confident and so independent. I found that incredibly sexy," Tim recalled when I asked him how their relationship had begun. "I had to know her better. It took me weeks, but I finally worked up the nerve to ask her out."

They had what Tim described as "great chemistry," and one date led to another and another. Soon things were serious, but they agreed to keep it all under wraps at work, apprehensive about how their coworkers and higher-ups might react. "Then we'd go to my place and tear each other's clothes off," he recalled with a laugh. Their emotional connection was as strong as their physical one. Lily was direct and honest, more so than any woman he'd ever been with, but she was also a great compartmentalizer, Tim told me. She liked to confront issues head-on, resolve them, and move forward. Lily wasn't a wallower; she was a realist. She was compassionate and loving and avid

about her life and their shared life but also tough and focused on res-
olutions in all matters, from work to scheduling their time together.
She was fun—Lily loved to dance, cook, and spend time with friends
and was often the party starter—but also calm under pressure and
rational. Tim was smitten. When they announced their engagement
after a year and a half of seeing each other, Tim's boss said, "It was so
obvious you guys were into each other and are meant to be," and that
everyone already knew and had been waiting for them to come forward about it.

A few weeks before their wedding, Lily told Tim, in effect, that
whatever his dreams were, he should follow them, and that he had
freedom to do as he wished:

"She said to me then and has always said to me, 'Whatever it is
that is a dream for you, you will be able to pursue your dreams if
you're married to me. And whether that's you want to be able to
bike across the country, or you need to have a relationship with
someone else, as long as it doesn't endanger the marriage, as long
as it's not distracting, that's okay.' Drinking, drugs, all the other
things that people do that end up ruining their relationships—I
think she was telling me, 'I want us to have freedom, but not the
freedom to wreck our marriage.'"

It never occurred to Tim to offer anything less than Lily had,
once she opened up the discussion. Tim knew it was going to be
a marriage of equals and, as he explained, of "respect for what we
each wanted, tempered by respect for each other's feelings. Lily
was always very independent and that was a *huge* part of her appeal
for me." They decided to be married by a judge, and they spoke
with him ahead of time about changing their marriage vows to re-
move "forsake all others."

Their understanding, Tim explained to me, was explicit, and its
bedrock was an agreement that their relationship had priority. "If
she ever asked me to stop seeing someone, I would, in a second,"
Tim said. Lily never asked him to. Tim never asked Lily to. Their
system worked—neither knew more than he or she wanted to, or

had less than they desired of each other and others. Several years after getting married, they had kids and decided it made sense for Lily to stay home with them for a time. "She loved being a mommy, but she really missed having a career and being with her colleagues" is how Tim described this period. Lily eventually became very down and then clinically depressed. The couple took a step that seemed logical to them, given Lily's love for her work and Tim's desire for more time with the kids. He would stay home.

Like their open marriage, their professional/domestic arrangement worked well for them, even in an era when it was rarer than it is now, and at the same time it raised some eyebrows. I asked him what that was like, how they dealt with judgment. "I never really cared what other people thought of us as a couple, whether they agreed or approved or disapproved of our choices. So we ended up having a group of friends that got us and supported the way we are," Tim explained, shrugging. "The ones who didn't get it or judged just kind of stepped away."

Soon after the kids started school, Tim noticed a change in his wife. Lily grew increasingly distant and preoccupied. It seemed to Tim they were talking less—Lily would come home from work, work some more, put the kids to sleep, and collapse into bed herself. Eventually some of Lily's girlfriends, concerned, came to Tim. They really cared about him and Lily and the marriage, they explained, and were concerned that she was very much in love with a man she was seeing. "You need to tell her she needs to end this! You need to kick her out!" one insisted to Tim.

Another friend told Tim she blamed him for "letting Lily have too long a leash." He told me, "I found the way they talked about it mind-boggling. Like Lily was my property and I had to control her. Like she was my horse!"

Lily had apparently fallen hard for someone else, and while Tim had no intention of trying to "rein her in," he knew he had to speak to his wife. So one night, after they had put the kids to bed, Tim asked her what was going on. Lily admitted that, yes, she was involved with someone. She told Tim that things had become serious and intense, and that this man made her happy in ways she hadn't felt before. Did this mean there was something wrong with her, and with their marriage? She didn't think so. She sobbed and apologized and said she loved both this man and Tim, in different ways, and that she didn't know what to do. "What should I do now?" she asked Tim over and over, crying.

Tim recalled, "She was in pain. She was being so raw and honest with me and saying, 'Now what?'" Tim wasn't sure either. He fought back his jealousy and a feeling of panic. He tried to be reasonable and thoughtful and considerate, something he and Lily had promised one another to strive for always. "I figured, 'My job as your husband is to be empathic, to say, "Okay, you are going through a painful thing. It's painful for both of us. What's next?"' And I just realized, *Okay, this is probably one of the most important decisions I'm ever going to make.* I thought, *I trust her, I do. And if I try to shut this down, she'll just want to be with him more.* I knew if I told her she had to cut him off—that's it. She'd be more in love with him than ever. I would make her long and pine for him if I forbade her to see him, and besides, that wasn't in our vocabulary."

To Lily's surprise, Tim told her that he thought she needed to continue the relationship with her boyfriend. "You need to figure it out," he advised her, "and think about what this is going to mean for you and me." Lily was enormously relieved, Tim said, when he reassured her, "I'm going to be cool. It's all going to be good. And it's not going to be a situation where I say, 'Oh yeah, Lily? Well, now watch what *I'm* going to go out and do!' No. I felt compassionate toward her, and toward me, and our marriage."

They had been together for ten years at this point. Reflecting on it, Tim said, "We weren't having sex that often anymore, because of the kids, and I think I talked to her about the kids a lot because I was the one taking care of them mostly, and we were in a rut in that way. Plus her father had a slow, lingering death that was really terrible for her, for our family. She was hurting."

Having agreed to weather the challenge of remaining open, they decided it was okay for Lily to go stay with her boyfriend one or two nights per week. She didn't stay more often than that. She didn't talk to Tim about him much; Tim didn't ask. But over time, Tim learned Lily's boyfriend was everything Tim was not—big and strapping, a physical laborer who also loved to cook. Eventually, after several months, the two men met. Tim was relieved that he did not dislike Lily's new boyfriend. He described him to me as "Not the kind of person I would seek out, but a nice and basically very decent guy." Eventually, Lily's boyfriend, whom I'll call Rick and who was divorced, began spending some time at their home. Many years later, when Tim was back at work and his career was booming and busy, Lily's boyfriend moved in to Lily and Tim's second home, where he became their caretaker, chef, and a kind of "uncle" to the twins.

On his end, Tim has long had relationships with other women. He says that what has kept things going in his marriage is a sense that he and Lily are allies. And he says the most important thing is that in their first conversation when things got difficult, "there was no feinting, no dodging, no machismo on my part. There wasn't room for it." He told me that there had been a learning curve to their open marriage: "During those early years, I started experimenting. I started having relationships, just little relationships is how I would describe them, with other people. I would say always with Lily's knowledge, one way or another. With her approval or her disapproval from time to time. And she's my friend, and she's a protector of me and of our marriage, and so sometimes she'll say, 'That's going to be a problem. Don't do it!'"

Fascinated, I asked Tim about whether he and Lily had ground rules, and he laughed. "The rules have morphed over the years. You change so much as you age, and age together. What's okay, what's appropriate or not appropriate. We had a thing about no secrets, and no siphoning time, energy, or money from each other and the kids. That's basic and has stayed in place. The rules at this point are nobody with children under a certain age. Nobody who has never had a child, unless they are no longer capable of having a child. That could just get way too messy." Lily's live-in boyfriend has no children and doesn't want any, so these rules mostly apply to Tim.

While Lily occasionally "fools around" with other men—she particularly enjoys that she is pursued by younger guys, according to Tim—she has remained committed to her marriage for more than twenty-five years, and to her boyfriend Rick for nearly a decade and a half. "It's not like she doesn't come sleep at home every night. She does," he explains. Meanwhile, although Tim has had multiple relationships, he has never wanted to have anyone live with them. I asked him how his relationships in particular had changed over time. He thought for a moment. "I was fairly inappropriate, looking back on it, because it was like, *Oh, this is fun,* expanding into some new universe where you can pretty much do whatever you want, within those agreed upon parameters. That's how you feel at first. But you *can't* do whatever you want, because you still have to have respect for every person involved, including your wife and children, even if your wife is the catalyst for all this going on. Then there's the person you're involved with. It's a lot of obligations."

"Respect" is a word that Tim uses a lot in our conversations. He mentions, at one of our meet-ups, that he has never seen Lily and Rick so much as hold hands. In fact, while the two of them go on vacation together twice a year and enjoy going to concerts together, he has never seen any physical contact between them. He explained, "She's not a PDA person. So it's that, but it's partially out of respect to me, and bigger respect even for our kids. My kids don't want to feel like they live or have ever lived in a commune. Even though they kind of do! But it doesn't feel like that. To any of us. He's a chef. He cooks, he takes care of our house, he drives the kids where they want to go, so for them it's always been more like 'Rick is our family friend.' Whatever goes on between Rick and Lily happens offscreen.

"It's more a question for Rick, I guess," Tim muses when I ask how he feels about "sharing" his wife with another man. "Rick has a bedroom; Lily sleeps with me—it's just the way we do it. There's a hierarchy there. Our marriage is at the top. He seems okay with it." The domestic arrangement seems to suit them all, after all this time. Tim describes it as "cozy."

Tim is well aware that not everyone is accepting of how they live. Gossipy neighbors have plenty of opinions and questions. "They'll come over to me and say, 'This is none of my business, but how can you have another man living in your house? I mean, you're a nice guy. How do you put up with this?'" Tim shrugs it off and tells them Rick, too, is a nice guy. He lets them draw their own conclusions. He once heard someone refer to their home as "that weird orgy house," which made him laugh. "Our life is boring! We sit on the deck and have friends over. We play board games sometimes! We cook big meals. Well, Rick does. That's about as fascinating and decadent as it gets."

The conversations that really matter to Tim and Lily are the ones with their kids, who are now young adults. As soon as he sensed that they were picking up on gossip about their mom and dad, Tim told them that they could ask anything at all about their parents' living arrangement and their relationship. They said it all felt normal enough to them, and that they understood it just fine and didn't need to know more. "Do your kids want to know what goes on in your bedroom [with your spouse]? Heck no," Tim observed. "So what makes you think your kids want to know about your relationship with the person who is not your spouse?" Tim told me he believed that his children felt "Whatever you guys do in there, don't make us live with it, and we'll all be fine."

I got the impression that Tim loves Lily as much as ever, perhaps in part because she presented him not only with freedom but with an ongoing challenge, one that keeps them linked but separate. He agreed, adding, "Lily is one of a kind. She's the one who taught me that marriage is not being each other's property. Not in any way, shape, or form. She set that as the platform of our future together, when we got married."

Tim feels convinced that being open is the right way for him and for Lily. He has little in the way of advice for others, and unlike many people in open marriages I spoke to, he never talks about monogamy as "impossible" or "hypocritical" or even "difficult." He is beyond that point in the process, and when it came to his marriage, he seems to have very little to prove. He prefers to keep his private life private, to the extent that he can, but he is in no sense embarrassed by it, and he seems to enjoy thinking through what it all might mean and why it works for them.

During one of our talks, Tim told me that he himself was emerging from the very sudden and bruising crack-up of a longish relationship with a married woman. I was surprised; I had never heard about her before. Tim explained that he had entered into the affair believing that the woman's husband knew about it. He did not. And when he found out, he told his wife to end the relationship immediately via text. She did. "This was someone I spoke to daily for nearly three years," Tim said, shaking his head. He spoke of feeling tremendously guilty and said, "I can only imagine what was happening on the other side of that text. The anger. The fireworks." He said he felt this breakup had altered him at the cellular level, and that he would never again be involved with a woman if he wasn't sure her husband knew. I wondered about the logistics of confirming such a thing, how it could be done. With a permission slip? A conversation between The Guys? Tim wasn't sure. This breakup was fresh, though, and what upset him most, he said, was that he had caused pain, and that his ex-girlfriend's husband would hold this over her forever as punishment. "This will be how he controls the relationship," Tim explained, shaking his head again. "And I bear some responsibility for that. It makes me feel ill." He says he would rather be open. "I have struggled with it sometimes. But it means that something like this—the breakup of a family over a deception, or a long terrible stalemate in a marriage with kids because someone was dishonest—won't happen."

Maybe what those in the self-described "poly community" are trying to achieve is a hedge against these types of disasters. Perhaps their path confers the benefits of pair-bonding to their children and in some cases themselves while shielding everyone from the unrealistic expectations of monogamy and the painful effects when the fragile concept shatters. When I tell Tim about polyamory, how it is a relatively new, emerging cultural practice and identity for people who join groups like Open Love, Polyamory Society, and Loving More for support, I presume he will see them as kindred spirits. Instead, he is somewhat incredulous. "I don't think of myself or my marriage as *polyamorous,*" he says tactfully, deliberately. He clearly wants me to understand where he's coming from.

"That Lily and I decided to be in an open marriage is not an identity for me. What would I have in common with a bunch of people, just because they happened to not be monogamous with their spouses?"

Lily did not want to speak to me. Tim explained that she was very private, that she agreed that Tim could talk about her, and that she trusted his version of events and didn't want or feel the need to chime in. There is a level of trust between Tim and Lily that struck me as pure. If someone had described their situation to me before I began work on this book—"They're open. It was her idea. He has girlfriends too"—I might have thought it indicated that something was wrong with each of them, that they had a fear of intimacy or had attachment issues, or that there was something sleazy about what they were doing. In short, I would likely have presumed they were "troubled." Or had troubled pasts. Now I saw them as creative and committed. And I saw Lily as deeply, thoroughly true.

A FEMALE PHILOSOPHER OF POLY

Lily may be something of an iconoclast, but she is far from alone. The philosopher Carrie Jenkins has turned her considerable intellectual energy and acumen toward analyzing arrangements like

Lily's. Jenkins is a tenured professor of philosophy at the University of British Columbia in Vancouver, where she holds a coveted Canada Research Chair, figurative real estate that in the academic world packs a punch not unlike having a beachfront property in Malibu or living in the fancy part of town in Anywhere, USA. Her areas of expertise are heady stuff: epistemology, metaphysics, and the philosophy of language, math, and romantic love. As an undergraduate and graduate student at Trinity College, Cambridge, Jenkins immersed herself in the works of Ludwig Wittgenstein, G. E. Moore, and Bertrand Russell. In addition to her teaching and research duties, Jenkins has been an editor of the prestigious journal of academic philosophy *Thought*. Her 2008 book *Grounding Concepts: An Empirical Basis for Arithmetical Knowledge* was well received and well reviewed by her peers but did not exactly create shockwaves, gain her a mass following, or earn her many impassioned detractors.

But lately and more often than she can possibly keep track of, Jenkins—who wears her medium-length dark hair in a smooth, well-kempt longish bob, sports round, owlish glasses, and is often photographed in conservative jackets—is as likely to be called a whore, a slut, "a walking sexually transmitted infection," "everything that is wrong with women," "a selfish cunt," and "a fucking cumdumpster" as she is to be addressed with the honorific "Professor."

These names were first hurled at her—in online comments, emails, anonymous letters to her department, and all the contemporary equivalents of degrading graffiti on the walls of a men's room reeking of piss—after she wrote a blog piece for *Slate,* and even more intensely following the 2017 publication of her book *What Love Is: And What It Could Be.* Jenkins's crossover work of nonfiction is an accessible philosophical treatise on love, including an exploration of the fact that love is often neither exclusionary nor exclusive. Jenkins was driven to write *What Love Is* in part because she wants philosophy to be something everyday and in the service of real people, applied to subjects that matter to them: who isn't interested in love? When we spoke, she told me she is inspired by exemplars of politically engaged philosophy like Socrates ("He'd just walk around and try to get anyone who'd listen to talk with him about philosophical concepts!" she enthuses), Simone de Beauvoir ("She wrote *The Second Sex* for every woman. She just *knew* it mattered"), and her beloved Bertrand Russell ("He dared to write not just analytic philosophy but explorations of sex and love. And he really paid a price for it. A very high price"). Jenkins also wrote *What Love Is* for deeply personal reasons: she herself is in a polyamorous relationship with two men, her husband, with whom she's been for "about nine years" as of this writing, and her boyfriend, whom she met in 2012. She wanted to engage with the theoretical and lived implications of her own arrangement, one she knew to be gaining popularity, and explore and critique our deep and often unspoken but profoundly powerful cultural expectations around monogamy.

"If the history of popular culture in the last half century is anything to go by, questions about the nature of romantic love are very important" is how she sums up the why of her book in its introduction, alluding to sex scandals (from Clinton to Mitterrand), popular song lyrics ("I Want to Know What Love Is," "What Is This Thing Called Love?"), and shows like *The Affair*. Of her own life, she writes:

> On the mornings when I walk from my boyfriend's apartment to the home I share with my husband, I sometimes find myself reflecting on the disconnects between my own experiences with romantic love and the way romantic love is normally understood in the time and place in which I live (Vancouver, Canada, in 2016). Sometimes this starts out in my mind as a replay of an awkward conversation, one of those where someone's asked me a perfectly innocent question— "So how do you two know each other?"—and unwittingly forced me to choose between giving a deceptive answer and providing what I know will be *too much information*. If I tell the truth—"He's my

boyfriend"—to people who know me and my husband, it's inevitably going to cause embarrassment—the kind of embarrassment that comes with suddenly being made to acknowledge the existence of something awkward, something abnormal, something that makes people feel icky. Deceptive answers—"Oh, he used to work in the office upstairs from mine"—are easy and comfortable.

Jenkins told me she spends one night a week with her boyfriend, Ray, and the six other nights with her husband, Jonathan. The three of them are very good with shared Google calendars. Part of being successfully polyamorous, Jenkins told me, is being organized. She and her husband had decided from the outset of their marriage that they wanted to be non-monogamous. But Jenkins, a stickler for accuracy, wasn't sure, initially, that she wanted to use the term "polyamory." Then she fell in love with her boyfriend, and it became the right label: *poly* meaning "many," and *amore* meaning "love." Loving more than one. With her commitment to philosophy being part of the real world, and her commitment to non-monogamy, Jenkins had considered writing about her personal life in a philosophical way for some time, but she'd sensed she should wait until she had tenure, which she figured would help buffer her to some extent from any negative attention she might garner.

Jenkins is an unlikely lightning rod. She describes herself as "an approval junkie" and "Hermione Granger-ish, never in trouble" and says she is "the world's worst rebel. I always just wanted straight As." She didn't know she was drawing a line in the sand until the hate began. Her book came out in early 2017, "Just in time for Valentine's Day," she joked when I asked. It was no love fest. The name calling and demeaning, the criticisms and threats, began almost immediately.

Simply going public with her day-to-day life was threatening to the order of things—monogamy for women, if not for men—and incited violent threats, mostly to control her if she won't control herself. Underneath the attacks is a teeming, roiling sense of entitlement, a feeling that something sacred has been disturbed or desecrated and must be returned to rights. "Get herpes and die, slut. Sharia law looks more attractive by the day" is how some have expressed it, their anger a good indication that her "wayward" or "disobedient" behavior is in their minds an affront not only to Jenkins's husband, and all of civilization, but to the commenters themselves.

Jenkins has a calm, even, and open demeanor that's very much in evidence as we FaceTime one summer afternoon: she is equanimity itself when my nine-year-old and his friend burst noisily onto the scene and I drop my laptop and have to switch rooms, and again when a huge truck near her balcony begins its deafening *beep-beep-beep* backup routine (like nails on a chalkboard to this high-strung New Yorker). Indeed, Jenkins strikes you as the kind of person who can hear just about anything, at any pitch or frequency, and then proceed to make sense of its underlying meaning with the kind of deep, grounded intelligence and authentic curiosity that set your favorite college professor apart from the rest. She does just this with the very public and often histrionic threats and insults she has received since the publication of *What Love Is.* "The idea that women are naturally monogamous makes it 'worse' when we are 'unfaithful,'" she observes. "That's why words like 'slut' and 'whore' are gendered female, of course." And at the bottom of all that, she says, here invoking Bertrand Russell, "is an historical vision of women as the reproductive property of men."

But property with a will and volition, I note.

"Yes!" Jenkins agrees, really warming to her topic. Because it's property with a will, "you must control it, and if it's *out* of control, if it's *beyond* control, it's extremely dangerous to you personally, and also socially dangerous. It can basically bring down the world." I thought of the Plymouth and Massachusetts Bay colonies, and the persistence of the legacy of the plough, the wide, deep rows it had tilled in the history of women's lived experience. The "walking sexually transmitted infection" insult—with its implication that women like Jenkins who cross the line are at once polluted and polluting in their very essence, at once abject and contagious, like lepers, but lepers who want to drag you down into the gutter with them and infect you too—expresses this rage and anxiety all at once, while wrapping it up neatly in a container of fantasized control.

When I ask her whether stigma against polyamory and against women like her who are autonomous and assertive is lessening, Jenkins gives a quick and definitive "No." Sure, there are shows about polyamory, and terms related to "consensual non-monogamy" are being searched with such frequency on Google that it may indicate a new openness to the idea. But Jenkins isn't buying it. She's haunted especially by the overt racism of many of her critics, who have plenty to say about her being with two men of Asian descent. "There might be some TV series about it and a cultural conversation about it, but there are plenty of people for whom polyamory is not okay, especially for a woman to be with two non-white men," Jenkins notes. She told me she uses comments she has received—taunts like "gook lover," "Asian fuck whore," and "Jap double penetration cum bucket"—projecting them in huge letters onto a large screen when she gives lectures to underscore the fact of their intersection. Invoking the work of bell hooks, whose writing she greatly admires, she says, "Anti-poly, misogyny, and racist commentary and beliefs are deeply tied to each other, and to other cultural prejudices."

In this context, other seemingly willful misconstruings of what Jenkins writes about and believes and how she lives seem almost quaint—or at least comparatively innocuous. Except they aren't. One article about Jenkins and her book, published by *New York* magazine's *The Cut,* went into great detail about her life with her husband and her boyfriend. The article headline suggested, "Maybe Monogamy Isn't the Only Way to Love." Next to it was a stock photo of a triad—a man with his arm around one woman while surreptitiously holding the hand of another. It doesn't take a doctorate in cultural studies to read that message: "Even when our publication runs a story about a polyamorous woman, we will reassert that having multiple sexual partners is an essentially *male* privilege."

These coercive tactics—subtly undermining stock photos, explicitly racist epithets, overt threats—work. Many women told me they avoid using hashtags like #feminism on Twitter during periods when misogynist trolls are out in full force—basically always. Until *Wonder Woman* and *Hidden Figures,* studios had little interest in making movies with female protagonists for female audiences—and were more reluctant still to bankroll films with black female protagonists. Indeed, a hacked email from Marvel's CEO to a Sony exec in 2014 argued that investing in female viewers would be a mistake, cementing the impression that Hollywood likes to bet on teenaged boys and men. Hillary Clinton was defeated by a wave of conviction that we had to "Trump that bitch, crooked Hillary," or the entire world would fall apart; white women fell in line. Leslie Jones got back to the business of comedy and was tapped as an Olympic commentator after being subjected to viciously racist, misogynist trolling for having the audacity to defend the right of women to an imaginary job previously reserved for men—ghostbusting—but she did take a brief Twitter break, citing the toll taken on her by haters.

Jenkins can deconstruct and understand the rageful words directed at her and others who step outside the narrow lane women are supposed to stay in, whether by refusing sexual exclusivity or by not shutting up about male coercion or by running for president. But the words sting, every single time. "I have wildly optimistic days and terribly dark pessimistic days," she summarizes when I ask her how she is taking the controversy around her book. "Saying women are people, not property, is deeply threatening, even to people who say they believe in equality," she observed, mentioning the deep and unexamined current of misogyny among not just Trump supporters but also some Bernie Sanders fans.

"I'm in a position to represent the non-weirdness of poly in that I present as quite a boring human being," she continues. "And I threaten the slutty stereotype because I write as a philosopher and have institutional creds and prestige, plus look how I dress for my photos! Dowdy!" She pauses for a moment and then summarizes: "The whole combination makes me at once threatening and hard to dismiss. But the status quo reaches so far down. So much is built on top of it. It's the foundation." On her best days, Jenkins sees the backlash against her lifestyle, against her book, against women who aren't monogamous and aren't apologizing about it, and against women who feel entitled to sexual self-determination and autonomy more generally as a kind of extinction burst event. "Maybe the backlash is this spectacular, last-gasp thing we have to get through. And it's actually a sign that the prejudices are dying this dramatic death because they run so deep," she posits.

Jenkins has lately been thinking a lot about kindness, and the polarity between kindness and cruelty. In a deep, philosophical way. Being poly, she says, means working very hard at allowing someone else to do something that might be hurtful to you: to see someone else. On the other side of the coin, it means being exquisitely sensitive to your spouse or long-term partner with whom you are being open, if you have that type of arrangement. Or being sensitive to everyone's needs equally if you are part of a "throuple." Whatever the specific poly arrangement, it requires kindness that is deliberate and painstaking. "You can learn about communication. You can learn about yourself and others. You can learn empathy too. But kindness may not be learnable," Jenkins muses. Being polyamorous and writing about it, she says, has been a learning experience in many regards. "You have to work at forgiveness, both interpersonally and in a larger sense," she says. "I think one thing that has really become clear to me is that social change and social justice are not just about large-scale politics. It's about how we respond to and police one another."

And how we police ourselves. For in addition to all the threats and roadblocks women like Jenkins are up against when they decide monogamy is not for them and choose to be open about it, or when they decide to be non-monogamous without disclosing it (they might create incredible unhappiness in their home lives, or be divorced, or be harassed as Jenkins was by infuriated total strangers, or be subjected to physical violence, raped, or even killed), they mirror and intensify society's contempt for the woman who is untrue, doubling it back onto themselves. Subjected to slut-shaming, many women join in and pile on themselves. With the exception of Annika, most women I interviewed were like thirty-three-year-old Mara. She had an older, possessive ex-Marine boyfriend who would not or could not have sex with her and refused to seek treatment for his erectile dysfunction. Eventually, Mara had an affair. "I can't tell you what it meant to me, to be desired," she said, as if reading from a script written by Marta Meana's study participants. It was like a tonic for Mara to be wanted, finally. She was a beautiful young woman in her late twenties at the time, and it struck me as healthy and normal that she had wanted and sought out sexual and emotional satisfaction, that she got the latter from the former. But years later, happily married, the fact that she had "cheated" on her then-boyfriend—who found out because he invaded her privacy by opening her mail—brought her to tears. Her guilt hung in the diner where I interviewed her, and I wished I could wave a magic wand to absolve her of it.

In Alicia Walker's words, "When it comes to sexual autonomy, women are up against external and internal constraints in ways that men just aren't." In some instances, as with Walker's study participants, the social script about women not caring as much as men about sex led them to believe they were "weird" or "just jacked up" not only for wanting sex so badly that they sought it outside their marriages but for wanting it period. Meanwhile, the proscription against extra-pair sex and particularly female infidelity is so comprehensive that one woman I interviewed, whom I'll call Michelle, was unable to forgive herself—not for cheating but for having been with a married woman.

MICHELLE

Michelle is a self-confident, independent, and inspiring person. She runs a nonprofit and has a prominent profile, speaking often on national news shows and writing for popular publications with huge readerships. She is a thought leader on Serious Topics, beautiful and smart. But she is also approachable and funny and fun, and her sense of humor is vast and wicked. I wasn't aware she was gay until, at her prompting, I found myself talking to her about my book at a mutual friend's party. Forthright and wry, Michelle said, "You know I'm a lez, right? Well, anyway, I am and now you know, and at some point I have to tell you about this woman I was involved with. I am still trying to understand it and how it happened and why I did what I did."

Michelle was soon off traveling for a series of speaking engagements, but we continued to be in touch. We exchanged some emails about her situation and her thoughts about it, but she kept things very general. Eventually we sat down together at a café when I was visiting the town where she lives. Michelle described the woman she was involved with for a time, Delia, as "very married, publicly married, you might say, and sort of a rock star in the lesbian community in my town." They met at a cocktail party—"the kind that starts off very civilized but becomes a rager," in Michelle's words. Delia, whom Michelle found endearingly self-conscious, was there without her wife. When they spoke, they realized they had sons the same age, and after a couple of drinks, Delia told Michelle, "My wife is out of town, and I'm so happy about it."

"I took that in," Michelle told me as we sat in the café. "I mean, I didn't realize yet that she was flirting with me and that I was attracted to her, because it never crossed my [mind] that I'd allow myself to be interested in someone who's married." I asked her why, and without pausing, Michelle told me, "Because I want to be more than someone's affair." Still, the fact that Delia had dropped an unsubtle hint that she was unhappy in her marriage lodged in Michelle's brain and stayed there.

A few days later they ran into each other at the playground with their kids. They ended up all going to a family-style restaurant after. Their boys fell in together like long-lost friends. So did Michelle and Delia, with Delia again mentioning that she found her marriage lonely and difficult. She told Michelle she had tried to leave her wife once before but hadn't been able to follow through. Delia was clearly hurting. She was also beautiful and alluring, with a sly sense of humor like Michelle's and a taut runner's body. Delia invited Michelle and her son over to the house that evening for dinner; Delia's wife was still out of town. "I really wanted to, but I also wanted to be upstanding. So I said, 'I can't, it's not a good idea, because you're married.'" Delia nodded and said she understood, and that Michelle was right.

They started emailing and texting the next day. They texted about what they were up to, how their kids were. And then, after that first week, about their mutual attraction. "I knew it was wrong. Mostly I told myself that she was married and this would not lead anywhere for me. But the truth is, I just lived for her next text." Delia's texts were funny. And honest. And raw. "She really was just so miserable about her relationship with her wife. She said there was zero communication and that her wife was a workaholic." Not long after their texts took a turn for the intimate, they saw each other at a get-together at a mutual friend's, and Delia's wife was there. "The sexual tension was just impossible. It was so thick you could *see* it," Michelle recalls. "And it continues that way to this day. Still."

A week or so after that awkward get-together and continued texting, late one evening Michelle's doorbell rang. When she opened it, Delia stood in front of her. Her wife was away and she just had to see Michelle, she said. She walked in and pushed Michelle up against the wall, pressing into her, and they kissed, a long, hot kiss. "There was a line there, and I crossed it," Michelle says in retrospect. "That is very, very me." She told Delia to leave, and she did, but Michelle couldn't stop thinking about her—that kiss, the way it felt to have Delia's body pressed up against hers—and soon they were seeing each other. It was secretive and exciting, but it didn't feel right to Michelle. "She'd sometimes come over while she was out on a run. Once we met in a park. Other times I'd wait for her in a parking garage and we'd go to a hotel. It was all very covert; it was terrible," Michelle recalls, shaking her head. "From the get-go I told her, 'Look, we can't do this unless you leave your wife.' I was clear about that. I said, 'You have to at least be on your way out.' And she said, 'I'm doing it.' And to her credit she tried." A few months after Delia and Michelle's first kiss, Delia and her wife separated, and she moved into her own place. She and Michelle spent a few weeks together, though no sleepovers "because of the kids." They were weeks Michelle still describes as "incredibly sexy but also deep. We had and still have a very real connection and an incredible attraction to each other."

They were getting into a groove, talking about how to integrate their lives and what to tell their children when all hell broke loose. Delia's wife discovered a love letter Michelle had written to Delia and put the timeline together. She realized Delia had cheated on her with Michelle, and she was devastated and very angry. She came to Delia's job and created a scene that was humiliating to Delia. And then Delia decided to go back to her wife. "She told me she felt so guilty and that she didn't deserve to be happy when her partner was so miserable. She's just utterly codependent on this woman she's desperately unhappy with, but it wasn't my place to get into that with her."

Michelle had her son and her work to keep her busy during the days, but as soon as her head hit the pillow at night, she began her guilty ruminations and went over her list of regrets. "Initially my belief was, I'm not married, and this woman's marriage is broken, and she says she's leaving her wife so this is fair game. In the beginning when I was blinded by love and lust, I had no capacity to think about the morality of my choices. Now that I'm more awake and not blinded by my choices, I feel bad about having an affair with a married person and hurting her family. I wasn't the primary source of hurt, but I like her child and I know he suffered." Michelle felt another, perhaps more abstract sense of guilt as well. "I'm a gay woman who wanted marriage equality because I respect the institution. I desire the right to be married as a gay person and then I carelessly invade another person's marriage. I feel ashamed about that."

The love story was not over, though. After months of therapy with her wife, Delia told her that she wanted to date Michelle. Her wife agreed. Michelle was hesitant, but they all sat down and discussed it. "It was a little surreal. But her wife said she understood that there was a lot Delia was not getting out of the marriage and that she wanted her to be happy, that she was on board." Still, after an initial period of euphoria about being back with Delia, Michelle began to feel increasingly anxious. A few months into their second attempt at a relationship, Delia's wife "fell apart," in Michelle's words, and demanded that Delia stop seeing her. Delia seemed frozen and conflicted about what to do. Michelle, feeling agonized, decided to break things off herself. "It wasn't good for anyone. But I miss her so much. I am just so in love with her." She shook her head. It had been over a year since their breakup, and she didn't feel any less adrift or broken about it. Part of her pain, she said, was that her relationship with Delia began illicitly.

Michelle began to cry as she tried to explain: "You're a secret when you love someone who's married. You don't matter, and you're under a shroud of secrecy and shame. We had an amazing love, and you have to hide this beautiful thing." The fact that Delia had eventually been open with her wife about wanting to get back together with Michelle didn't seem to make a difference. Michelle was shunted to the side again anyway, and it was devastating, even if technically she had been the one to call it off. She had done so to protect herself and do the right thing, not because she wanted to. In a sense, she had been a pawn in Delia and her wife's relationship, and it stung horribly. Not long before she and I sat down to talk, Michelle told me, she had received a letter from Delia.

"I need you to know, in case I die, or in case I just don't find a time or a way to tell you, that I think about you every single day," the letter began. It was a beautiful letter, a letter about love and sex and connection. But after she read it, after she sobbed and wondered whether she had made the right choice, whether she should have fought harder for a chance to make something permanent with Delia, Michelle found herself wondering, *Life is so short. Why am I making myself miserable?* She ended it for good with Delia in her mind then. She still sees her sometimes at events and makes a point of walking in the other direction. It isn't easy. She is sure that she and Delia could be happily married. But she senses it's impossible. After all, Delia wants to end her marriage, but she doesn't. She wants freedom, and she wants Michelle, but she feels too guilty to demand it, to take it. Michelle wept for a few moments more telling me about it. I told her I was sorry to be dredging up these memories and that I appreciated her sharing this very painful story with me. Michelle nodded. She was busy. She had a speaking engagement, and she had to be going. "I have to thank you," she said. "Because these aren't things you can really talk about. My whole issue with what Delia and I had was that it couldn't be public, it couldn't see the light of day. And now it kind of can." Michelle said she wanted to honor the intense sexual, romantic, and emotional connection she felt with Delia. I felt honored to listen.

MEN WHO LOVE (MARRIED) WOMEN TOO MUCH

Some people just happen to love someone who is with someone else. That was the case with Michelle. She fell for Delia, and Delia was already partnered, and it was an inconvenience and a heartbreak to have fallen for her. Michelle didn't have a history of going for married women—it "just happened."

But some people are drawn to women who are already partnered, for various reasons—because it's convenient, because it's a little dangerous, or because they have a "thing" for married women. I spoke and emailed with a few men for whom these factors seemed to be in play. Robert, sixty, told me the story of being with a married woman when he was younger. It was a sexy story (this anecdote draws from both an email and a phone conversation) with an unhappy ending. "A married woman is responsible for one of the worst scares of my life. Her name was Sally. I was in my mid-twenties, and we had a once a week or so thing going on in my apartment that was quite wonderful…I liked that she was attracted to me, and that she went for it. I liked her independence in that regard. That she wanted to do this, and she did. That was appealing. And there were no strings attached. I didn't have to take her out, or wonder. It wasn't a serious thing for me—she showed up and we had our fun. But it got to the point where we were too indiscreet. I was young and stupid…and she was only a few years older than I was. We went out to a bar one time, and a friend of hers saw us…One Friday night I got a call [from a man] at about 7:00 asking if Sally was there. I thought it was an innocent wrong number. An hour later, the phone rang again. Same voice telling me that he knows where I live and if I ever touch her again he'll know and he'll kill me."

A shaken Robert walked into the bathroom and caught sight of his reflection in the mirror. All the blood had drained from his face. He had been reminded—with a death threat—that he lived in a world where women were the property of men and that his transgression against Sally's husband could be lethal. It worked. He saw himself as a dead man. Like Walter Neff in *Double Indemnity*, he knows a cheating woman is as dangerous as she is alluring. Unlike Neff, Robert got out before he was in too deep. He told me, "I stayed away but good. I waited a few weeks to call and explain what had happened and that we were over. Not long after that she called one night to tell me that she loved me and had planned to leave her husband for me. I explained that she was lovely but I wasn't up for getting shot. After that I limited my fun and games to unwed women."

It's hard to ignore that one of the things that drew Robert to Sally was what he called her "independence." She was married, and it didn't stop her. And it was clear that sex was on the agenda. These factors also draw the utterly witting and willing Walter Neff into Phyllis Dietrichson's orbit and are his ultimate undoing as she (barely) backseat drives him into killing her wealthy husband. "That's a honey of an anklet," Walter says to Phyllis at their first, sexually charged meeting rife with double entendre. At the time, anklets were known to connote that a woman was possibly "loose," having long been associated with courtesans and prostitutes. Thus we know who has the power, and how it will end.

Meanwhile, Robert ultimately heeded the cultural script that married women belong to their husbands. That script remained very much in place when Sally told Robert that she wanted to be *his* wife. She basically wanted to switch up the players. Robert's fear made sense to me, and Sally's husband's rage is all too familiar, the endless repetition of the same old song. But I was surprised to learn, as I interviewed and read, that there are men utterly unlike Sally's husband, men who want to be Robert and Sally's husband at the same time. These men don't merely tolerate their wives stepping out or look the other way when it happens. They want and frequently beg them to do so. These men have a particular and fascinating fetish: a deep need to watch their wives cheat. They are the antithesis of Peter the Great, who beheaded his wife's supposed lover, then is rumored to have ordered that the unfortunate man's head, preserved in alcohol in a jar, be displayed in the faithless woman's bedroom, where she would be forced to contemplate it every night. No, these men are not possessive, and they are not driven to violence by their women straying. In fact, nothing excites them more than being married to an adulteress. They welcome, celebrate, and engineer female infidelity for their own sexual delectation. I first learned about such men and partnerships via social media, and it was an education.

CUCKOO FOR CUCKOLDS

"You look like a classic hotwife," the direct message to my Instagram account read. *Well, maybe,* I thought, deleting it without giving it much thought. After all, who hasn't received unwanted direct messages, sometimes with sexual content or innuendo? "Are you a hotwife?" another DM from yet another stranger asked later that week. *Duh,* I thought, deleting that one too. And then a third message: "Hi. Are you into the cuckold lifestyle?" This one gave me pause. The cuckold lifestyle? I looked at the profile of the guy who had DM'd me. Ex-military. Clean-cut. His feed was all about sports. He looked macho. But the term "cuckold lifestyle" conjured up the Chaucer I had read as a student—stories like "The Miller's Tale" and "The Merchant's Tale," in which younger women have sex right under the noses of their unsuspecting older and ineffectual in every sense husbands. In both stories, the wife goes unpunished, and the joke is on her clueless spouse, for whom she, the reader, and the narrator alike have contempt.

After a bit of Googling, I was back in the realm of Chaucer, except in this case, the husbands are no dupes. They aren't blind like the knight, the husband in the merchant's story, or hapless like the carpenter, the husband in the miller's story. Men into the "cuckold lifestyle" or "hotwifing" are fully in the know. In fact, they actively engineer their own cuckolding, because they are turned on by hearing about or witnessing firsthand their wives' infidelity. Bucking the script of masculine possession, the man into this practice embraces being married to a woman who is untrue—his hotwife—egging her on to "betrayal" after betrayal because he likes it. And it seems there is no short supply of these men—or the men who fantasize about doing what these men do. This fascinating subset of swinging and kink is the second most commonly searched term by heterosexual porn users on English-language search engines, and researcher Justin Lehmiller found in a survey of four thousand men that 58 percent of them had fantasies about sharing their partner with other men, or being "cucked." Some men like to be present for the act, even participate in it, while others just like to help set it up and hear about it after.

In her Nerve.com article "Take My Wife, Please," Kai Ma provides a great introduction to and overview of what practitioners call "cucking" and "hotwifing." She observes that a husband who wants to watch his wife have sex with another man or encourages her to "goes against the grain" of the institution of marriage, the ideology of masculinity, and even patriarchy "in a radical way." Many of these men, according to Ma—who interviewed several and dove into the world of online cuckold life via websites like Chatzy.com and CuckoldPlace.com—are what we might consider "alphas" in their day-to-day lives, hyper-masculine types who enjoy playing a decidedly beta role in their sex lives with their wives. One couple she spent time with, Kurt and Christina, walked her through their sessions with a "bull"—the term for the other man who has sex with the married hotwife—named Claudio, with whom they "played" regularly. Kurt and Christina found Claudio on Craigslist. They had specified that their bull needed to have a penis that was larger than Kurt's. Kurt, who is a former Army man, gets very turned on when Christina says things like "[Claudio] is hitting spots in me that [you aren't]." Even more, he loves watching Christina while she actually has sex with Claudio or any of the other bulls they have invited into their bedroom and their relationship, all of whose penises are larger than his. Kurt says that he enjoys that bulls loom large over him, physically and psychologically, making him feel less than in every sense. "This is the one area in life where I can choose to be submissive," he told Ma. There is a deep and abiding belief in our society that "a real man controls his wife." Kurt and his cuck confreres relish ceding that control. Many get off on not being the "biggest" man in the room.

Men who identify as cucks and like to hotwife may hide to watch the action or observe via video camera. Still others are far away when the sex between their hotwife and the bull takes place but are there for the lead-up. These men enjoy helping their wives get ready for their dates: a man might shave his wife's legs for her, make the dinner and hotel reservation for her, shop for the sexy outfit she will wear on the date, and buy the condoms she will bring along. Still other men enjoy being told about it after the fact, in great detail. And then there are cucks who enjoy performing oral sex on their "cheating" wives or girlfriends after the fact—this is called "clean up." "What makes it erotic," one such man explained, "is that my woman is really enjoying herself [with the bull]. Then she comes back to me and humiliates me by saying, 'Now it's your turn to have me. You can taste what the other guy left behind.'" To these men, submitting to female infidelity is delicious.

Not all men married to hotwives are cucks, though. On her hotwife lifestyle blog, Alexis McCall, a hotwife and self-described "hotwife lifestyle coach," clears up what she believes are some misconceptions, describing her relationship with her husband, who enjoys it when she has sex with other men but is not sexually submissive. It turns him on to hear about it, but he doesn't like to watch, and he doesn't like to be humiliated like the men Ma interviewed. McCall defines a hotwife as "a married woman whose marriage is open on her end only, so that she can date other men and have sex with them, with both the permission and encouragement of her husband, in order to fulfill his fantasy of sharing her with other men, to the benefit of their marriage." If the marriage is not open and a woman is having sex with another man, McCall says, she is a "cheater" (it's remarkable when women who are considered sluts by the mainstream slut-shame women they consider to be "worse" than they are, but that's for another day), and if the marriage is open on both ends, she's a "swinger." Hotwives are something else again. Many hotwives like McCall wear an anklet, linking them to Phyllis Dietrichson and an entire world of women who are alluring and dangerous. The anklets are a way to advertise their availability to other men who are in the lifestyle. They also help hotwives find one another. McCall describes seeing a woman in a grocery store parking lot and knowing immediately that she was in the lifestyle—she could tell from her jewelry, including the way she wore rings on nearly all but her ring finger, and the way she noticed Lexi's anklet.

McCall confesses in one of her posts she had been miserable in her previously sexless marriage, and considered having an affair, before her husband told her of his interest in hotwifing. That turned things around. "I was committed in my own mind just as soon as I found out it was going to give me a personal sex life outside my marriage, which I had been planning on doing anyway," she explains. It sounds like a disaster in the offing, but not for McCall and her husband. She says that hotwifing counterintuitively built intimacy and better communication skills in her marriage. Essentially, stepping out for sex with her husband's encouragement saved their relationship, helping them talk to each other and connect more deeply than ever before. Female infidelity, fetishized and performed, became the glue that held this couple together, requiring them to speak honestly and leading them to desire each other as nothing else ever had.

In his remarkably comprehensive and readable *Insatiable Wives,* clinical psychologist and sex therapist David Ley made similar discoveries—couples who were into the cuckold/hotwife lifestyle, he found, varied in how exactly they practiced it, but what the successful ones had in common was impressive levels of connection and intimacy, enviable communication skills, and high levels of desire for each other compared to couples in monogamous unions. When he first stumbled across this lifestyle while reading responses to an online sex survey he had sent out, Ley (who is also the author of *Ethical Porn for Dicks,* which demonstrates that he really has a way with titles) thought people were having him on. There was virtually no academic literature on the topic. But exploring further, he connected with some hotwifing and cuckold-life practitioners and interviewed them at length. What he discovered surprised him. "I initially thought, *This can't be healthy,*" he told me when I interviewed him via Skype one morning. "And then I had to stop myself. Why did I assume that these couples, often in decades-long marriages, were necessarily unhealthy for engaging in sex behaviors outside the norm? I was allowing my social biases around monogamy, promiscuity, and female sexuality to intrude into my clinical judgment." Instead, Ley decided to listen. He found more participants to interview and was further surprised to learn that, like Alexis McCall and her husband, many of these couples had quite extraordinary levels of commitment, showed deep mutual respect, and communicated skillfully. Not a few also reported very high levels of marital satisfaction and sexual satisfaction after decades of being together, a rather unusual state of affairs.

According to Ley, there is variation within the lifestyle. For example, a couple he saw named Bobby and Richard don't even really discuss Bobby's extracurriculars, which she conducts on her own, with people they know, for safety's sake. But Ley also interviewed couples in which the man participated in his wife's sexual experiences with other men, and he told me that "quite a few men into this lifestyle have bisexual leanings." They wouldn't feel comfortable going to a gay club, but they might give a man oral sex in the context of cucking, if their wives directed them to as part of their play, Ley explained. One man Ley interviewed— married for twenty-two years and deeply in love with his wife— identified as bisexual and said he enjoyed "silky seconds" with her after she had had sex with another man because "his presence lingers in her." In cases like this, men in the lifestyle can explore their sexual fluidity, though Ley told me they don't always admit that to themselves. In this respect they are not unlike Alfred Kinsey, the father of American sex research and founder of the famed Kinsey Institute. Kinsey reportedly enjoyed sharing his wife, Clara, with other men, including his mentee Clyde Martin, with whom he may or may not have been involved sexually.

Meanwhile, in a study of gay men into cuckolding that Ley undertook with Dan Savage and Justin Lehmiller, the researchers discovered that the lifestyle is also popular with gay men in the age of marriage equality. It may be that, once gay men can get married, they are increasingly interested in being cucks and hothusbands. "It seems that when your relationship is codified and legalized, it is more erotic to cuckold within it, because it becomes more taboo," Ley explained. As one of the straight couples he interviewed put it, "For the grass to be greener on the other side of the fence...there has to be a fence...If there's no fence it's all just grass." Marriage creates a fence or line to cross. For some of us, crossing that line is a sin; for others, it is a fetish, a transgression with tremendous erotic charge.

On many cuck websites, including MySlutWife.com and Blacked Wives.com, it's evident that race often plays a disquieting role in the cuckold and hotwife lifestyle. There is an almost overwhelming fixation on "Mandingos," or well-endowed black men. One might argue that in these scenarios everyone is getting something out of it. But if hotwifing is radical in the agency it gives women, who seemingly have free rein to fuck with abandon, it is reactionary in its reliance on and reification of stereotypes—of the "hypersexual" black man and the "BBC," or big black cock. One bull told Kai Ma he refuses to respond to white couples' ads because they have "rigid" and stereotypical and just plain racist criteria. "To some of these people, a black guy is necessarily a corn-row-wearing thug or a basketball player...the big black Mandingo." Sighing, he mentioned an ad that said, "We want you to look like Usher." "The typical bull on Craigslist is not going to look like Allen Iverson or Usher, so get over your stereotype and deal with it."

Mireille Miller-Young, the historian and porn scholar, has a nuanced take on the figure of the Mandingo and what she calls "cuckold sociality." She and her co-author Xavier Livermon emphasize the importance of acknowledging that there are "mobile desires at play" in the racial fetishism of Mandingo cuckolding, which they say is on the one hand full of "productive possibilities and queer potential" for all the actors in the triad. At the same time, it demands the sexual labor of black men, turning them into stereotypically menacing beasts of burden. Miller-Young and Livermon suggest that pornography in general and Mandingo cucking in particular "are among the few places where our most privately held societal views about race are most revealed." In "eroticiz[ing] the sexual powerlessness" and humiliation of the (usually) white head of household and performing the threat that the black man, with his sexual prowess, will displace the white husband, this genre of cuckolding also allows for the possibility of white men being sexual with black men by proxy, reframing anxiety and threat as thrill. Meanwhile, the white wife's body acts "as a conduit of white male desires for racial purity and also for the black man's body." In this sense, she is less a woman coloring outside the lines and more an actress in her husband's complex, racialized, and heteronormativity-bending passion play.

If being a hotwife sounds enlightened and perhaps even empowering, it might not be. Some men into the cuckold/hotwife lifestyle give the impression that when it comes down to it, they are a whole lot less interested in their wives' sexual freedom and much more into rigidly choreographing their own pleasure. In some instances, a wife may not enjoy being a character in her husband's scripts. Or the partners may find they have agendas that are no longer in alignment. "You sometimes get these situations where the guy is very upset that his wife is doing it wrong," David Ley told me wryly. "They'll say, 'No, no, no, *this* is the way you need to do it, *this* is the kind of man I fantasize about you being with!'" Ley seemed flat-out amused, gunning for the girls, when he further observed, "What I saw was a number of women who, as they start initially to engage in this to fulfill their husband's fantasies and needs, gradually they themselves begin to develop more sexual autonomy and independence. These women will say, 'I'm interested in doing this, in developing relationships' or just in doing it their own way, without the men's controls placed on it." To paraphrase a saying among swingers, be careful what you wish for when you yourself are a guy who can have perhaps several orgasms per day but are married to a woman who can have many times that per *hour*. The fear and the fantasy is that one's wife will be "set loose." As Alexis McCall puts it, "Once your genie is out of the bottle, she's not going back in."

Ultimately, Ley thinks that the cuckold and hotwife relationships he studied may be about many things for men: bisexuality, an interest in being submissive, wanting control, wanting to cede control, being masochistic. Miller-Young might add: accessing the black male body while warding off "gayness." What strikes Ley most, he told me, is the incredible resourcefulness and creativity of the arrangements he witnessed. "It's like these guys understand the very real sexual power of the women they're partnered with," he marveled, "and so they're saying, 'Okay, female sexuality is "insatiable" in ways male sexuality is not. So let's ride this engine together.' They get vicarious fulfillment, these men, from revving the engine of female sexuality."

The cuck elects to join forces with his hotwife, knowing that her capacity for pleasure, unlike his, is nearly limitless. Standing apart from the tradition of men who have tried to contain or exterminate or diminish the female libido, or force it into the confines of fidelity, he knows better. He embraces it, because it can take him everywhere.

CHAPTER NINE

LIFE IS SHORT.
SHOULD YOU BE UNTRUE?

There is no shortage of research about why people cheat. Perhaps the most common belief, one we've embraced and built an entire culture and gender script around, is a neat binary asserting that men want sex and women want connection and intimacy. You can't Google "affair" without eventually running into this supposedly "universal truth" about lust and commitment. But tell it to Alicia Walker's study participants, the ones who went on Ashley Madison to find and audition men who could provide them with what they didn't have in their marriages: sex. And the ones in avowedly heterosexual marriages who seek out other women online for one-time sexual encounters. Tell it to couples therapists like Tammy Nelson, author of *The New Monogamy,* who says that in her experience, "men and women basically want the same things when they're having an affair. They want sex and connection. I wish I had known that earlier in my life and career—that when it comes to motivation, men and women are really very similar." Too often study participants are asked questions that lead them to answer a certain way, or they feel pressured by an overarching cultural script to do so. Women told they seek intimacy and emotional connection are likely to internalize that that's how women are, so that's how they should be, and then researchers hear what they expect, and so there is little incentive for them to ask the kind of questions Lisa Diamond and Sarah Hrdy did about male and female sexual motivations, identities, and desires. Such self-reporting is a slippery slope when ideology looms so large.

But like the women in Walker's studies, some women apparently buck the dogma. Of the 2,000 surveyed female users of the Victoria Milan website for married people seeking affairs, most responded "to add excitement to my life" (35 percent) when asked why they cheated (and a whopping 22.5 percent, more than one in five, reported doing so because they were unsatisfied in their marital beds). In a 2011 Kinsey study of infidelity and "sexual personality," researchers found that the 506 men and 412 women surveyed online cheated at a statistically comparable rate. They also found that fear of sexual performance failure upped the chances that both men and women would have extra-pair sex—maybe because a new, one-time partner was a chance to pretend there wasn't an issue, or presented an opportunity to be so excited that there wouldn't be an issue. Finally, those women who reported being in sexually incompatible marriages or relationships were 2.9 times as likely to cheat as women who didn't. In her Good in Bed survey of 1,923 women and 1,418 men, sex researcher Kristen Mark discovered that men and women were equally likely to consider infidelity due to "boredom" in a relationship, and that in the first three years of a relationship, women were roughly twice as likely as men to become bored.

Some women have extra-pair involvements because they can. Having access to resources, and particularly being the breadwinner or main provider of one's household, frees up women in the industrialized West to be sexually autonomous just as it did Wyandot women, who lived in a society where women had high status because they provisioned the group. I heard at least a dozen stories from women telling me about friends or friends of friends who were independently wealthy, had their own homes and trust funds or accumulated or earned wealth, and so were in a position to call the shots about their sex lives. In this category, Tilda Swinton comes to mind. Rich, beautiful, and powerful, for a time she reportedly lived in a castle in Scotland with her life partner, with whom she had twins, and also with her nearly twenty-years-younger boyfriend (in an interview with Katie Couric, among others, Swinton denied being in a "dual relationship" with the men, though did not deny having an arrangement that might appear unusual to some). A woman told me about an acquaintance, an heiress who lived in a fabulous house with her husband—and also had a relationship with the father of her young child in Europe. She shuttled back and forth between men and continents. In the absence of intensive kin support, money can act as a buffer against restrictive ideology and the threat of consequences for female sexual autonomy, including male reprisals like withdrawal of support and even violence. It is harder to imagine raising your hand against a woman who owns the house you live in and puts food in the pantry than it is against one you yourself support.

Other women are "untrue" because they have to be, are expected to be, or because it is practical. In many partible paternity cultures of South America, a monogamous woman may be considered both stingy and a bad mother. Closer to home, the anthropologist Arline Geronimus has demonstrated in her work and her article "What Teen Mothers Know" that in areas of the US where sex ratios are skewed against women—that is, where there are notably fewer men than women—delaying childbearing and monogamy are reproductive and social strategies women can ill afford. In neighborhoods where there are high rates of incarceration, for example, women and children may benefit from serial relationships and depending on extended family and other kin support to raise their children. Contrary to what social conservatives assert, this has less to do with morality and more to do with material circumstances and the kind of maternal strategizing and trade-offs in a sometimes hostile environment—in this instance, one ravaged by institutionalized racism—that helped *Homo sapiens* thrive.

There are other drivers that may be difficult to "feel." Some evolutionary biologists believe that we step out in search of a partner with whom we are compatible on a genetic level. Who can forget the famous T-shirt test? In case you have, it presented forty-nine women with T-shirts that had been worn for two days by men who didn't use any cologne or deodorant or soap. When asked to sniff the tees and rate the sexiness of the smells, women chose the shirts of guys with something called major histocompatibility complex most different from their own. In general, the more different the MHC of both parents, the healthier the offspring. The T-shirt test suggests that smell may well be at work in mate choice, and that we are attracted to mates through olfaction based on how good a genetic match they are, which is to say, how different certain of their genes are. Specifically, the genes that make molecules that allow the immune system to recognize invaders. Leslie Vosshall, a neurobiologist who studies olfaction, says, "It seems unlikely that humans would *not* use this system, given how many animals clearly demonstrate responses to MHC odortype." So there's that. (The study findings were reversed in women who took the pill. Block our hormones and our noses don't work right and we are more likely to pick the wrong fellow. You may be used to hearing that hormones "drive" men, but this study suggests that women are hormonally driven too.) Another study of Hutterites found that those with closely matched MHC had longer interbirth intervals (that is, it was harder for the women to get pregnant) and more miscarriages. This body of research would suggest that the hard-to-describe attraction you feel for someone, that irresistible pull they exercise over you, might be that they are a better genetic match. Woe to the woman who marries a man who isn't—she might forever be sniffing around for a guy with the ineffable je ne sais quoi (well, MHC) she craves.

So we know something about who the women who have affairs are. They're you and me. They're bored in their marriages, or sexless and orgasmless in their marriages, or happy in their marriages but eager for sex with someone other than their spouses, or they have money and power so they can do what they want, or they live in a culture that dictates that monogamy is stingy, or where monogamy isn't an option. Or they have a particular sexual "personality." Not unlike men, they often do it simply because they feel like it. For fun or for payback or because they are out of town or they had one drink too many and succumbed to their feelings for that woman at work. Whatever the reason, for that window in time, whether the encounter is under an hour or an affair that extends for years, when they are doing it they are not mothers or wives or employees. They are not honest and they are not self-sacrificing. They are not good; they are not admirable. But make no mistake, they are being themselves. Part of female sexuality, part of its legacy and its present and its future is that it is assertive, pleasure centered, and selfish. No amount of pathologizing can change the deep lessons we glean from the Wyandot and the Himba, from Amy Parish's bonobos and Sarah Hrdy's langurs, from the laboratories of Meredith Chivers and Marta Meana and Lisa Diamond's twenty years of interviews: that when ecological circumstances are right, women are just as likely to step out as men are. Our dearest held binary cannot hold. The world is being rewritten. But certain rules and formulas adhere, and the lesson from cultures across the world and the women you know is clear: there can be no autonomy without the autonomy to choose, without coercion or constraint, or in spite of it, who our lovers will be.

AFTERWORD

FEMALE CHOICES

After the better part of two and a half years writing, researching, and being a participant-observer on the topic of women who are "untrue" and all the untruths we have promulgated about them—in science, literature, and pop culture—I feel most of all a sense of amazement at how vast the terrain is. This book only scratches the surface of the history and evolutionary prehistory of female infidelity and female sexual autonomy, which are complex, surprising, and in many instances an upending of everything we have been taught about men and women. Meanwhile, the sex research data is copious, sometimes contradictory, and emerging at a quick pace from a number of committed female researchers whose findings will ultimately re-form many of our deeply held assumptions about who and how women are. Similarly, it seems that every time I mention that I am writing on female infidelity, someone shares another "must-include" node on the cultural landscape—from *Big Little Lies* to the brilliant and deceptively "simple" Florynce Kennedy quips that reframed our sexual consciousness in the 1970s to Rihanna lyrics. My research could have gone on many years more and I still wouldn't be anywhere near qualified to write *The Big Book of Female Infidelity* with any comprehensiveness or authority. This stopping point and the scope of *Untrue* itself are, of necessity, arbitrary. May we continue to be inundated with ever-new challenges to received notions of female sexuality, in the form of groundbreaking research as well as songs, movies, Netflix series, social movements, hashtags, and more.

Some readers may wonder about the choices I have made or where my research and this journey have led me. Writing about female infidelity and female sexual autonomy enriched my thinking and my marriage in ways I couldn't have imagined. My husband and I discussed issues—how we felt about sexual exclusivity and "forever," for starters—that we hadn't before. Learning the legacy of female African American "hidden figures" of sex research like Gail E. Wyatt and June Dobbs Butts; delving into topics like hotwifing and polyamory; researching and observing female bonobo sexuality; going to sex parties; interviewing women who had affairs or consensually non-monogamous arrangements; immersing myself in the social science, science, and popular literature on female extra-dyadic behaviors; and interviewing experts in fields as various as primatology, doula care, and social activism were all adventures that not only reshaped my ideas about women, sex, and relationships but also shook up my comfortable assumptions about my own practices, beliefs, and life.

The decision a woman makes to be monogamous or not has everything to do with her own environment, ecology, and sexual self—that amalgam of desires, risk tolerance, the decisions and agreements she may have made with her partner, kin support, social support, culture, access to resources, in a word, *context*. For that reason, my own path is not relevant to other women's situations, and I haven't shared it on the chance that my choices might somehow be misconstrued as a recommendation or imply some "best choice." There is none, because there is no one context. What we think of as female "promiscuity" is a reproductive and social strategy with a long tail, one that I among others believe was, at certain times and under specific yet far-from-rare conditions, an efficacious, adaptive, and smart choice for non-human female primates, early hominin females, and women. For some women, it still is. For others, stepping outside monogamy may be lethal. As feminist thinkers and primatologists including Sarah Hrdy, Barbara Smuts, and Meredith Small have suggested, we still don't know what kind of breeding systems and social-sexual practices women might choose if they are actually free to do so. But what we learn from our closest primate relatives and the hunter-gatherers and nomadic pastoralistis who impart lessons about our own legacy and Skirt Club partiers and participants in the polyamory movement like Mischa Lin and Carrie Jenkins, for example, is that we certainly cannot presume it would continue to be heterosexual sexual exclusivity.

Like the stories of Annika and Sarah in chapter three, the story of Virginia, a ninety-three-year-old woman I interviewed at her assisted living facility in the American Southwest in 2017, illustrates just how important context, culture, and constraint have been in our experience of our sexuality and specifically our sexual autonomy, and in the choices we make.

Virginia was married once, for more than six decades, and had six children. This alone made me think she would be a marvelous interview subject. But of course there was more: her life had spanned the Great Depression, World War II, the moon landing, the sexual revolution, the election of our nation's first black president, the campaign of a female candidate for president, the backlash against her, and the tech revolution. Virginia had seen a lot. Raised Catholic, she was taught that kissing was wrong, that birth control other than the rhythm method was a sin, and that premarital sex was a mortal sin. Her parents, she told me, were strict, particularly her mother. When Virginia sat down for a two-hour-long interview at Indiana University Bloomington in 1944, she was a sheltered freshman who wanted to improve her grade in her psychology course. Her professor had intimated to the class, she recalled, that participation in a study by someone named Dr. Kinsey would be looked upon favorably.

Virginia and her family told me they believed she had likely been interviewed not by Kinsey himself but by one of his colleagues— perhaps Clyde Martin or Wardell Pomeroy? Virginia wasn't sure. The questions started off reasonably enough, she thought: things like how often she smoked, danced, and played cards. Then came a question about whether she had ever played strip poker (she certainly hadn't!), and things just got stranger after that. She was asked, among other things, "How old were you when / When was the first time you ever had sex with an animal?" and "How old were you when / When was the first time you had sex with a dead body?" (Kinsey researchers framed their questions this way in order to make it more likely that interviewees would feel comfortable disclosing stigmatized practices.)

Virginia, who had learned about the birds and bees from her girlfriends in high school, told me she nearly fainted. "I said— I didn't use the word s-e-x, that wasn't polite—so I said 'affair.' I asked him, 'Do people really have *affairs* with a dead body?!'" At this point in our interview, Virginia's two daughters in attendance and I burst into gales of laughter. So did Virginia.

"Mom," one of them managed to get out, "when we were young you and Dad told us you never even kissed before you got married. You said you *shook hands*!" We laughed even harder.

Virginia told me that she had felt very important, like a celebrity, after the interview with the Kinsey researcher. The other girls in her dorm wanted to know all about the questions. The few who had also been interviewed wanted to compare. "Did you get the animal question? Oh, I nearly *died*!" said one. "Oh, I *did* die!" another exclaimed.

The next time she went home to see her parents, Virginia, no doubt fascinated and thrilled by her experience, told her mother all about it. Her mother, whom Virginia described as "just horrified," called the school. According to an archived note about her call to the university, Virginia's mother did not so much object to the questions as she did to the way they were framed, along the lines of: "Lots of young women your age are sexually active. When did you first…"

"And I didn't go to that school again!" Virginia told us as we sat together, eating fruit salad in her living room. She reenrolled, at her parents' wishes, in a nearby Catholic college and lived at home until graduation. We laughed again.

Our laughter underscored our surprise at how unrecognizable the world was only half a century ago. Virginia still believed, when I interviewed her, that premarital sex was a bad idea. Her daughters in the room didn't agree; neither did Virginia's grandchildren, presumably. *My, how things have changed,* our laughter said.

And yet. Had they really? We have a sense that we simply get more liberated in a straight march forward through time. And we are wrong. Virginia's mother had been a vaudeville performer, it turns out, and had played in an all-girl band. But as a mother, Virginia explained, she had become a stickler for table manners and later the guardian of her daughter's virtue. "My mom had a much more interesting life than I did! But there was no trace of vaudeville left in her by the time I came around," Virginia told me with a chuckle. Maybe not that Virginia, or anyone else for that matter, could see. But "the vaudeville" was in there, like it is in all of us— the parts that biology and evolution built, the wants and the wildness that have been tamed, constrained, and repackaged, if you will, as Virginia's mother had been.

When Virginia was young, living in a World War II landscape without young men around, she and her girlfriends played "ridiculous games."

"We'd get a Pepsi after school—it was a nickel. And then we'd just [joke] around. We'd say things like 'You've had my husband, and I'll never speak to you again!'" They played out the dramas they saw and heard, the stories around them. The naïve, observant Catholic girls were observant in other ways too.

That was a long time ago. It was also just yesterday, and tomorrow. We have never been wholly innocent. It seems reasonable to hope that, one day, we will not automatically and unthinkingly judge ourselves guilty, or will at least develop the capacity to absolve ourselves of sin.

AUTHOR'S NOTE

To bring statistics and research findings to life, I interviewed thirty women and two men about their experiences of female infidelity. Stay-at-home parent, student, artist, business owner, receptionist, teacher, and retiree are just some of the ways they might describe themselves. Five of the interview participants were African American; four were Latina; and the remainder were white. They ranged in age from twenty to ninety-three, and lived in nine states. This was not intended to be a representative sample, obviously; the point was to hear people tell stories about female infidelity in their own words to complement the studies, surveys, and other data from which I draw in *Untrue*.

The semi-structured interviews were designed to encourage interviewees to feel comfortable discussing their motivations and subjective experiences, and were conducted in person or over the phone. They generally lasted between just under an hour and two hours.

In presenting their stories, I have changed many specifics regarding the individuals portrayed, including all their names (whether or not I call this out in the text) and other potentially identifying details. What I have not changed is the way in which their stories reveal their authentic experience. My personal experiences are recounted as I recall them.

ACKNOWLEDGMENTS

It was a privilege to speak to the thirty women (and two men) who shared their stories and secrets with me. I am honored by their trust, grateful for their honesty, and hope to have done justice to them and their experiences in these pages.

In addition to the experts who appear in *Untrue*, others enriched my understanding of the topic either by patiently speaking or emailing with me, by writing works that inform and inspire, or simply by their example: Suzanne Iasenza, Katie Hinde, Sofia Jawed-Wessel, Sari Cooper, Helen Fisher, Lori Brotto, Jon Marks, Stephen Glickman, Henry Kyemba, Robert Martin, Emily Nagoski, Jeff Nunokawa, Ian Kerner, Mal Harrison, Latham Thomas, and Cynthia Sowers. Special thanks to Dr. Michelle Bezanson and her field assistant, Allison McNamara, for generously inviting me to their field site in Costa Rica, and to Allison for her invaluable assistance with the primatological literature. Victor P. Corona and Bethany Saltman did excellent research and more—they offered insight. Victor suggested the chapter title "Significant Otherness" and the subtitle "Cuckoo for Cuckolds." Thanks to my assistants, Florence Katusiime, Melissa Tan, and Jerrod MacFarlane, and my intern, Hannah Park.

I am indebted to my editor, Tracy Behar, for her magical touch, humor, and unflagging enthusiasm and support, and to everyone at Little, Brown—from publisher Reagan Arthur to the art department to editorial assistant Ian Straus—who helped shepherd *Untrue* into being. My deep gratitude to my literary agent, Richard Pine, who with characteristically remarkable generosity read, aided, and advised from the book's inception to its last word. Thanks also to Eliza Rothstein for her assistance.

My mother, the first feminist I ever met, taught me to love biology and anthropology, and was factual about sex when I was young and full of questions. Beyoncé was the book's soundtrack as I wrote, and Mary Gaitskill and Roxane Gay gave the gift of their language.

Thank you to my good girlfriends for encouraging me. Your enthusiasm for this project buoyed me every day, and I love you. Thank you to my children, Eliot and Lyle, who said, "Oh no, Mom, now you're writing about *sex*?!" and then endured. Thanks to my stepdaughters, Lexi and Katharine, for their friendship, and to my goddaughters, Sylvie and Willa, for being themselves and the future of feminism.

My final and most heartfelt thanks are for my husband, Joel Moser, with whom married life and married love are the world's greatest adventures. This book is for him.

NOTES

EPIGRAPH

vii **We do not even in the least know:** C. R. Darwin, "On the Two Forms, or Dimorphic Condition, in the Species of *Primula*, and on Their Remarkable Sexual Relations," *Journal of the Proceedings of the Linnean Society of London (Botany)* 6 (1862): 94–95.

vii **Our worldviews:** K. DeRose, "UCLA Biologists Reveal Potential 'Fatal Flaw' in Iconic Sexual Selection Study," Science + Technology, UCLA Newsroom, June 25, 2012, http://newsroom.ucla.edu/releases/ucla-biologists-reveal-potential-235586.

vii **Every sensible woman:** S. Martin, vocalist, "Strange Lovin' Blues," by S. Martin, Okeh Records, General Phonograph Corp., 1925, 45 rpm.

INTRODUCTION: MEET THE ADULTERESS

4 **Many psychologists, anthropologists, and scientists:** B. Chapais, *Primeval Kinship: How Pair-Bonding Gave Birth to Human Society* (Cambridge, MA: Harvard University Press, 2008); R. D. Alexander, *Darwinism and Human Affairs* (Seattle: University of Washington Press, 1979), 159; R. B. Lee and I. DeVore, eds., *Man the Hunter* (Chicago: Aldine De Gruyter, 1968); R. J. Quinlan, "Human Pair-Bonds: Evolutionary Functions, Ecological Variation, and Adaptive Development," *Evolutionary Anthropology* 17, no. 5 (2008): 227–38; and W. Tucker, *Marriage and Civilization: How Monogamy Made Us Human* (Washington, DC: Regnery, 2014).

4 **males who benefit from having more than one partner:** S. B. Hrdy, "The Optimal Number of Fathers: Evolution, Demography, and History in the Shaping of Female Mate Preferences," *Annals of the New York Academy of Sciences* 907, no. 1 (2000): 75–96; M. Daly and M. Wilson, "The Reluctant Female and The Ardent Male," in *Sex, Evolution, and Behavior* (North Scituate, MA: Duxbury Press, 1978); D. Symons, *The Evolution of Human Sexuality* (New York: Oxford University Press, 1979), ix, cited in *The Woman That Never Evolved*, by S. B. Hrdy (Cambridge, MA: Harvard University Press, 1999): xx; and M. Mills, "Why Men Behave Badly: Causality vs. Morality," *Psychology Today*, June 22, 2011,

https://www.psychologytoday.com/us/blog/the-how-and-why-sex-differences/201106/
why-men-behave-badly-causality-vs-morality.

4 **received death threats:** S. Hite, "Why I Became a German," *New Statesman*, November 17, 2003, https://www.newstatesman.com/node/194881.

4 **suggesting that 70 percent of us do:** S. Hite, *The Hite Report: Women and Love—A Cultural Revolution in Progress* (New York: Knopf, 1987), 410.

4 **as low as 13 percent to as high as 50 percent:** D. C. Atkins, D. H. Baucom, and N. S. Jacobson, "Understanding Infidelity: Correlates in a National Random Sample," *Journal of Family Psychology* 15, no. 4 (2001): 735–49; General Social Survey (1993), cited in "Adultery Survey," *New York Times*, http://www.nytimes.com/1993/10/19/us/adultery-survey-finds-i-domeans-i-do.html; A. M. Walker, *The Secret Life of the Cheating Wife: Power, Pragmatism, and Pleasure in Women's Infidelity* (Unpublished manuscript, 2017), PDF p. 22; "Adultery Survey Finds 'I Do' Means 'I Do,'" *New York Times*, http://www.nytimes.com/1993/10/19/us/adultery-survey-finds-i-do-means-i-do.html; M. W. Wiederman, "Extramarital Sex: Prevalence and Correlates in a National Survey," *Journal of Sex Research* 34, no. 2 (1997): 167–74; P. Drexler, "The New Face of Infidelity," *Wall Street Journal*, October 19, 2012, https://www.wsj.com/articles/SB10000872396390443684104578062754288906608; A. Vangelist and M. Gerstenberger, "Communication and Marital Infidelity," in J. Duncombe, K. Harrison, G. Allan, and D. Marsden, eds., *The State of Affairs: Explorations of Infidelity and Commitment* (New York: Routledge, 2014): 59–78; and W. Wang, "Who Cheats More? The Demographics of Infidelity in America," *IFS Blog*, Institute for Family Studies, January 10, 2018, https://ifstudies.org/blog/who-cheats-more-the-demographics-of-cheating-in-america.

4 **closing the infidelity gap:** E. Perel, *The State of Affairs: Rethinking Infidelity* (New York: Harper-Collins, 2017), 18–19 (author worked from unpublished manuscript, and checked against published book); and Z. Schonfeld, "Wives Are Cheating 40% More Than They Used To, but Still 70% as Much as Men," *The Atlantic*, July 2, 2013, https://www.theatlantic.com/national/archive/2013/07/wives-cheating-vs-men/313704/.

6 **As the sociologist Alicia Walker has suggested:** Alicia Walker, interview with the author, September 25, 2017.

8 **as experts who work with them have pointed out:** Michael Moran, interview with the author, May 25, 2017; Mark Kaupp, interview with the author, June 23, 2017; C. C. Hoff, S. C. Beougher, D. Chakravarty, L. A. Darbes, and T. B. Neilands, "Relationship Characteristics and Motivations Behind Agreements Among Gay Male Couples: Difference by Agreement Type and Couple Serostatus," *AIDS Care* 22, no. 7 (2010): 827–35; and S. Mcnaughton, "Sleeping with Other People: How Gay Men Are Making Open Relationships Work," *The Guardian*, July 22, 2016, https://www.theguardian.com/lifeandstyle/2016/jul/22/gay-dating-open-relationships-work-study.

8 **woman in her late thirties:** Anonymous, interview with the author, 2017.

9 **bipedal, semicontinuously sexually receptive:** S. B. Hrdy, *Mother Nature: Maternal Instincts and the Shaping of the Species* (New York: Ballantine, 2000), xi.

9 **Under particular, not uncommon ecological circumstances:** Sarah Hrdy, interview with the author, October 25, 2016; and E. M. Johnson, "Promiscuity Is Pragmatic," *Slate*, December 4, 2013.

13 **Pure's tagline is:** Pure website, www.pure.dating.

13 **Sex tech expert Bryony Cole:** Bryony Cole, interview with the author, May 5, 2017.

13 **"My whole life changed…hookups":** Anonymous, interview with the author, 2017.

13 **in large part driven and led by women:** Mischa Lin, interview with the author, May 17, 2017; David Ley, interview with the author, June 27, 2017; and Christopher Ryan and Cacilda Jethá, interview with the author, October 17, 2017.

13 **A woman with access to resources:** "Tilda Swinton on Rumors of Her Love Life," interview with Katie Couric, YouTube, published June 16, 2010; and K. Roiphe, "Liberated in Love: Can Open Marriage Work?" *Harper's Bazaar* online, July 13, 2009.

CHAPTER ONE: FREE YOUR MIND

17 **Freud's *Civilization and Its Discontents:*** S. Freud, *Civilization and Its Discontents* (London: Hogarth Press and Institute of Psycho-analysis, 1949).

20 **"the Tenderloin":** L. Elsroad, "Tenderloin," in T. K. Jackson, ed., *The Encyclopedia of New York City* (New Haven, CT: Yale University Press, 1995), 1161.

20 **a row of brothels**: E. Burrow and M. Wallace, *Gotham: A History of New York City to 1898* (London: Oxford University Press, 2000), 1148–49.

20 **"Satan's Circus" and "modern Gomorrah":** Elsroad, "Tenderloin," 1161.

21 **"Is an Open Marriage a Happier Marriage?":** S. Dominus, "Is an Open Marriage a Happier Marriage?," *New York Times Magazine,* May 11, 2017, www.nytimes.com/2017/05/11/magazine/is-an-open-marriage-a-happier-marriage.html.

22 **"dispatch a surveillance team...partner":** *Cheaters* website, http://www.cheaters.com.

22 ***Opening Up:*** T. Taormino, *Opening Up: A Guide to Creating and Sustaining Open Relationships* (New York: Cleis Press, 2008).

22 ***The Ethical Slut:*** D. Easton and C. A. Liszt, *The Ethical Slut: A Guide to Infinite Sexual Possibilities* (San Francisco: Greenery Press, 1997).

22 ***The New Monogamy:*** T. Nelson, *The New Monogamy: Redefining Your Relationship After Infidelity* (Oakland, CA: New Harbinger, 2013).

22 **"You can't look at porn...":** Tammy Nelson, interview with the author, July 5, 2017.

22 ***Mating in Captivity* and *The State of Affairs:*** E. Perel, *Mating in Captivity* (New York: HarperCollins, 2006); and E. Perel, *The State of Affairs: Rethinking Infidelity* (New York: HarperCollins, 2017).

23 **"segmented model":** M. Scheinkman, "Beyond the Trauma of Betrayal: Reconsidering Affairs in Couples Therapy," *Family Process* 44, no. 2 (2005): 232.

23 **"dogmatic no secrets policy":** Scheinkman, "Beyond the Trauma of Betrayal," 230.

23 **coined the term "monogamish":** D. Savage, "Monogamish," *Savage Love* (blog), The Stranger, July 20, 2011, https://www.thestranger.com/seattle/SavageLove?oid=9125045; and D. Savage, "Meet the Monogamish," *Savage Love* (blog), The Stranger, January 4, 2012, https://www.thestranger.com/seattle/SavageLove?oid=11412386.

23 **roughly 95 percent of respondents:** J. Treas and D. Giesen, "Sexual Infidelity Among Married and Cohabiting Americans," *Journal of Marriage and Family* 62, no. 1 (2000): 48–60, cited in A. M. Walker, *The Secret Life of the Cheating Wife: Power, Pragmatism, and Pleasure in Women's Infidelity* (Unpublished manuscript, 2017), PDF p. 17.

23 **Australian researchers presented:** "Who's Cheating? Agreements About Sexual Exclusivity and Subsequent Concurrent Partnering in Australian Heterosexual Couples," *Sexual Health* 11 (2014): 524–531.

23 **Sociologist Alicia Walker:** Walker, *The Secret Life,* 17 (page references throughout are to an earlier version of the manuscript and have been checked against the published work).

25 ***Hold Me Tight:*** S. Johnson, *Hold Me Tight: Seven Conversations for a Lifetime of Love* (New York: Little, Brown, 2008).

31 **Sometimes those who practice it:** R. Morin, "Up for Polyamory? Creating Alternatives to Marriage," *The Atlantic,* February 19, 2014, https://www.theatlantic.com/health/archive/2014/02/up-for-polyamory-creating-alternatives-to-marriage/283920/.

31 **Although there is no hard data:** David Ley, interview with the author, June 27, 2017; Mischa Lin, interview with the author, May 17, 2017; and Christopher Ryan and Cacilda Jethá, interview with the author, October 17, 2017.

31 **poly peeps, as I came to think of them:** C. Bodenner, "When Polyamory Isn't Really About Sex," *The Atlantic,* January 19, 2016, https://www.theatlantic.com/notes/2016/01/when-polyamory-isnt-really-about-sex/424653/; C. Camacho, "Polyamory Is About Way More Than Just Having Sex with Multiple People," MSN Lifestyle, August 22, 2017, https://www.msn.com/en-us/lifestyle/family-relationships/polyamory-is-about-way-more-than-just-having-sex-with-multiple-people/ar-AAqyBbx; and C. Jenkins,

"Dear Media: Stop Acting Like Polyamory Is All About the Sex," The Establishment, July 27, 2016, https://theestablishment.co/dear-media-polyamory-is-not-all-about-sex-6216830b9d39.

32 **As polyamory activist and educator Mischa Lin:** Mischa Lin, interview with the author, May 17, 2017.

34 **"generally report high levels...do monogamists":** A. N. Rubel and A. F. Bogaert, "Consensual Nonmonogamy: Psychological Well-Being and Relationship Quality Correlates," *Journal of Sex Research* 52, no. 9 (2015): 961–82.

34 **The psychiatrist, sex therapist, and author:** S. Snyder, *Love Worth Making* (New York: St. Martin's Press, 2018); and Stephen Snyder, email correspondence with the author, August 20, 2017.

35 **"the non-negotiable admission price to liberation":** H. Schwyzer, "How Marital Infidelity Became America's Last Sexual Taboo," *The Atlantic*, May 29, 2013, https://www.theatlantic.com/sexes/archive/2013/05/how-marital-infidelity-became-americas-last-sexual-taboo/276341/.

35 **more than 20 percent of single US adults:** M. L. Haupert, A. N. Gesselman, A. C. Moors, H. E. Fisher, and J. R. Garcia, "Prevalence of Experiences with Consensual Non-monogamous Relationships: Findings from Two National Samples of Single Americans," *Journal of Sex and Marital Therapy* 43, no. 5 (2017): 424–40.

36 **According to researcher and historian of CNM:** E. Sheff, "Three Waves of Non-Monogamy: A Select History of Polyamory in the United States," Sheff Consulting, September 9, 2012, https://elisabethsheff.com/2012/09/09/three-waves-of-polyamory-a-select-history-of-non-monogamy/; and L. A. Hutchins, "Erotic Rites: A Cultural Analysis of Contemporary United States Sacred Sexuality Traditions and Trends" (PhD dissertation, Cultural Studies, Union Institute and University, 2001).

36 **there were only three thousand:** Bureau of Labor Statistics, "Occupational Employment and Wages, May 2016, 21-1013 Marriage and Family Therapists," US Department of Labor, last modified March 31, 2017, https://www.bls.gov/oes/current/oes211013.htm.

36 **the term "consensual non-monogamy":** C. Bergstrand and J. B. Williams, "Today's Alternative Marriage Styles: The Case of Swingers," *Electronic Journal of Human Sexuality* 3, no. 10 (2000). Mention of "consensual sexual non-monogamy" is in the "Discussion" section, paragraph 5.

37 **writers and experts are giving us provocative pieces:** D. Baer, "Maybe Monogamy Isn't the Only Way to Love," The Cut, *New York*, March 6, 2017, http://nymag.com/scienceofus/2017/03/science-of-polyamory-open-relationships-and-nonmonogamy.html; I. Kerner, "Rethinking Monogamy Today," CNN.com, April 12, 2017, http://www.cnn.com/2017/04/12/health/monogamy-sex-kerner/index.html; B. J. King, "A Cultural Moment for Polyamory," National Public Radio, March 23, 2017, http://www.npr.org/sections/13.7/2017/03/23/521199308/a-cultural-moment-for-polyamory; N. Little, "Black Folks Do: A Real Look at Consensual Non-Monogamy in the Black Community," *Griots Republic*, June 6, 2017, http://www.griotsrepublic.com/black-folks-do/; Z. Vrangalova, "Is Consensual Non-Monogamy Right for You?," Dr. Zhana, March 10, 2017, http://drzhana.com/2017/03/10/is-consensual-non-monogamy-right-for-you/; and V. Safronova, "Dating Experts Explain Polyamory and Open Relationships," *New York Times*, October 26, 2016, https://www.nytimes.com/2016/10/25/fashion/dating-experts-explain-polyamory-and-open-relationships.html.

37 **Sex researcher and Kinsey Institute fellow:** A. C. Moors, "Has the American Public's Interest in Information Related to Relationships Beyond 'The Couple' Increased Over Time?," *Journal of Sex Research* 54, no. 6 (2017): 677–84.

37 **said infidelity is "always wrong":** General Social Survey stats cited in A. J. Cherlin, "Americans Prefer Serial Monogamy to Open Relationships," *New York Times*, May 21, 2013, https://www.nytimes.com/roomfordebate/2012/01/20/the-gingrich-question-cheating-vs-open-marriage/americans-prefer-serial-monogamy-to-open-relationships?mcubz=3.

37 **And 91 percent of over 1,500 adults:** Schwyzer, "America's Last Sexual Taboo," https://www.theatlantic.com/sexes/archive/2013/05/how-marital-infidelity-became-americas-last-sexual-taboo/276341/; and Gallup poll, 2013, https://news.gallup.com/poll/162689/record-high-say-gay-lesbian-relations-morally.aspx.

38 **between 20 and 37.5 percent of us:** Walker, *The Secret Life,* 22; D. C. Atkins, D. H. Baucom, and N. S. Jacobson, "Understanding Infidelity: Correlates in a National Random Sample," *Journal of Family Psychology* 15, no. 4 (2001): 735–49; M. W. Wiederman, "Extramarital Sex: Prevalence and Correlates in a National Survey," *Journal of Sex Research* 34, no. 2 (1997): 167–74; and S. Luo, M. Cartun, A. Snider, "Assessing Extradyadic Behavior: A Review, a New Measure, and Two New Models," *Personality and Individual Differences* 49/3 (2010): 155–63.

38 **suggests that up to 60 percent of men:** Walker, *The Secret Life,* 22; A. L. Vangelisti and M. Gerstenberger, "Communication and Marital Infidelity," in J. Duncombe, *The State of Affairs,* 59–78, cited in Walker, *The Secret Life,* 22, 285.

38 **One survey found:** Herbenick et al., "Sexual Diversity in the US," e0181198.

38 **while our cultural norm is monogamy:** M. Brandon, "The Challenge of Monogamy: Bringing It Out of the Closet and into the Treatment Room," *Sexual and Relationship Therapy* 26, no. 3 (2011): 271–77, cited in Walker, *The Secret Life,* 22.

38 **One study characterizes infidelity:** J. S. Hirsch, H. Wardlow, D. J. Smith, H. M. Phinney, S. Parikh, and C. A. Nathanson, *The Secret: Love, Marriage, and HIV* (Nashville: Vanderbilt University Press, 2009): 22, cited in Walker, *The Secret Life,* 3.

38 **"Cheating is as common as fidelity…monogamy":** E. Anderson, "Five Myths About Cheating," *Washington Post,* February 13, 2012, https://www.washingtonpost.com/opinions/five-myths-about-cheating/2012/02/08/gIQANGdaBR_story.html?utm_term=.ed749d677958.

39 **"People wonder…a *lot*":** Tammy Nelson, interview with the author, July 5, 2017.

39 **numerous studies tell us:** The Austin Institute for the Study of Family and Culture, "Relationships in America," survey, 2014, p. 43, http://relationshipsinamerica.com/; L. Betzig, "Causes of Conjugal Dissolution: A Cross-Cultural Study," *Current Anthropology* 30, no. 5 (1989): 654–76; and R. E. Emery, ed., *Cultural Sociology of Divorce: An Encyclopedia* (Thousand Oaks, CA: SAGE Publications, 2013), 36.

39 **Not a few anthropologists:** S. B. Hrdy, "Empathy, Polyandry, and the Myth of the Coy Female," in E. Sober, ed., *Conceptual Issues in Evolutionary Biology* (Cambridge, MA: MIT Press, 1994), 131–59; M. F. Small, *Female Choices* (Ithaca, NY: Cornell University Press, 1993), 193–95; and B. A. Scelza, "Choosy but Not Chaste: Multiple Mating in Human Females," *Evolutionary Anthropology* 22, no. 5 (2013): 269.

39 **one sixteen-year longitudinal study:** M. Kalmijn, "The Ambiguous Link Between Marriage and Health: A Dynamic Reanalysis of Loss and Gain Effects," *Social Forces* 95, no. 4 (2017): 1607–36.

39 **two-fifths of Americans polled:** D. Cohn, J. S. Passel, W. Wang, and G. Livingston, "Barely Half of US Adults Are Married—A Record Low," Social and Demographic Trends, Pew Research Center, December 14, 2011, http://www.pewsocialtrends.org/2011/12/14/barely-half-of-u-s-adults-are-married-a-record-low/.

39 **a mere 51 percent of US adults:** Cohn et al., "Barely Half of US Adults," http://www.pewsocialtrends.org/2011/12/14/barely-half-of-u-s-adults-are-married-a-record-low/. See also Pew Research Center's *The Decline of Marriage and Rise of New Families,* report, November 18, 2010, http://www.pewsocialtrends.org/2010/11/18/the-decline-of-marriage-and-rise-of-new-families/6/.

39 **today we are less tolerant of infidelity:** E. Barkhorn, "Cheating on Your Spouse Is Bad; Divorcing Your Spouse Is Not," *The Atlantic,* May 23, 2013, https://www.theatlantic.com/sexes/archive/2013/05/cheating-on-your-spouse-is-bad-divorcing-your-spouse-is-not/276162/; and GSS Data Explorer, "Is It Wrong to Have Sex with Person Other Than Spouse," https://gssdataexplorer.norc.org/trends/Gender%20&%20Marriage?measure=xmarsex.

40 **we think cheating is worse:** Schwyzer, "America's Last Sexual Taboo," https://

www.theatlantic.com/sexes/archive/2013/05/how-marital-infidelity-became-americas -last-sexual-taboo/276341/.

CHAPTER TWO: WOMEN WHO LOVE SEX TOO MUCH

41 In 2013, some new data emerged: NORC's General Social Survey, http:// www.norc.org/pages/search-all.aspx#k=female%20infidelity%2040%25; and National Data Program for the Social Sciences, *General Social Surveys, 1972–2016: Cumulative Codebook* (NORC, University of Chicago, September 2017), http://gss.norc.org/ documents/codebook/GSS_Codebook.pdf.

41 women were roughly 40 percent more likely: Sources reporting the GSS data include J. Ohikuare, "The Fate of Today's TV Mistresses: Not Death, but Shame," *The Atlantic,* July 17, 2013, https://www.theatlantic.com/sexes/archive/2013/07/the-fate-of-todays-tv-mistresses-not-death-but-shame/277874/; Z. Schonfeld, "Wives Are Cheating 40% More Than They Used to but Still 70% as Much as Men," *The Atlantic,* June 2, 2013, https://www.theatlantic.com/national/archive/2013/07/wives-cheating-vs-men/313704/; F. Bass, "More Wives in the US Are Having Affairs," *Boston Globe,* July 3, 2013, https://www.bostonglobe.com/news/nation/2013/07/02/wives-narrow-infidelity-gap-with-increase-cheating/kkwYp8P2Q3jcXKwR7YAKYP/story.html; and V. Taylor, "Cheating Wives Narrowing the Infidelity Gap: Report," *The Daily News,* July 3, 2013, http://www.nydailynews.com/life-style/wives-narrowing-infidelity-gap-report-article-1.1389687.

41 In 1993, across the Atlantic: P. Druckerman, *Lust in Translation: Infidelity from Tokyo to Tennessee* (New York: Penguin, 2008), 59; and "Telling Tales Explain the Discrepancy in Sexual Partner Reports," *Nature 365* (1993): 437–40.

41 And in four national surveys: D. C. Atkins, D. H. Baucom, and N. S. Jacobson, "Understanding Infidelity: Correlates in a National Random Sample," *Journal of Family Psychology* 15, no. 4 (2001): 735–49, cited in Druckerman, *Lust in Translation,* 54.

41 a 1992 survey: Atkins et al., "Understanding Infidelity," cited in Druckerman, *Lust in Translation,* 54; and W. Wang, "Who Cheats More? The Demographics of Infidelity in America," *IFS Blog,* Institute for Family Studies, January 10, 2018, https://ifstudies.org/blog/who -cheats-more-the-demographics-of-cheating-in-america.

41 a 2017 study shows: D. Herbenick, J. Bowling, T-C. (J.) Fu, B. Dodge, L. Guerra-Reyes, and S. Sanders, "Sexual Diversity in the United States: Results from a Nationally Representative Probability Sample of Adult Women and Men," *PLoS One* 12, no. 7 (2017): e0181198.

42 "closing the infidelity gap": E. Perel, *The State of Affairs: Rethinking Infidelity* (New York: HarperCollins, 2017), 18 (page references are to an earlier version of the manuscript and have been checked against the published book).

42 what science writer Natalie Angier: N. Angier, *Woman: An Intimate Geography.* (Boston: Houghton Mifflin Harcourt, 1999), 389.

43 Rosemary Basson's concept of "responsive desire": R. Basson, "The Female Sexual Response: A Different Model," *Journal of Sex and Marital Therapy* 26, no. 1 (2000): 51–65.

45 the author of *What Do Women Want?*: D. Bergner, *What Do Women Want? Adventures in the Science of Female Desire* (New York: HarperCollins, 2013): 5; and E. Blair, "I'll Have What She's Having," review of *What Do Women Want?,* by D. Bergner, *New York Times,* June 13, 2013, http://www.nytimes.com/2013/06/16/books/review/what-do -women-want-by-daniel-bergner.html.

45 In a 2014 study: S. J. Dawson and M. L. Chivers, "Gender Differences and Similarities in Sexual Desire," *Current Sexual Health Reports* 6, no. 4 (2014): 211–19.

45 "There is this fairly monolithic idea…another woman": Meredith Chivers, interview with the author, April 21, 2017.

46 "That people like to hang their hats on…true": Chivers, interview, April 21, 2017.

46 **"might give women permission...woman":** Chivers, interview, April 21, 2017.

47 **"Why do we think that two people...It's *work*!":** Chivers, interview, April 21, 2017.

48 **In a qualitative study of nineteen women:** K. E. Sims and M. Meana, "Why Did Passion Wane? A Qualitative Study of Married Women's Attributions for Declines in Sexual Desire," *Journal of Sex and Marital Therapy* 36, no. 4 (2010): 360–80.

48 **"We have plenty of data telling us...an impact!":** Marta Meana, interview with the author, April 22, 2017.

49 **a 2017 study:** C. A. Graham, C. H. Mercer, C. Tanton, K. G. Jones, A. M. Johnson, K. Wellings, and K. R. Mitchell, "What Factors Are Associated with Reporting Lacking Interest in Sex and How Do These Vary by Gender? Findings from the Third British National Survey of Sexual Attitudes and Lifestyles," *BMJ Open* 7, no. 9 (2017): e016942.

49 **a headline in *Newsweek*:** L. Borreli, "Moving in with Your Boyfriend Can Kill Your Sex Drive, Study Finds," *Newsweek*, September 14, 2017, http://www.newsweek.com/moving-boyfriend-kill-sex-drive-study-665071.

50 **"But so many women experiencing low desire...":** Meana, interview, April 22, 2017.

50 **homing in on "female erotic self-focus":** M. Meana and E. Fertel, "It's Not You, It's Me: Exploring Erotic Self-Focus" (PowerPoint presentation, Society for Sex Therapy and Research 41st Annual Meeting, Chicago, April 16, 2016).

50 **"It's Not You, It's Me":** Meana and Fertel, "It's Not You, It's Me."

51 **"That doesn't mean she's not turned on...":** Meana, interview, April 22, 2017.

52 **In her SSTAR talk:** M. Meana, "Sexual Desire Issues in Women" (lecture, Society for Sex Therapy and Research 42nd Annual Meeting, Montréal, April 20, 2017).

52 **Alicia Walker—an assistant professor of sociology:** "About," Alicia M. Walker website, https://www.alicia-walker.com/.

52 **and her own study of forty-six female users:** A. M. Walker, *The Secret Life of the Cheating Wife: Power, Pragmatism, and Pleasure in Women's Infidelity* (Unpublished manuscript, 2017), PDF p. 61.

53 **"These women weren't just falling into it...":** Alicia Walker, interview with the author, September 25, 2017.

53 **"My goal is to contribute...world":** P. Bourdieu and L. J. D. Wacquant, *An Invitation to Reflexive Sociology* (Chicago: University of Chicago Press, 1992), 53.

54 **Erica (forty-six and married) said:** Walker, *The Secret Life,* 64–65.

54 **Regina, thirty-eight:** Walker, *The Secret Life,* 65.

54 **"[A] lack of sex":** Walker, *The Secret Life,* 64.

54 **"I finally decided":** Walker, *The Secret Life,* 64.

54 **Walker calls "concurrent relationships":** Walker, *The Secret Life,* 64.

54 **Avery, forty-five, explained:** Walker, *The Secret Life,* 82.

54 **Heather, thirty-three...told Walker:** Walker, *The Secret Life,* 93.

54 **thirty-three-year-old Trudy explained:** Walker, *The Secret Life,* 99.

55 **Priscilla, thirty-seven, said:** Walker, *The Secret Life,* 104.

55 **Heather noted:** Walker, *The Secret Life,* 104.

55 **"Oh, they felt no...promised!":** Walker, interview, September 25, 2017.

55 **As Darcy, forty-eight, explained:** Walker, *The Secret Life,* 85.

55 **Jordan, thirty-four, said:** Walker, *The Secret Life,* 97.

55 **many "found they enjoyed the boost in self-esteem...brings":** Walker, *The Secret Life,* 74.

56 **"relationships of sexual utility":** Walker, *The Secret Life,* 242.

56 **"That's very different...marriages":** Walker, interview, September 25, 2017.

56 **"infidelity workaround":** Walker, *The Secret Life,* 44.

56 **"You're a fat cow":** Walker, *The Secret Life,* 80.

57 **"dismantling my life and breaking my husband's heart":** Walker, *The Secret Life,* 87.

57 **"These women were unwilling to toss the dice...into the sunset":** Walker, interview, September 25, 2017.

57 **findings of a pilot study she did in 2014:** A. M. Walker, "'I'm Not a Lesbian; I'm Just a Freak': A Pilot Study of the Experiences of Women in Assumed-Monogamous Other-Sex Unions

Seeking Secret Same-Sex Encounters Online, Their Negotiation of Sexual Desire, and Meaning-Making of Sexual Identity," *Sexuality and Culture* 18, no. 4 (2014): 911–35.

58 **Numerous studies, for example, have found:** D. C. Atkins, D. H. Baucom, and N. S. Jacobson, "Understanding Infidelity: Correlates in a National Random Sample," *Journal of Family Psychology* 15, no. 4 (2001): 735–49; J. Treas and D. Giesen, "Sexual Infidelity Among Married and Cohabiting Americans," *Journal of Marriage and Family* 62, no. 1 (2000): 48–60; Walker, *The Secret Life*, 19; D. Selterman, J. R. Garcia, and I. Tsapelas, "Motivations for Extradyadic Infidelity Revisited," *Journal of Sex Research*, published online ahead of print (December 15, 2017); and S. Glass and T. Wright, "Sex Differences in Type of Extramarital Involvement and Marital Dissatisfaction," *Sex Roles* 12 (1985): 1101–1120, cited in H. Fisher, *The Anatomy of Love* (New York: Norton, 2016).

58 **when women are guaranteed a pleasurable experience:** T. D. Conley, "Perceived Proposer Personality Characteristics and Gender Differences in Acceptance of Casual Sex Offers," *Journal of Personality and Social Psychology* 100, no. 2 (2011): 309–29.

58 **women choose potential mates:** P. W. Eastwick and E. J. Finkel, "Sex Differences in Mate Preference Revisited: Do People Know What They Initially Desire in a Romantic Partner," *Journal of Personality and Social Psychology* 94, no. 2 (2008): 245–64.

58 **Studies in 1997 and 2018 found:** M. W. Wiederman, "Extramarital Sex: Prevalence and Correlates in a National Survey," *Journal of Sex Research* 34, no. 2 (1997): 167–74; and Wang, "Who Cheats More?," https://ifstudies.org/blog/who-cheats-more-the-demographics -of-cheating-in-america.

58 **Men create profiles; women follow through:** L. Wolfe, "The Oral Sex Void: When There's Not Enough at Home," *Electronic Journal of Human Sexuality* 14 (2011): 1–14.

CHAPTER THREE: HOW FREE ARE WE?

61 **Sarah seemed wistful as we sat at a diner:** Sarah, interview with the author, 2016.

64 **assertive anthems of female sexual autonomy:** S. Shange, "A King Named Nicki: Strategic Queerness and the Black Femmecee," *Women and Performance: A Journal of Feminist History* 24, no. 1 (2014): 29–45.

64 *Cosmo* **articles:** L. Moore, "8 Ways to Get What You Want in Bed," *Cosmopolitan*, October 23, 2014, http://www.cosmopolitan.com/sex-love/a32424/ways-to-get-what-you-want-in-bed/.

64 **episodes of** *Veep:* H. Havrilesky, "Thank God for Selina Meyer's Unapologetic 50-Something Sex Drive," The Cut, *New York,* June 6, 2016, https://www.thecut.com/ 2016/06/thank-god-for-selinas-sex-life-on-veep.html.

64 **the pill was legalized for unmarried women:** K. M. J. Thompson, "A Brief History of Birth Control in the U.S.," Our Bodies Ourselves website, December 14, 2013, https://www.ourbodiesourselves.org/health-info/a-brief-history-of-birth-control/.

64 **a year later, Isadora Wing:** E. Jong, *Fear of Flying* (New York: Holt, Rinehart and Winston, 1973).

64 **PsychologyToday.com, where an article blares:** R. F. Baumeister, "The Reality of the Male Sex Drive," *Psychology Today,* December 8, 2010, https://www.psychologytoday.com/ blog/cultural-animal/201012/the-reality-the-male-sex-drive.

65 **some data contradict this:** M. Gerressu, C. H. Mercer, C. A. Graham, K. Wellings, and A. H. Johnson, "Prevalence of Masturbation and Associated Factors in a British National Probability Survey," *Archives of Sexual Behavior* 37, no. 2 (2008): 226–78; correspondence from Dr. Cynthia Graham with the author, October 13, 2017; H. Leitenberg and K. Henning, "Sexual Fantasy," *Psychological Bulletin* 117, no. 3 (1995): 469–96, cited in N. Wolf, *Promiscuities: The Secret Struggle for Womanhood* (New York: Random House, 1997), 161; and J. Jones and D. Barlow, "Self-Reported Frequency of Sexual Urges, Fantasies, and Masturbatory Fantasies in Heterosexual Males and Females," *Archives of Sexual Behavior* 19, no. 3 (1990): 269–79.

65 women propositioned by handsome male strangers: R. D. Clark and E. Hatfield, "Gender Differences in Receptivity to Sexual Offers," *Journal of Psychology and Human Sexuality* 2, no. 1 (1989): 39–55.

65 as critics of this study have already pointed out: T. Conley, "Perceived Proposer Personality Characteristics and Gender Differences in Acceptance of Casual Sex Offers," *Journal of Personality and Social Psychology* 100, no. 2 (2011): 309–29; T. D. Conley, A. C. Moors, J. L. Matsick, and A. Ziegler, "The Fewer the Merrier?: Assessing Stigma Surrounding Consensually Non-Monogamous Romantic Relationships," *Analyses of Social Issues and Public Policy* 13, no. 1 (2013): 1–30; and A. M. Baranowski and H. Hecht, "Gender Differences and Similiarities in Receptivity to Sexual Invitations: Effects of Location and Risk Perception," *Archives of Sexual Behavior* 44, no. 8 (2015): 2257–65.

65 Some studies suggest that men: D. J. Ley, *Insatiable Wives* (Lanham, MD: Rowman and Littlefield, 2009), 34. In addition, a 2000 review of the Registrar General on Marriages, Divorces, and Adoptions in England and Wales suggests that 29 percent of men presented "adultery" as a cause of the breakdown of a marriage while 21 percent of women did, according to K. Smedley, "Why Men Can Never Forgive a Wife's Affair…Even Though They'd Expect YOU to Forgive Them," *Daily Mail*, December 17, 2009, http://www.dailymail.co.uk/femail/article-1236435/Why-men-forgive-wifes-affair-theyd-expect-YOU-forgive-them.html.

66 Other experts tell us: I. Kerner, "Female Infidelity: It's Different from the Guys," *The Chart* (blog), CNN, April 7, 2011, http://thechart.blogs.cnn.com/2011/04/07/female-infidelity-its-different-from-the-guys/; P. Hall in Smedley, "Why Men Can Never Forgive a Wife's Affair"; and D. Buss et al., "Jealousy: Evidence of Strong Sex Differences Using Both Forced Choice and Continuous Measure Paradigms," *Personality and Individual Differences* 86 (2015): 212–16.

66 In *The Times of Their Lives:* J. Deetz and P. S. Deetz, *The Times of Their Lives* (New York: W. H. Freeman, 2000).

66 In the first codification of the law in 1636: Deetz and Deetz, *Times of Their Lives*, 143.

66 In 1658, it was decreed: Deetz and Deetz, *Times of Their Lives*, 144.

66 when Mary Mendame of Duxbury: Deetz and Deetz, *Times of Their Lives*, 143.

66 This was punishable by: Deetz and Deetz, *Times of Their Lives*, 148.

66 "adultery was viewed as the breaking…constraints": Deetz and Deetz, *Times of Their Lives*, 148.

66 While some historians suggest this belief: K. Thomas, "The Double Standard," *Journal of the History of Ideas* 20, no. 2 (1959): 195–216.

67 "The unfaithfulness of the wife…": R. von Krafft-Ebing, *Psychopathia Sexualis, with Especial Reference to Contrary Sexual Instinct: A Medico-Legal Study*, trans. C. G. Chaddock (New York: G. P. Putnam, 1965), 9, cited in Ley, *Insatiable Wives*, 3.

67 Cacilda Jethá, a psychiatrist: Cacilda Jethá, interview with the author, October 17, 2017.

68 In a 2008 study: S. P. Jenkins, "Marital Splits and Income Changes over the Longer Term" (working paper, no. 2008-07, Institute for Social and Economic Research, University of Essex, Colchester, UK, 2008).

69 a 20 percent drop in income when their marriages end: D. Cunha, "The Divorce Gap," *The Atlantic*, April 28, 2016, https://www.theatlantic.com/business/archive/2016/04/the-divorce-gap/480333/.

69 the poverty rate for women who are separated: Cunha, "Divorce Gap," https://www.theatlantic.com/business/archive/2016/04/the-divorce-gap/480333/.

69 women's incomes tend never to reach: Jenkins, "Marital Splits and Income Changes over the Longer Term," cited in A. Hill, "Men Become Richer After Divorce," *The Guardian*, January 24, 2009, https://www.theguardian.com/lifeandstyle/2009/jan/25/divorce-women-research.

69 One Australian report found that divorced women: L. Brown, *Divorce: For Richer, for Poorer*, AMP.NATSEM Income and Wealth Report, Issue 39 (2016), https://www.amp.com.au/content/dam/amp/digitalhub/common/Documents/Insights/News/December%2013%20-%20AMP.NATSEM39%20-%20For%20Richer%20For%20Poorer%20-%20Report%20-%20FINAL%20(1).pdf; and D. Dumas, "Women with Children

Biggest Financial Losers of Divorce: Report," *Sydney Morning Herald,* December 13, 2016, http://www.smh.com.au/lifestyle/news-and-views/news-features/women-with-children-biggest-financial-losers-of-divorce-report-20161212-gt92op.html.

69 **"It seemed selfish…":** Sarah, interview, 2016.

70 **in an early episode of** *Divorce:* A. Breslaw, *"Divorce* Recap: A Tough Time," Vulture, *New York,* October 16, 2016, http://www.vulture.com/2016/10/divorce-recap-season-1-episode-2.html.

70 **anthropologists call these "life-history trade-offs":** S. C. Stearns, "Trade-Offs in Life-History Evolution," *Functional Ecology* 3 (1989): 259–68.

71 **As Marta Meana had explained:** Marta Meana, interview with the author, April 22, 2017.

72 **In her book** *Lust in Translation:* P. Druckerman, *Lust in Translation: Infidelity from Tokyo to Tennessee* (New York: Penguin, 2008), 71–77.

72 **"Yvonne had an affair…":** Druckerman, *Lust in Translation,* 72–73.

73 **The story of Druckerman's interviewee Elaine:** Druckerman, *Lust in Translation,* 74–78.

74 **We didn't have guilt:** Druckerman, *Lust in Translation,* 71.

74 **I'm talking about:** Druckerman, *Lust in Translation,* 75.

75 **"Having an affair may allow a woman…current one":** B. A. Scelza, "Choosy but Not Chaste: Multiple Mating in Human Females," *Evolutionary Anthropology* 22, no. 5 (2013): 259–69; and E. M. Johnson, "Promiscuity Is Pragmatic," *Slate,* December 4, 2013, http://www.slate.com/articles/health_and_science/science/2013/12/female _promiscuity_in_primates_when_do_women_have_multiple_partners.html.

75 **The bridging, or mate-switching, strategy:** D. M. Buss, C. Goetz, J. D. Duntley, K. Asao, and D. Conroy-Beam, "The Mate Switching Hypothesis," *Personality and Individual Differences* 104 (2017): 143–49.

75 **from the protection of their fathers:** Druckerman, *Lust in Translation,* 75.

76 **Contemporary titles like** *How Can I Forgive You?:* J. A. Spring, *How Can I Forgive You?* (New York: HarperCollins, 2004).

77 **In** *Lust in Translation,* **Druckerman writes about:** Druckerman, *Lust in Translation,* 17–18.

77 **Another woman who is engaged to be married:** Druckerman, *Lust in Translation,* 18.

78 **"I was used to a high level of…":** Annika, interview with the author, 2016.

81 **Carmen Rita Wong's novel:** C. R. Wong, *Never Too Late* (New York: Kensington, 2017).

81 **what Marta Meana calls "erotic self-focus":** M. Meana and E. Fertel, "It's Not You, It's Me: Exploring Erotic Self-Focus" (PowerPoint presentation, Society for Sex Therapy and Research 41st Annual Meeting, Chicago, April 16, 2016).

85 **passages from Daniel Bergner's book:** D. Bergner, *What Do Women Want?* (New York: HarperCollins, 2013), 44–50.

85 **the work the anthropologist Beverly Strassmann:** B. I. Strassmann, "Menstrual Hut Visits by Dogon Women: A Hormonal Test Distinguishes Deceit from Honest Signaling," *Behavioral Ecology* 7, no. 3 (1996): 304–15; and Brooke Scelza, interview with the author, March 22, 2017.

CHAPTER FOUR: PLOUGHS, PROPERTY, PROPRIETY

87 **approximately ten to twelve thousand years ago:** C. S. Larsen, "Our Last 10,000 Years: Agriculture, Population, and the Bioarchaeology of a Fundamental Transition," chap. 13 in *Our Origins: Discovering Physical Anthropology* (New York: W. W. Norton, 2010), retrieved from http://www.wwnorton.com/college/anthro/our-origins2/ch/13/answers.aspx; K. Nair et al., "Origins of Agriculture," *Encyclopædia Britannica,* last modified March 10, 2017, https://www.britannica.com/topic/agriculture; and L. Evans, "Early Agriculture and the Rise of Civilization," in *Science and Its Times: Understanding the Social Significance of Scientific Discovery,* vol. 1, ed. N. Schlager (Farmington Hills, MI: Gale Group, 2001), on Encyclopedia.com, http://www.encyclopedia.com/science/encyclopedias-almanacstranscripts-andmaps/early-agriculture-andrise-civilization.

88 **"As societies learned to produce...fundamental":** Evans, "Early Agriculture," http://www.encyclopedia.com/science/encyclopedias-almanacs-transcripts-and-maps/early-agriculture-and-rise-civilization.

88 **they had less osteoarthritis:** Larsen, "Our Last 10,000 Years."

89 **Archaeological evidence and human remains suggest:** Larsen, "Our Last 10,000 Years."

89 **Jared Diamond, pulling no punches:** J. Diamond, "The Worst Mistake in the History of the Human Race," *Discover*, May 1987, 64–65, http://discovermagazine.com/1987/may/02-the-worst-mistake-in-the-history-of-the-human-race.

89 **Especially for women:** H. Fisher, "Why We Love, Why We Cheat," TED video, 9:00–9:33 (of 23:24), filmed February 2006, https://www.ted.com/talks/helen_fisher_tells _us_why_we_love_cheat/transcript#t-576310.

90 **Farming made women more sedentary and easier to control:** M. Shostak, *Nisa: The Life and Words of a !Kung Woman* (Cambridge, MA: Harvard University Press, 1981), 195.

90 **shortened interbirth intervals:** Shostak, *Nisa*, 195.

90 **There is growing consensus among anthropologists:** S. B. Hrdy, *Mothers and Others: The Evolutionary Origins of Mutual Understanding* (Cambridge, MA: Belknap Press, 2011), passim; S. B. Hrdy, "Evolutionary Context of Human Development: The Cooperative Breeding Model," chap. 2 in C. S. Carter, L. Ahnert, K. E. Grossmann, S. B. Hrdy, M. E. Lamb, S. W. Porges, and N. Sachser, eds., *Attachment and Bonding: A New Synthesis* (Cambridge, MA: MIT Press, 2006), http://citeseerx.ist.psu.edu/viewdoc/download? doi=10.1.1.207.8922&rep=rep1&type=pdf; A. V. Bell, K. Hinde, and L. Newson, "Who Was Helping? The Scope for Female Cooperative Breeding in Early *Homo*," *PLoS One* 8, no. 12 (2013): e83667; K. Hawkes, "The Grandmother Effect," *Nature* 428, March 11, 2004, 128–29, http://radicalanthropologygroup.org/sites/default/files/pdf/class_text_002.pdf; K. Hawkes, "Grandmothers and the Evolution of Human Longevity," *American Journal of Human Biology* 15 (2003): 380–400; and K. L. Kramer, "Cooperative Breeding and Its Significance to the Demographic Success of Humans," *Annual Review of Anthropology* 39 (2010): 417–36.

90 **Enhanced cooperation meant all were more likely:** C. Ryan and C. Jethá, *Sex at Dawn: How We Mate, Why We Stray, and What It Means for Modern Relationships* (New York: HarperCollins, 2012), 94.

90 **our cherished, 1950s-inflected:** C. O. Lovejoy, "The Origin of Man," *Science* 211, no. 4480 (1981): 341–50; R. B. Lee and I. DeVore, eds., *Man the Hunter* (Chicago: Aldine De Gruyter, 1968), passim; and S. B. Hrdy, *Mother Nature: Maternal Instincts and the Shaping of the Species* (New York: Ballantine, 2000), 253.

90 **favored by natural selection and characterized early *Homo* life history:** Bell, Hinde, and Newson, "Who Was Helping?," e83667; Ryan and Jethá, *Sex at Dawn;* Hrdy, *Mother Nature*, 64–65, 90–93, 266–77; and Hrdy, *Mothers and Others*, 30–31, 197–203, 276–80.

91 **As Saint Louis University associate professor:** Katherine MacKinnon, interview with the author, August 2015.

91 **early hominin ancestors:** Hrdy, *Mother Nature*, 248, 252.

91 **Captain Samuel Wallis, who traveled to Tahiti in 1767:** Ryan and Jethá, *Sex at Dawn*, 95.

91 **Two years later, James Cook:** Ryan and Jethá, *Sex at Dawn*, 95.

92 **in 1623, a Recollect friar:** G. Sagard, *The Long Journey to the Country of the Hurons*, ed. G. McKinnon Wrong (Toronto: Champlain Society, 1939).

92 **"There are also assemblies...concluded":** Quoted in J. Steckley, "For Native Americans, Sex Didn't Come with Guilt," *Fair Observer*, March 30, 2015, www.fairob server.com/region/north_america/for-native-americans-sex-didnt-come-with-guilt -21347/; and Sagard, *The Long Journey to the Country of the Hurons*, 120.

93 **"The Huron considered...other friends":** B. G. Trigger, *The Children of Aataentsic: A History of the Huron People to 1660*, vol. 2 (Kingston, Ontario: McGill-Queen's University Press, 1987), 49, cited in C. Tindal, "The Sex-Positive Huron-Wendat," *Acres of Snow* (blog), February 11, 2017, https://acresofsnow.ca/the-sex-positive-huron-wendat/.

94 **"vote with her feet":** Hrdy, *Mother Nature*, 231.

94 **nearly 70 percent:** Hrdy, *Mother Nature,* 252.

95 **"The Division of Work According to Sex in African Hoe Culture":** H. Baumann, "The Division of Work According to Sex in African Hoe Culture," *Africa* 1, no. 3 (1928): 290.

96 **In some parts of Southeast Asia:** R. L. Blumberg, "'Dry' Versus 'Wet' Development and Women in Three World Regions," *Sociology of Development* 1, no. 1 (2015): 91–122.

96 **Rae Blumberg:** Quoted in A. E. Bromley, "Patriarchy and the Plow," *UVA Today,* August 23, 2016, https://news.virginia.edu/content/patriarchy-and-plow.

96 **"[In these places]...system":** Quoted in Bromley, "Patriarchy and the Plow," https://news.virginia.edu/content/patriarchy-and-plow.

97 **sixth millennium BC:** K. Kh. Kushnareva, *The Southern Caucasus in Prehistory: Stages of Cultural and Socioeconomic Development from the Eighth to the Second Millennium BC,* University Museum monograph 99, trans. H. N. Michael (Philadelphia: University Museum, University of Pennsylvania, 1997), 170.

97 **Egyptians and then the Romans and Greeks:** S. Hornblower, A. Spawforth, E. Eidinow, eds., *The Oxford Classical Dictionary,* 4th ed. (Oxford, UK: Oxford University Press, 2012), 708.

98 **Agustín Fuentes tells us that one study:** A. Fuentes, *Race, Monogamy, and Other Lies They Told You: Busting Myths About Human Nature* (Berkeley: University of California Press, 2012), 178; and J. S. Hyde, "The Gender Similarities Hypothesis," *American Psychologist* 6, no. 6 (2005): 581–92.

98 **"natural role of women...":** A. F. Alesina, P. Giuliano, and N. Nunn, "On the Origins of Gender Roles: Women and the Plough," *Quarterly Journal of Economics* 128, no. 2 (2013): 470–71.

98 **Shere Ortner has observed:** Cited in N. Angier, *Woman: An Intimate Geography* (Boston: Houghton Mifflin Harcourt, 1999), 313.

99 **According to Stephanie Coontz:** S. Coontz, *Marriage, a History: From Obedience to Intimacy or How Love Conquered Marriage* (New York: Penguin, 2006), 47.

99 **Separation of the sexes:** Coontz, *Marriage, a History,* 47.

99 *Beware:* Y. Thomas, "Fathers as Citizens of Rome, Rome as a City of Fathers," in A. Burguière, C. Klapisch-Zuber, M. Segalen, and F. Zonabend, eds., *A History of the Family, Vol. I: Distant Worlds, Ancient Worlds,* trans. S. H. Tenison, R. Morris, and A. Wilson (Cambridge, UK: Polity Press, 1996), 265, cited in Coontz, *Marriage, a History,* 46.

100 **Lesley Hazleton has suggested:** L. Hazleton, *Jezebel: The Untold Story of the Bible's Harlot Queen* (New York: Doubleday, 2009).

101 **"Now when Jehu had come...'lies Jezebel'":** "II Kings 9:30–37 NKJV," Bible.com, www.bible.com/bible/114/2KI.9.30-37.

102 **prior world order:** Hazleton, *Jezebel,* 157.

102 **high priestesses:** G. W. Bromiley, ed., *The International Standard Bible Encyclopedia,* vol. 2 (Grand Rapids, MI: William. B. Eerdmans, 1979), 1058.

102 **"seed of an adulteress and a harlot":** Hazleton, *Jezebel,* 66–67.

102 **"infatuated by profligates...stallions":** Hazleton, *Jezebel,* 67.

102 **"Let her rid...":** Hazleton, *Jezebel,* 68–69.

103 **use of the term "jezebel" to mean:** "Jezebel," *Merriam-Webster's Collegiate Dictionary,* 10th ed. (Springfield, MA: Merriam-Webster, 1993), 629.

104 **In ancient Greece:** M. Cartwright, "Food and Agriculture in Ancient Greece," *Ancient History Encyclopedia,* July 25, 2016, https://www.ancient.eu/article/113/food-agriculture-in-ancient-greece/.

104 **According to Aristotle:** S. Forsdyke, "Street Theatre and Popular Justice in Ancient Greece: Shaming, Stoning, and Starving Offenders Inside and Outside the Courts," *Past and Present* 201, no. 1 (2008): 3n2.

104 **Clytemnestra as told by Aeschylus in *The Oresteia*:** L. Mastin, "Ancient Greece—Aeschylus—Agamemnon," Classical Lecture, accessed February 8, 2018, www.ancient-literature.com/greece_aeschylus_agamemnon.html.

105 Ancient Romans: M. C. Nussbaum, "The Incomplete Feminism of Musonius Rufus, Platonist, Stoic, and Roman," in M. C. Nussbaum and J. Sihvola, eds., *The Sleep of Reason: Erotic Experience and Sexual Ethics in Ancient Greece and Rome* (Chicago: University of Chicago Press, 2002), 283–326; and C. Edwards, *The Politics of Immorality in Ancient Rome* (Cambridge, UK: Cambridge University Press, 2002), 34–35.

106 Virgil composed his: Virgil, "The Georgics," Internet Classics Archive, http://classics.mit.edu/Virgil/georgics.html; and Virgil, *The Bucolics, Æneid, and Georgics of Virgil,* ed. J. B. Greenough (Boston: Ginn and Company, 1900), www.perseus.tufts.edu/hopper/text?doc=Perseus%3Atext%3A1999.02.0058.

106 Augustus had his own daughter, Julia: Editors, "Julia," *Encyclopædia Britannica,* May 3, 2013, www.britannica.com/biography/Julia-daughter-of-Augustus.

106 When asked why all her children: M. Lefkowitz and M. Fant, *Women's Life in Greece and Rome* (Baltimore: Johns Hopkins University Press, 2016), 196.

106 "a disease in my flesh": "Julia," *Encyclopædia Britannica,* www.britannica.com/biography/Julia-daughter-of-Augustus.

106 in the words of Natalie Angier: Angier, *Woman,* 316.

107 In a uniquely comprehensive analysis: Alesina, Giuliano, and Nunn, "On the Origins of Gender Roles," 469–530.

109 the Women's Land Army: A. Mason, "What Was the Women's Land Army?," Imperial War Museums website, January 30, 2018, www.iwm.org.uk/history/what-was-the-womens-land-army; and S. R. Grayzel, "Nostalgia, Gender, and the Countryside: Placing the 'Land Girl' in First World War Britain," *Rural History* 10, no. 2 (1999): 155–70.

110 47th of the 181 countries: Alesina, Giuliano, and Nunn, "On the Origins of Gender Roles," 477.

110 The Harvard and UCLA study authors note: Alesina, Giuliano, and Nunn, "On the Origins of Gender Roles," 477.

110 the International Labour Organization tells us: International Labour Organization, "Labor Force Participation Rate, Female," November 2017, retrieved from Index Mundi, https://www.indexmundi.com/facts/indicators/SL.TLF.CACT.FE.ZS/rankings.

111 for political participation: Catalyst, "Women in Government," report, February 15, 2017, http://www.catalyst.org/knowledge/women-government.

111 In another study: A. Lenhardt, L. Wise, G. Rosa, H. Warren, F. Mason, and R. Sarumi, *Every Last Girl: Free to Live, Free to Learn, Free from Harm,* Save the Children, 2016, https://www.savethechildren.org.uk/content/dam/global/reports/advocacy/every last-girl.pdf. See also A. MacSwan, "US Ranks Lower Than Kazakhstan and Algeria on Gender Equality," *The Guardian,* October 11, 2016, https://www.theguardian.com/global-development/2016/oct/11/us-united-states-ranks-lower-than-kazakhstan-algeria-gender-equality-international-day-of-the-girl.

111 Black women are: L. Villarosa, "Why America's Black Mothers and Babies Are in a Life-or-Death Crisis," *New York Times Magazine,* April 11, 2018.

111 Fifty-two or -three percent of white female voters: "Election 2016: Exit Polls," CNN Politics, November 23, 2016, www.cnn.com/election/2016/results/exit-polls (Nate Silver believed the correct figure was 53 percent); and C. Malone, "Clinton Couldn't Win Over White Women," November 9, 2016, https://fivethirtyeight.com/features/clinton-couldnt-win-over-white-women/.

111 "Part of the importance of the plough...beliefs": Alesina, Giuliano, and Nunn, "On the Origins of Gender Roles," 473.

112 our cycle was more of a quarterly event: B. I. Strassmann, "The Biology of Menstruation in *Homo sapiens:* Total Lifetime Menses, Fecundity, and Nonsynchrony in a Natural-Fertility Population," *Current Anthropology* 38, no. 1 (1997): 123–29.

112 In 2012, the World Health Organization: C. Garcia-Moreno, A. Guedes, and W. Knerr, "Understanding and Addressing Violence Against Women: Sexual Violence," World Health Organization, 2012, http://apps.who.int/iris/bitstream/10665/77434/1/WHO_RHR_12.37_eng.pdf.

114 **"they are loose 'down there'":** A. Mulholland, "Increase in 'Vaginal Tightening' Surgeries Worries Doctors," CTVNews, May 20, 2014, https://www.ctvnews.ca/health/increase-in-vaginal-tightening-surgeries-worries-doctors-1.1829041.

114 **The American Congress of Obstetricians and Gynecologists:** American College of Obstetricians and Gynecologists, "Vaginal 'Rejuvenation' and Cosmetic Vaginal Procedures," ACOG Committee Opinion no. 378, *Obstetrics and Gynecology* 110 (2007): 737–38, https://www.acog.org/Clinical-Guidance-and-Publications/Committee-Opinions/Committee-on-Gynecologic-Practice/Vaginal-Rejuvenation-and-Cosmetic-Vaginal-Procedures.

115 **Cheryl Iglesia, MD:** American College of Obstetricians and Gynecologists, "Expanding Cosmetic Gynecology Field Draws Concern," 2017 annual meeting update, May 17, 2017, http://annualmeeting.acog.org/expanding-cosmetic-gynecology-field-draws-concern/.

115 **Dr. Dennis Gross, a cosmetic dermatologist:** D. Gross, correspondence with the author, September 4, 2017, and September 20, 2017.

116 **"Men Want Beauty...":** I. Ting, "Men Want Beauty, Women Want Money: What We Want from the Opposite Sex," *Sydney Morning Herald,* October 1, 2015, http://www.smh.com.au/lifestyle/life/family-relationships-and-sex/men-want-beauty-women-want-money-what-people-want-in-a-sexual-partner-20151001-gjyyot.html.

117 **Rae Blumberg:** Quoted in A. E. Bromley, "Patriarchy and the Plow," *UVA Today,* August 23, 2016, https://news.virginia.edu/content/patriarchy-and-plow.

117 **Mbuti women in the Ituri rainforest and Aka women of the Central African Republic:** IResearchNet.com, "Anthropology Research Topics: 338. Mbuti Pygmies," accessed February 8, 2018, www.iresearchnet.com/topics/anthropology-research-topics.html; and A. J. Noss, and B. S. Hewlett, "The Contexts of Female Hunting in Central Africa," *American Anthropologist,* 103, no. 4 (2001): 1024–40.

CHAPTER FIVE: BEING HIMBA

119 **live the Himba:** B. A. Scelza, "Female Choice and Extra Pair Paternity in a Traditional Human Population," *Biology Letters* 7, no. 6 (2011): 889–91.

119 **Only an estimated 30,000 to 50,000 Himba remain:** M. Bollig and H. Lang, "Demographic Growth and Resource Exploitation in Two Pastoral Communities," *Nomadic Peoples* 3, no. 2 (1999): 17.

120 **Himba women cover their skin:** A. S. Cameron, "The Influence of Media on Himba Conceptions of Dress, Ancestral, and Cattle Worship, and the Implications for Culture Change" (master's thesis, Brigham Young University, 2013), 24.

120 **Himba women wear:** Cameron, "The Influence of Media," 25.

120 **dependent upon one another:** Katie Hinde, interview with the author, January 27, 2017.

120 **In the twenty-three Himba compounds:** Scelza, "Female Choice," 889–91; and B. A. Scelza, "Jealousy in a Small-Scale, Natural Fertility Population: The Roles of Paternity, Investment, and Love in Jealous Response," *Evolution and Human Behavior* 35, no. 2 (2014): 103–8.

121 **"There exists no culture...philandering":** M. Norman, "Getting Serious About Adultery; Who Does It and Why They Risk It," *New York Times,* July 4, 1998, http://www.nytimes.com/1998/07/04/arts/getting-serious-about-adultery-who-does-it-and-why-they-risk-it.html.

121 **Spouses expect:** Scelza, "Jealousy in a Small-Scale," 103–8.

121 **"I don't like it when...away":** Brooke Scelza, interview with the author, March 22, 2017.

121 **As Scelza explained to me:** Brooke Scelza, interview with the author, March 22, 2017.

121 **Himba women actually improve their lot in life:** Scelza, "Female Choice," 889–91.

122 She began her career: Brooke Scelza, interview with the author, October 11, 2016.

122 "a form of parent-offspring conflict...": Scelza, "Female Choice," 889–91.

124 Darwin introduced this idea: C. Darwin, *The Descent of Man, and Selection in Relation to Sex* (New York: D. Appleton and Company, 1896); and A. G. Jones and N. L. Ratterman, "Mate Choice and Sexual Selection: What Have We Learned Since Darwin?," *Proceedings of the National Academy of Sciences* 106, suppl. 1 (2009): 10001–8.

124 Darwin also noted: Darwin, *The Descent of Man;* and Jones and Ratterman, "Mate Choice and Sexual Selection," 10001–8.

124 "The female...with the rarest exception...selfishness": Darwin, *The Descent of Man,* 222, 557, 563.

125 Sarah Hrdy observed: S. B. Hrdy, *The Woman That Never Evolved* (Cambridge, MA: Harvard University Press, 1981), xiii.

125 William Acton, author of the ambitious and influential: W. Acton, *The Functions and Disorders of the Reproductive Organs in Childhood, Youth, Adult Age, and Advanced Life, Considered in the Physiological, Social, and Moral Relations,* first edition, 1857, British Library Archive, https://www.bl.uk/romantics-and-victorians/articles/victorian-sexualities.

125 "the majority of women (happily for them)...": Acton, *Functions and Disorders of the Reproductive Organs,* 112; and Hrdy, *The Woman That Never Evolved,* 165. Also cited by S. B. Hrdy, correspondence with the author, January 19, 2017.

126 Krafft-Ebing's apocalyptic vision: R. von Krafft-Ebing, *Psychopathia Sexualis, with Especial Reference to Contrary Sexual Instinct: A Medico-Legal Study,* trans. C. G. Chaddock (Philadelphia: F. A. Davis: 1894), 13.

126 We call them "socially monogamous": Alexander G. Ophir, Steven M. Phelps, Anna Bess Sorin, and Jerry O. Wolff, "Social but Not Genetic Monogamy Is Associated with Greater Breeding Success in Prairie Voles," 2008, https://pdfs.semanticscholar.org/526d/c2781f6094002810f8eeb0b604e5ad155486.pdf; and M. C. Mainwaring and S. C. Griffith, "Looking After Your Partner: Sentinel Behavior in a Socially Monogamous Bird," *PeerJ* 1, e83 (2013), https://doi.org/10.7717/peerj.83.

126 female Muscovy ducks: "Ballistic Penises and Corkscrew Vaginas—The Sexual Battles of Ducks," *Discover,* December 22, 2009.

127 Lillie Langtry: J. Ridley, *Bertie: A Life of Edward VII* (New York: Penguin Random House, 2013), 200–12.

127 Consider the twenty: C. Groneman, *Nymphomania: A History* (New York: W. W. Norton, 2001), 13–16.

127 In her book *Nymphomania:* Groneman, *Nymphomania,* 14.

128 "The patient was ordered...writing": Groneman, *Nymphomania,* 16.

128 even working outside the home was suspect: J. Beach, "Limits to Women's Rights in the 1930s," Classroom, September 29, 2017, https://classroom.synonym.com/limits-to-womens-rights-in-the-1930s-12082808.html; L. K. Boehm, "Women, Impact of the Great Depression On," in R. S. McElvaine, ed., *Encyclopedia of the Great Depression,* vol. 2 (New York: Macmillan Reference USA, 2004), 1050–55, http://link.galegroup.com/apps/doc/CX3404500550/UHIC?u=vol_h99hs&xid=73687bb3; and L. Hapke, *Daughters of the Great Depression: Women, Work, and Fiction in the American 1930s* (Athens: University of Georgia Press, 1997).

129 Making matters still more difficult: Beach, "Limits to Women's Rights," https://classroom.synonym.com/limits-to-womens-rights-in-the-1930s-12082808.html.

129 Between 1940 and 1944: US Department of Labor, Women's Bureau, *Women Workers in Ten War Production Areas and Their Postwar Employment Plans,* Bulletin 209 (Washington, DC: US Government Printing Office, 1946); and M. Schweitzer, "World War II and Female Labor Force Participation Rates," *Journal of Economic History* 40 (1980): 89–95.

129 Historians, cultural critics who study gender, and sex researchers: B. Kahan, "The Walk-In Closet: Situational Homosexuality and Homosexual Panic," *Criticism* 55, no.

2 (2013): 177–201; J. L. Jackson, "Situational Lesbians and the Daddy Tank: Women Prisoners Negotiating Queer Identity and Space, 1970–1980," *Genders* 53 (2011); and E. Kennedy and M. Davis, *Boots of Leather, Slippers of Gold* (New York: Routledge, 1993).

129 **notes historian Jessica Toops:** J. Toops, "The Lavender Scare: Persecution of Lesbianism During the Cold War," *Western Illinois Historical Review* 5 (2013): 91–107, http://www.wiu.edu/cas/history/wihr/pdfs/Toops-LavenderScareVol5.pdf.

129 **"female sexual fluidity":** L. Diamond and R. C. Savin-Williams, "Explaining Diversity in the Development of Same-Sex Sexuality Among Young Women," *Journal of Social Issues* 56, no. 2 (2000): 297–313; and L. M. Diamond, *Sexual Fluidity* (Cambridge, MA: Harvard University Press, 2008).

130 **an English botanist and geneticist named Angus Bateman:** A. J. Bateman, "Intra-sexual Selection in *Drosophila*," *Heredity* 2 (1948): 349–68.

130 **Bateman assembled:** D. A. Dewsbury, "The Darwin-Bateman Paradigm in Historical Context," *Integrative and Comparative Biology* 45, no. 5 (2005): 831–37.

130 **nearly 96 percent of the females:** Bateman, "Intra-sexual Selection in *Drosophila*," 362.

131 **"fertility is seldom likely to be limited…him":** Bateman, "Intra-sexual Selection in *Drosophila*," 364.

131 **"There is nearly always a combination…rule":** Bateman, "Intra-sexual Selection in *Drosophila*," 365.

132 **"The message to women was clear…citizens":** M. E. Murray, "Whatever Happened to G. I. Jane?: Citizenship, Gender, and Social Policy in Postwar Era," *Michigan Journal of Gender and Law* 9, no. 1 (2002): 123.

132 **"Intra-sexual Competition in *Drosophila*":** Dewsbury, "The Darwin-Bateman Paradigm," 831–37.

132 **Donald Dewsbury notes:** Dewsbury, "The Darwin-Bateman Paradigm," 831–37.

132 **Harvard sociobiologist Robert Trivers popularized Bateman:** R. L. Trivers, "Parental Investment and Sexual Selection," in B. Campbell, ed., *Sexual Selection and the Descent of Man, 1871–1971* (Chicago: Aldine, 1972), 136–79; and R. L. Trivers and D. E. Willard, "Natural Selection of Parental Ability to Vary the Sex Ratio of Offspring," *Science* 179, no. 4068 (1973): 90–92.

133 **his theory of Parental Investment:** Trivers, "Parental Investment and Sexual Selection," passim.

133 **She wanted *quality, not quantity:*** S. B. Hrdy, "Quality vs. Quantity," in *Mother Nature: Maternal Instincts and the Shaping of the Species* (New York: Ballantine, 2000), 8–10.

133 **"the Bateman paradigm":** S. B. Hrdy, "Empathy, Polyandry, and the Myth of the Coy Female," in E. Sober, ed., *Conceptual Issues in Evolutionary Biology* (Cambridge, MA: MIT Press, 1994), 131–59.

134 **a 1977 cover of *Time:*** "Why You Do What You Do: Sociobiology: A New Theory of Behavior," *Time,* August 1, 1977, http://content.time.com/time/magazine/article/0,9171,915181,00.html.

134 **"In primitive times women…will be":** D. J. Trump and B. Zanker, *Think Big and Kick Ass in Business and Life* (New York: HarperLuxe, 2007), 270–71, cited in H. Dunsworth, "How Donald Trump Got Human Evolution Wrong," *Washington Post,* July 14, 2017, https://www.washingtonpost.com/news/speaking-of-science/wp/2017/07/13/human-evolutions-biggest-problems/?utm_term=.3215e2a12035.

135 **The anthropologist Holly Dunsworth:** Dunsworth, "How Donald Trump Got Human Evolution Wrong," https://www.washingtonpost.com/news/speaking-of-science/wp/2017/07/13/human-evolutions-biggest-problems/?utm_term=.3215e2a12035.

135 **whom Trump suggested he might "lock up":** "Lock Her Up Is Right," *Washington Post* video, Donald Trump campaign speech, October 10, 2016, https://www.washingtonpost.com/video/politics/trump-on-clinton-lock-her-up-is-right/2016/10/10/fd56d59e-8f51-11e6-bc00-1a9756d4111b_video.html?utm_term=.44a85887919e.

135 **"blood coming out of her wherever":** P. Rucker, "Trump Says Fox's Megan Kelly

Had 'Blood Coming Out of Her Wherever,'" *Washington Post*, August 8, 2015, https://www.washingtonpost.com/news/post-politics/wp/2015/08/07/trump-says-foxs-megyn-kelly-had-blood-coming-out-of-her-wherever/?utm_term=.caa657382a49.

136 **"I just wanted to study langurs":** Sarah Blaffer Hrdy, interview with the author, October 25, 2016.

136 **her doctoral dissertation:** S. B. Hrdy, "Male and Female Strategies of Reproduction Among the Langurs of Abu" (PhD thesis, Harvard University, 1975), retrieved from ProQuest Dissertations and Theses database (UMI no. 1295398).

136 **"sexually adventurous females were not supposed to exist":** Hrdy, interview, October 25, 2016.

136 **Hrdy did indeed witness males attacking:** S. B. Hrdy, "Male-Male Competition and Infanticide Among the Langurs (*Presbytis entellus*) of Abu, Rajasthan," *Folia Primatologica* 22, no. 1 (1974): 19–58.

137 **An infanticidal male "eliminated...males":** Sarah Blaffer Hrdy, correspondence with the author, January 19, 2017.

138 **"assiduously maternal":** Hrdy, interview, October 25, 2016, and correspondence with the author, January 19, 2017.

138 **"Those monkeys are deranged":** Hrdy, interview, October 25, 2016.

139 **In her 1981 book, *The Woman That Never Evolved*:** S. B. Hrdy, *The Woman That Never Evolved* (Cambridge, MA: Harvard University Press, 1981).

140 **"So, Sarah, put another way, you're saying you're horny, right?...":** Hrdy, interview, October 25, 2016.

140 **female macaques in captivity who craved sexual variety:** D. Bergner, *What Do Women Want? Adventures in the Science of Female Desire* (New York: HarperCollins, 2013), 43–51, 121.

140 **ostensibly "monogamous" female gibbons:** C. Barelli, K. Matsudaira, T. Wolf, C. Roos, M. Heistermann, K. Hodges, T. Ishida, S. Malaivijitnond, and U. H. Reichard, "Extra-Pair Paternity Confirmed in Wild White-Handed Gibbons," *American Journal of Primatology* 75, no. 12 (2013): 1185–95.

140 **female chimps who risked their lives:** M. F. Small, "Female Choice in Nonhuman Primates," *American Journal of Physical Anthropology* 32, no. S10 (1989): 103–27; and M. F. Small, "Female Choice and Primates," in *Female Choices: Sexual Behavior of Female Primates* (Ithaca, NY: Cornell University Press, 1993), 171.

140 **there was good reason:** Small, *Female Choices*, passim; A. Jolly, "Pair Bonding, Female Aggression, and the Evolution of Lemur Societies," *Folia Primatologica* 69, suppl. 1 (1998): 1–13; B. Smuts, *Sex and Friendship in Baboons* (New York: Aldine, 1985); B. Smuts, "The Evolutionary Origins of Patriarchy," *Human Nature* 6, no. 1 (1994): 1–32; and J. Altmann, and S. C. Alberts, "Variability in Reproductive Success Viewed from a Life-History Perspective in Baboons," *American Journal of Human Biology* 15, no. 3 (2003): 401–9.

140 **increase their chances of conceiving:** C. M. Drea, "Bateman Revisited: The Reproductive Tactics of Female Primates," *Integrative and Comparative Biology* 45, no. 5 (2005): 915–23.

141 **could deplete the sperm available to rival females:** J. Soltis, "Do Primate Females Gain Nonprocreative Benefits by Mating with Multiple Males? Theoretical and Empirical Considerations," *Evolutionary Anthropology* 11, no. 5 (2002): 187–97.

142 **including three- to four-inch-long paired legs:** S. Winston, "The Missing Female Pleasure Parts," Intimate Arts Center blog, September 20, 2016, https://intimateartscenter.com/the-missing-female-pleasure-parts/; and S. Winston, "Lost Sexy Bits," Intimate Arts Center blog, August 12, 2016, https://intimateartscenter.com/the-missing-sexy-pieces/.

142 **has more than eight thousand nerve endings:** N. Angier, *Woman: An Intimate Geography* (Boston: Houghton Mifflin Harcourt, 1999), 67.

142 **fourteen times the density of nerve receptor cells:** Angier, *Woman*, 65.

142 **"female erectile network" (FEN):** Winston, "The Missing Female Pleasure Parts," https://intimateartscenter.com/the-missing-female-pleasure-parts/; and S. Winston, "Lost Sexy Bits," https://intimateartscenter.com/the-missing-sexy-pieces/.

142 **says Rachel Carlton Abrams, MD:** L. R. Emery, "Here's [Why] Many Single Women Have Multiple Orgasms," *Bustle,* February 2, 2016, https://www.bustle.com/articles/139224-heres-many-single-women-have-multiple-orgasms.

143 **According to Manhattan psychiatrist and sex therapist Elisabeth Gordon, MD:** E. Gordon, correspondence with the author, April 8, 2018; and R. J. Levin and G. Wagner, "Orgasm in Women in the Laboratory—Quantitative Studies on Duration, Intensity, Latency, and Vaginal Blood Flow," *Archives of Sexual Behavior* 14, no. 5 (1985): 444.

143 **men come a hefty 22 percent more:** J. R. Garcia, E. A. Lloyd, K. Wallen, and H. E. Fisher, "Variation in Orgasm Occurrence by Sexual Orientation in a Sample of U.S. Singles," *Journal of Sexual Medicine* 11, no. 11 (2014): 2645–52; and L. Wade, "The Orgasm Gap," *AlterNet,* April 3, 2013.

143 **stimulation that leads to orgasm is *cumulative:*** S. B. Hrdy, "The Primate Origins of Human Sexuality," in G. Stevens and R. Bellig, eds., *The Evolution of Sex* (San Francisco: Harper and Row, 1988), 101–36.

144 **By now…various species of macaques:** Hrdy, interview, October 25, 2016.

144 **"Based on both clinical observations and interviews…":** Hrdy, "The Primate Origins of Female Sexuality," 122.

145 **female orgasm…has been best documented:** Hrdy, "The Primate Origins of Female Sexuality," 123.

145 **the story of a woman's cervix:** C. Ryan and C. Jethá, *Sex at Dawn: How We Mate, Why We Stray, and What It Means for Modern Relationships* (New York: HarperCollins, 2012), 265–67.

145 **human male's testicles:** J. E. Rodgers, *Sex: A Natural History* (New York: Henry Holt, 2002), 99; and Ryan and Jethá, *Sex at Dawn,* 222–32.

146 **Sperm plugs:** A. L. Dixson and M. J. Anderson, "Sexual Selection, Seminal Coagulation, and Copulatory Plug Formation in Primates," *Folio Primatologica* (Basel) 73, nos. 2–3 (2002): 63–69.

146 **the coronal ridge removed nearly three times:** G. G. Gallup, R. L. Burch, M. L. Zappieri, R. A. Parvez, M. L. Stockwell, and J. A. Davis, "The Human Penis as a Semen Displacement Device," *Evolution and Human Behavior* 27, no. 4 (2003): 277–89.

146 **And the final spurts:** Ryan and Jethá, *Sex at Dawn,* 228; and Amy Parish, interview with the author, March 13, 2017.

146 **our very cries of pleasure:** Z. Clay, S. Pika, T. Gruber, and K. Zuberbühler, "Female Bonobos Use Copulation Calls as Social Signals," *Biology Letters* 7, no. 4 (2011): 513–16.

147 **Barbara Smuts's unexpected observations:** Smuts, *Sex and Friendship in Baboons;* and Small, *Female Choices,* 6, 171.

148 **"—why, she would hang on him…woman!":** W. Shakespeare, *Hamlet,* ed. Cyrus Hoy (New York: W. W. Norton, 1996), 143–46.

148 **Mosuo practice of *sese,* or "walking marriage":** C. Hua, *A Society Without Fathers or Husbands: The Na of China,* trans. A. Hustvedt (New York: Zone Books, 2001).

148 **polyandrous arrangements in rural Tibet:** C. M. Beall and M. C. Goldstein, "Tibetan Fraternal Polyandry: A Test of Sociobiological Theory," *American Anthropologist* 83, no. 1 (1981): 5–12.

149 **Ethnographic evidence of such informal polyandry:** K. E. Starkweather and R. Hames, "A Survey of Non-Classical Polyandry," *Human Nature* 23, no. 2 (2012): 149–72.

149 **Meredith Small, in a survey of 133 societies:** Small, *Female Choices,* 214.

149 **"Why is polyandry so rare in humans?":** S. B. Hrdy, "The Optimal Number of Fathers: Evolution, Demography, and History in the Shaping of Female Mate Preferences," *Annals of the New York Academy of Sciences* 907, no. 1 (2000): 75–96; and M. Borgerhoff Mulder, "Serial Monogamy as Polygyny or Polyandry? Marriage in the Tanzanian Pimbwe," *Human Nature* 20, no. 2 (2009): 130–50.

149 **When men outnumber women:** J. F. Peters and C. L. Hunt, "Polyandry Among the Yanomama Shirishana," *Journal of Comparative Family Studies* 6, no. 2 (1975): 197–207.

149 **When it is difficult for a single man:** K. A. Haddix, "Leaving Your Wife and Your Broth-

ers: When Polyandrous Marriages Fall Apart," *Evolution and Human Behavior* 22, no. 1 (2001): 47–60.

150 **When there is a custom:** Hrdy, "The Optimal Number of Fathers," 75–96.

150 **When women can rely:** Borgerhoff Mulder, "Serial Monogamy," 130–50.

150 **When women have a high level of autonomy:** Hrdy, "The Optimal Number of Fathers," 75–96.

150 **When there are few accumulated or heritable:** Borgerhoff Mulder, "Serial Monogamy," 130–50.

150 **In her work among the Pimbwe of Tanzania:** Borgerhoff Mulder, "Serial Monogamy," 130–50.

151 **BorgerhoffMulder further concluded that:** Borgerhoff Mulder, "Serial Monogamy," 130–50.

151 **at least eighteen tribes:** S. Beckerman and P. Valentine, *Cultures of Multiple Fathers: The Theory and Practice of Partible Paternity in Lowland South America* (Gainesville: University of Florida Press, 2002).

151 **a total of 632 fathers:** K. Hill and A. M. Hurtado, *Aché Life History: The Ecology and Demography of a Foraging People* (New York: Aldine de Gruyter, 1996), cited in Hrdy, *Mother Nature*, 246.

151 *Miare* **is:** Hill and Hurtado, *Aché Life History*, cited in Hrdy, *Mother Nature*, 246.

151 **which "accumulates":** Beckerman and Valentine, *Cultures of Multiple Fathers*, 10.

151 **Anthropologist Stephen Beckerman:** S. Beckerman, R. Lizarralde, C. Ballew, S. Schroeder, C. Fingelton, A. Garrison, and H. Smith, "The Bari Partible Paternity Project: Preliminary Results," *Current Anthropology* 39, no. 1 (1998): 164–68, cited in Hrdy, *Mother Nature*, 247–48.

152 **The optimal number of fathers:** Hrdy, *Mother Nature*, 248.

152 **rethink the idea:** Z. Tang-Martínez, "Rethinking Bateman's Principles: Challenging Persistent Myths of Sexually Reluctant Females and Promiscuous Males," *Journal of Sex Research* 53, no. 4 (2016): 532–59; and Z. Tang-Martínez, "Data Should Smash the Biological Myth of Promiscuous Males and Sexually Coy Females," Phys.org, January 20, 2017, https://phys.org/news/2017-01-biological-myth-promiscuous-males-sexually.html.

153 **And since such a significant number:** Drea, "Bateman Revisited," 915–23.

153 *the range in male and female lifetime reproductive success:* Drea, "Bateman Revisited," 915–23.

154 **put Bateman to the test in 2012:** P. A. Gowaty, Y.-K. Kim, and W. A. Anderson, "No Evidence of Sexual Selection in a Repetition of Bateman's Classic Study of *Drosophila melanogaster*," *Proceedings of the National Academy of Sciences* 109, no. 29 (2012): 11740–45.

154 **Males don't have:** Drea, "Bateman Revisited," 915–23; and Gowaty, Kim, and Anderson, "No Evidence of Sexual," 11740–45.

155 **a woman informed Scelza:** Brooke Scelza, interview with the author, October 11, 2016.

156 **In the US and the industrialized West:** H. Greiling and D. M. Buss, "Women's Sexual Strategies: The Hidden Dimension of Extra-Pair Mating," *Personality and Individual Differences* 28, no. 5 (2000): 929–63, cited in Scelza, "Female Choice and Extra Pair Paternity," 889–91.

157 **She included 110 women:** Scelza, "Female Choice and Extra Pair Paternity," 889–91; and A. Saini, *Inferior: How Science Got Women Wrong—And the New Research That's Rewriting the Story* (Boston: Beacon, 2017), 129–31.

158 **"The Himba have few heritable resources...":** Scelza, interview, October 11, 2016.

159 **there were no** *omoka* **children born:** Scelza, "Female Choice and Extra Pair Paternity," 889–91.

159 **in nearly a quarter of arranged marriages:** Scelza, "Female Choice and Extra Pair Paternity," 889–91.

160 **"flexible and opportunistic individuals...options":** Hrdy, "The Optimal Number of Fathers," 246; and E. M. Johnson, "Promiscuity Is Pragmatic," *Slate,* December 4, 2013, http://www.slate.com/articles/health_and_science/science/2013/12/female_promiscuity_in_primates_when_do_women_have_multiple_partners.html.

160 **Scelza documented:** Scelza, "Female Choice and Extra Pair Paternity," 889–91.

CHAPTER SIX: BONOBOS IN PARADISE

163 **Linda Wolfe and Meredith Small tell us:** L. Wolfe, "Behavioral Patterns of Estrous Females of the Arashiyama West Troop of Japanese Macaques (*Macaca fuscata*)," *Primates* 20, no. 4 (1979): 525–34, cited in M. F. Small, *Female Choices: Sexual Behavior of Female Primates* (Ithaca, NY: Cornell University Press, 1993), 111.

163 **lion-tailed macaque female:** D. G. Lindburg, S. Shideler, and H. Fitch, "Sexual Behavior in Relation to Time of Ovulation in the Lion-Tailed Macaque," in P. G. Heltne, ed., *The Lion-Tailed Macaque: Status and Conservation*, vol. 7 (New York: Alan R. Liss, 1985), 131–48, cited in Small, *Female Choices*, 111–12.

163 **vocalizing and literally writhing:** Lindburg, Shideler, and Fitch, "Sexual Behavior in Relation to Time of Ovulation," cited in Small, *Female Choices*, 111–12.

163 **Female ruffed lemurs, meanwhile:** R. Foerg, "Reproductive Behavior in *Varecia variegata*," *Folia Primatologica* 38, nos. 1–2 (1982): 108–21, cited in Small, *Female Choices*, 112.

164 **female capuchins will chase males:** C. H. Janson, "Female Choice and Mating System of the Brown Capuchin Monkey *Cebus apella*," *Ethology* 65, no. 3 (1984): 177–200, cited in Small, *Female Choices*, 158.

164 **A capuchin female may be so busy:** Janson, "Female Choice and Mating System of the Brown Capuchin Monkey," 177–200, cited in Small, *Female Choices*, 158.

164 **Female chimps in one group:** Small, *Female Choices*, 174.

164 **an Indian female rhesus:** D. G. Lindburg, "Mating Behavior and Estrus in the Indian Rhesus Monkey," in P. K. Seth, ed., *Perspectives in Primate Biology* (New Delhi: Today and Tomorrow's Publishers, 1983), 45–61, cited in Small, *Female Choices*, 172.

164 **chacmas have been observed:** G. S. Saayman, "The Menstrual Cycle and Sexual Behavior in a Troop of Free-Ranging Chacma Baboons (*Papio ursinus*)," *Folia Primatologica* 12, no. 2 (1970): 81–110, cited in Small, in *Female Choices*, 173.

164 **Unconstrained, woolly spider monkey:** K. Milton, "Mating Patterns of Woolly Spider Monkeys, *Brachyteles arachnoides:* Implications for Female Choice," *Behavioral Ecology and Sociobiology* 17, no. 1 (1985): 53–59, cited in Small, *Female Choices*, 172–73; K. B. Strier, "New World Primates, New Frontiers: Insights from the Woolly Spider Monkey, or Muriqui (*Brachyteles arachnoides*)," *International Journal of Primatology* 11, no. 1 (1990): 7–19, cited in Small, *Female Choices*, 172–73; and K. B. Strier, "Causes and Consequences of Nonaggression in the Woolly Spider Monkey, or Muriqui (*Brachyteles arachnoides*)," in J. Silverberg and J. P. Gray, eds., *Aggression and Peacefulness in Humans and Other Primates* (New York: Oxford University Press, 1992), 100–16, cited in Small, *Female Choices*, 172–73.

164 **Barbary macaque females:** J. Kuester and A. Paul, "Female Reproductive Characteristics in Semifree-Ranging Barbary Macaques (*Macaca sylvanus*)," *Folia Primatologica* 43, nos. 2–3 (1984): 69–83, cited in Small, *Female Choices*, 172; M. F. Small, "Promiscuity in Barbary Macaques (*Macaca sylvanus*)," *American Journal of Primatology* 20, no. 4 (1990): 267–82, cited in Small, *Female Choices*, 172; and D. M. Taub, "Female Choice and Mating Strategies Among Wild Barbary Macaques (*Macaca sylvanus*)," in D. G. Lindburg, ed., *The Macaques: Studies in Ecology, Behavior, and Evolution* (New York: Van Nostrand Reinhold, 1980), cited in Small, *Female Choices*, 172.

164 **Female chimps leave their natal groups:** M. F. Small, "Female Choice in Nonhuman Primates," *American Journal of Physical Anthropology* 32, no. S10 (1989): 103–27; and Small, *Female Choices*, 171.

164 **Female patas monkeys:** Small, "Female Choice in Nonhuman Primates," 103–27; and Small, *Female Choices*, 171.

164 **Squirrel monkey females:** Small, "Female Choice in Nonhuman Primates," 103–27; and Small, *Female Choices*, 171.

164 **Kim Wallen and his colleagues:** D. Bergner, *What Do Women Want? Adventures in the Science of Female Desire* (New York: HarperCollins, 2013), 43–51, 121.

164 **"monogamous" gibbon females:** U. Reichard, "Extra-Pair Copulations in a Monogamous Gibbon (*Hylobates lar*)," *Ethology* 100, no. 2 (1995): 99–112; R. A. Palombit, "Extra-Pair Copulations in a Monogamous Ape," *Animal Behaviour* 47, no. 3 (1994): 721–23; and C. Barelli, K. Matsudaira, T. Wolf, C. Roos, M. Heistermann, K. Hodges, T. Ishida, S. Malaivijitnond, and U. H. Reichard, "Extra-Pair Paternity Confirmed in Wild White-Handed Gibbons," *American Journal of Primatology* 75, no. 12 (2013): 1185–95.

164 **a thirst for novelty:** Small, *Female Choices,* 171.

165 **"just how little importance":** Small, *Female Choices,* 164.

165 **Linda Wolfe discovered:** Wolfe, "Behavioral Patterns of Estrous Females," 525–34.

165 **Female langurs also have sexual encounters:** C. Srivastava, C. Borries, and V. Sommer, "Homosexual Mounting in Free-Ranging Hanuman Langurs (*Presbytis entellus*)," *Archives of Sexual Behavior* 20, no. 5 (1991): 487–516, cited in Small, *Female Choices,* 146.

165 **the bonobo, with whom we share:** A. L. Zihlman, J. E. Cronin, D. L. Cramer, and V. M. Sarich, "Pygmy Chimpanzee as a Possible Prototype for the Common Ancestor of Humans, Chimpanzees, and Gorillas," *Nature* 275, no. 5682 (1978): 744–46; K. Prüfer, K. Munch, I. Hellman, K. Akagi, J. R. Miller, B. Walenz, S. Koren, et al., "The Bonobo Genome Compared with the Chimpanzee and Human Genomes," *Nature* 486, no. 7404 (2012): 527–31; and A. Gibbons, "Bonobos Join Chimps as Closest Human Relatives," *Science,* June 13, 2012, https://www.sciencemag.org/news/2012/06/bonobos-join-chimps-closest-human-relatives.

165 **live under human care in seven zoos:** "Zoos," The Bonobo Project website, accessed 2018, https://bonoboproject.org/heroes-for-bonobos/zoos/.

167 **at which point we learned that bonobos:** Prüfer et al., "The Bonobo Genome Compared," 527–31; and Gibbons, "Bonobos Join Chimps," https://www.sciencemag.org/news/2012/06/bonobos-join-chimps-closest-human-relatives.

167 **"Bonobo muscles have changed the least...ancestor":** R. Diogo, J. L. Molnar, and B. A. Wood, "Bonobo Anatomy Reveals Stasis and Mosaicism in Chimpanzee Evolution, and Supports Bonobos as the Most Appropriate Extant Model for the Common Ancestor of Chimpanzees and Humans," *Scientific Reports* 7, article 608 (2017); and George Washington University, "Bonobos May Be Better Representation of Last Common Ancestor with Humans Than Chimps: Study Examined Muscles of Bonobos and Found They Are More Closely Related to Humans Than Common Chimpanzees," news release, *ScienceDaily,* April 29, 2017, https://www.sciencedaily.com/releases/2017/04/170429095021.htm.

167 **Like us, they have sex ventrally:** T. C. Nguyen, "Gorillas Caught in a Very Human Act," *Live Science,* February 13, 2008, https://www.livescience.com/2298-gorillas-caught-human-act.html; and Small, *Female Choices,* 175.

167 **bonobos follow the same "empathic gradient":** E. Palagi and I. Norscia, "Bonobos Protect and Console Friends and Kin," *PLoS One* 8, no. 11 (2013): e79290.

167 **human and bonobo babies have extraordinarily similar laughs:** F. B. M. de Waal and F. Lanting, *Bonobo: The Forgotten Ape* (Berkeley: University of California Press, 1997), 33.

168 **Meredith Small reports being in a room of three hundred:** Small, *Female Choices,* 175.

168 **Parish and her colleagues documented:** J. H. Manson, S. Perry, and A. R. Parish, "Nonconceptive Sexual Behavior in Bonobos and Capuchins," *International Journal of Primatology* 18, no. 5 (1997): 767–86.

168 **Younger bonobos, both male and female:** F. B. M. de Waal, "Bonobo Sex and Society," *Scientific American,* June 1, 2006, https://www.scientificamerican.com/article/bonobo-sex-and-society-2006-06/.

168 **Females equally or even more eagerly practice:** Manson, Perry, and Parish, "Nonconceptive Sexual Behavior in Bonobos and Capuchins," 767–86.

169 **It feels good enough:** J. P. Balcombe, *The Exultant Ark: A Pictorial Tour of Animal Pleasure* (Berkeley: University of California Press, 2011).

169 **Zanna Clay and colleagues noted:** Z. Clay, S. Pika, T. Gruber, and K. Zuberbühler,

"Female Bonobos Use Copulation Calls as Social Signals," *Biology Letters* 7, no. 4 (2011): 513–16.

169 **This is not a frequent occurrence, but it happens:** Amy Parish, interview with the author, March 16, 2017.

172 **certainly true among bonobos' closest relatives:** A. R. Parish, "Sex and Food Control in the 'Uncommon Chimpanzee': How Bonobo Females Overcome a Phylogenetic Legacy of Male Dominance," *Ethology and Sociobiology* 15, no. 3 (1994): 157–79.

172 **males often "patrol":** D. P. Watts, M. Muller, S. J. Amsler, G. Mbazazi, and J. C. Mitani, "Lethal Intergroup Aggression by Chimpanzees in Kibale National Park, Uganda," *American Journal of Primatology* 68, no. 2 (2006): 161–80.

172 **chimp males and females alike:** A. C. Arcadi and R. W. Wrangham, "Infanticide in Chimpanzees: Review of Cases and a New Within-Group Observation from the Kanyawara Study Group in Kibale National Park," *Primates* 40, no. 2 (1999): 337–51.

173 **bonobos as pacific, "Make love not war" "swingers":** I. Parker, "Swingers," *New Yorker,* July 30, 2007, https://www.newyorker.com/magazine/2007/07/30/swingers-2; P. Raffaele, "The Smart and Swinging Bonobo," *Smithsonian Magazine,* November 2006, https://www.smithsonianmag.com/science-nature/the-smart-and-swinging-bonobo-134784867/; and "The Make Love, Not War Species," *Living on Earth,* PRI, radio broadcast, 14:47, aired the week of July 7, 2006, https://loe.org/shows/segments.html?programID=06-P13-00027&segmentID=2.

174 **She realized that in spite of male philopatry:** A. R. Parish, "Female Relationships in Bonobos (*Pan paniscus*): Evidence for Bonding, Cooperation, and Female Dominance in a Male-Philopatric Species," *Human Nature* 7, no. 1 (1996): 61–96; Parish, "Sex and Food Control in the 'Uncommon Chimpanzee,'" 157–79; A. R. Parish, F. B. M. de Waal, and D. Haig, "The Other Closest Living Relative: How Bonobos (*Pan paniscus*) Challenge Traditional Assumptions About Females, Dominance, Intra- and Intersexual Interactions, and Hominid Evolution," *Annals of the New York Academy of Sciences* 907 (2000): 97–113; and T. Furuichi, "Female Contributions to the Peaceful Nature of Bonobo Society," *Evolutionary Anthropology: Issues, News, and Reviews* 20, no. 4 (2011): 131–42.

174 **a senior keeper at the San Diego Zoo, Mike Bates:** J. D. Roth, "Ape Bites Off Keeper's Finger, Returns It," Animal Intelligence, March 26, 2007, http://www.animalintelligence.org/2007/03/26/ape-bites-off-keepers-fingerreturns-it/.

175 **when a female bonobo is solicited simultaneously:** M. F. Small, "Casual Sex Play Common Among Bonobos," *Discover,* June 1, 1992, cited in Small, *Female Choices,* 144 .

176 **females using G-to-G contact:** G. Hohmann and B. Fruth, "Use and Function of Genital Contacts Among Female Bonobos," *Animal Behavior* 60, no. 1 (2000): 107–20; Furuichi, "Female Contributions to the Peaceful Nature of Bonobo Society," 131–42; and Parish, De Waal, and Haig, "The Other Closest Living Relative," 97–113.

177 **Girls and Sex:** P. Orenstein, *Girls and Sex: Navigating the Complicated New Landscape* (New York: Oneworld, 2016).

177 **Blurred Lines:** V. Grigoriadis, *Blurred Lines: Rethinking Sex, Power, and Consent on Campus* (Boston: Houghton Mifflin Harcourt, 2018).

177 **What if all our presumptions of alpha males:** B. Smuts, "The Evolutionary Origins of Patriarchy," *Human Nature* 6, no. 1 (1995): 1–32; and Z. Tang-Martínez, "Rethinking Bateman's Principles: Challenging Persistent Myths of Sexually Reluctant Females and Promiscuous Males," *Journal of Sex Research* 53, no. 4 (2016): 532–39.

177 **what if bonobo-ness is one of the drivers:** M. A. Fischer, "Why Women Are Leaving Men for Other Women," *O, The Oprah Magazine,* April 2009, http://www.oprah.com/relationships/why-women-are-leaving-men-for-lesbian-relationships-bisexuality/all.

177 **the powerful, polymorphous, perverse fantasies:** M. L. Chivers, M. C. Seto, and R. Blanchard, "Gender and Sexual Orientation Differences in Sexual Response to Sexual Activities Versus Gender of Actors in Sexual Films," *Journal of Personality and Social*

Psychology 93, no. 6 (2007): 1108–21; M. L. Chivers and A. D. Timmers, "Effects of Gender and Relationship Context in Audio Narratives on Genital and Subjective Sexual Response in Heterosexual Women and Men," *Archives of Sexual Behavior* 41, no. 1 (2012): 185–97; and M. L. Chivers, G. Rieger, E. Latty, and J. M. Bailey, "A Sex Difference in the Specificity of Sexual Arousal," *Psychological Sciences* 15, no. 11 (2004): 736–44.

178 **wide and unambiguous swerves:** A. M. Walker, "'I'm Not a Lesbian; I'm Just a Freak': A Pilot Study of the Experiences of Women in Assumed-Monogamous Other-Sex Unions Seeking Secret Same-Sex Encounters Online, Their Negotiation of Sexual Desire, and Meaning-Making of Sexual Identity," *Sexuality and Culture* 18, no. 4 (2014): 911–35.

178 **article by Mackenzie Dawson:** M. Dawson, "This Sex Club Gives Men Major FOMO," *New York Post*, March 3, 2016, https://nypost.com/2016/03/03/men-are-dying-to-get-into-this-all-female-sex-club/.

180 **Cole declared we had entered a new era of "vaginomics":** Bryony Cole, interview with the author, May 5, 2017.

186 **two-decade longitudinal study:** L. M. Diamond, *Sexual Fluidity: Understanding Women's Love and Desire* (Cambridge, MA: Harvard University Press, 2008).

187 **I reached out to Diamond via Skype:** Lisa Diamond, interview with the author, September 28, 2017.

189 **But a recent study of 180 men:** Diamond, interview, September 28, 2017.

189 **when avowedly heterosexual women have dalliances:** W. Martin, "Gay Until Labor Day: Stretching Female Sexuality in the Hamptons," *Observer*, May 18, 2016, http://observer.com/2016/05/gay-until-labor-day-stretching-female-sexuality-in-the-hamptons/.

190 **"Whoops! I Married a Lesbian":** *Saturday Night Live*, season 40, "Forgotten TV Gems: Whoops! I Married a Lesbian," aired May 16, 2015, on NBC, http://www.nbc.com/saturday-night-live/video/forgotten-tv-gems-whoops-i-married-a-lesbian/2866702?snl=1.

192 **a *Rolling Stone* article called it:** B. Kerr, "Inside the Sex Party That Lets Straight Women Be Gay for a Night," *Rolling Stone*, February 23, 2017, https://www.rollingstone.com/culture/features/inside-a-sex-party-where-straight-women-are-gay-for-a-night-w467015.

192 **In Lesotho:** J. Gay, "'Mummies and Babies' and Friends and Lovers in Lesotho," *Cambridge Journal of Anthropology* 5, no. 3 (1979): 32–61, cited in E. Blackwood, ed., *The Many Faces of Homosexuality: Anthropological Approaches to Homosexual Behavior* (New York: Harrington Park Press, 1986), 97–116.

192 **Among the !Kung:** M. Shostak, *Nisa: The Life and Words of a !Kung Woman* (Cambridge, MA: Harvard University Press, 1981), 99, 103.

192 ***mati* is a widespread institution:** G. Wekker, "'What's Identity Got to Do with It?' Rethinking Identity in Light of the *Mati* Work in Suriname," in E. W. E. Blackwood and S. E. Wieringa, eds., *Female Desires: Same-Sex Relations and Transgender Practices Across Cultures* (New York: Columbia University Press, 1999), 119–38, 232.

193 **women are uniquely designed:** H. E. Fisher, *Anatomy of Love: A Natural History of Marriage, Mating, and Why We Stray* (New York: W. W. Norton, 2016); and H. E. Fisher, *The Sex Contract: The Evolution of Human Behavior* (New York: William Morrow, 1982).

193 **A Boise State University study of 333 women:** E. M. Morgan and E. M. Thompson, "Processes of Sexual Orientation Questioning Among Heterosexual Women," *Journal of Sex Research* 48, no. 1 (2011): 16–28.

193 **In a *Glamour* survey:** A. Tsoulis-Reay, "Are You Straight, Gay, or Just…You?," *Glamour*, February 11, 2016, https://www.glamour.com/story/glamour-sexuality-survey.

193 **As Lisa Diamond commented:** Diamond, interview, September 28, 2017.

CHAPTER SEVEN: SIGNIFICANT OTHERNESS

195 **Deesha Philyaw's "Eula":** D. Philyaw, "Eula," *Apogee* 9 (Summer 2017).

198 **"The black church is an institution...":** Tiffany Dufu, interview with the author, January 25, 2018.

199 **"Milk for Free":** D. Philyaw, "Milk for Free," *Brevity* 49 (May 2015).

200 **Tamara Winfrey Harris, the cultural critic and author of *The Sisters Are Alright*:** T. Winfrey Harris, *The Sisters Are Alright: Changing the Broken Narrative of Black Women in America* (Oakland, CA: Berrett-Koehler, 2015).

200 **Philyaw told me when we spoke:** Deesha Philyaw, interviews with the author, July 26, 2017, and November 9, 2017.

202 **"[s]tereotypes of black women...protection":** Winfrey Harris, *The Sisters Are Alright*, 3–4.

203 **these "controlling images":** P. Hill Collins, *Black Feminist Thought: Knowledge, Consciousness, and the Politics of Empowerment* (New York: Routledge, 2002), 98.

203 **when Don Imus calls:** Collins, *Black Feminist Thought*, 19.

203 **Bill O'Reilly goes after Beyoncé:** Winfrey Harris, *The Sisters Are Alright*, 32–33.

203 **sociologist of gender and sexuality Victor Corona:** Victor Corona, correspondence with the author, summer 2017.

203 **According to experts:** J. K. Williams, G. E. Wyatt, H. F. Myers, K. N. Presley Green, and U. S. Warda, "Patterns in Relationship Violence Among African American Women," *Journal of Aggression, Maltreatment, and Trauma* 16, no. 3 (2008) 296–310; G. Pollard-Terry, "For African American Rape Victims, a Culture of Silence," *Los Angeles Times*, July 20, 2004, http://articles.latimes.com/2004/jul/20/entertainment/et-pollard20; and N. G. Alexander-Floyd, "Beyond Superwoman: Justice for Black Women Too," *Dissent*, Winter 2014, https://www.dissentmagazine.org/article/beyond-superwoman-justice-for-black-women-too.

204 **one study found:** J. Katz, C. Merrilees, J. C. Hoxmeier, and M. Motisi, "White Female Bystanders' Responses to Black Women at Risk for Incapacitated Sexual Assault," *Psychology of Women Quarterly* 41, no. 2 (2017): 273–85.

204 **In her article "No Disrespect":** T. Winfrey Harris, "No Disrespect: Black Women and the Burden of Respectability," Bitch Media, May 22, 2012, https://www.bitchmedia.org/article/no-disrespect.

204 **"work to counter negative views of blackness...":** Winfrey Harris, *The Sisters Are Alright*, 7.

204 **"I had a lot of fears in the beginning":** Philyaw, interview, July 26, 2017.

205 **"I recognize as a black woman...":** Winfrey Harris, *The Sisters Are Alright*, 79.

205 **"George Clooney just got married...nobody's calling *him* a ho!":** Issa Rae interview with Larry Wilmore, "Issa Rae from 'Insecure' on the 'Hoe Phase' and Finding Her Voice," *Black on the Air*, episode 10, August 3, 2017, found on The Ringer podcast network, https://www.theringer.com/2017/8/4/16100040/issa-rae-on-the-hoe-phase-and-finding-her-voice.

206 **black women who worked as porn actresses:** F. Chideya, "Sex Stereotypes of African Americans Have Long History," interview with H. Samuels and M. Miller-Young, *News and Notes*, National Public Radio, aired May 7, 2007, https://www.npr.org/templates/story/story.php?storyId=10057104.

206 **"show that the titillation of pornography...tells":** M. Miller-Young, *A Taste for Brown Sugar: Black Women in Pornography* (Durham, NC, and London: Duke University Press, 2014), 9.

206 **Desiree West plays Jill:** Miller-Young, *A Taste for Brown Sugar*, 90–98.

207 **"Between my *thighs* is where my rhythm *lies*":** Miller-Young, *A Taste for Brown Sugar*, 91.

207 **"animated and transgressive performance...'spoken soul'":** Miller-Young, *A Taste for Brown Sugar*, 97.

207 **"about slavery...it's actually a continuing legacy...":** "6.9 Questions with Dr Mireille Miller-Young," video interview of M. Miller-Young by K. Shibari, 14:55, posted April 10, 2013, by hotmoviesforher, https://www.youtube.com/watch?time_continue=2&v=DmZzLFznr-0.

207 **"One is from people of color…everyone else":** "6.9 Questions with Dr Mireille Miller-Young," interview, https://www.youtube.com/watch?time_continue=2&v=DmZzLFznr-0.

208 **During an interview:** Chideya, "Sex Stereotypes of African Americans," https://www.npr.org/templates/story/story.php?storyId=10057104.

208 **have "said that by showing these images…":** "6.9 Questions with Dr Mireille Miller-Young," interview, https://www.youtube.com/watch?time_continue=2&v=DmZzLFznr-0.

208 **porn industry maintains a segregated, niche market:** Miller-Young, *A Taste for Brown Sugar,* 110, 243.

208 **"the stuff a white guy might presume…":** Anonymous, interview with the author, 2017.

209 *New York Times* **op-ed:** T. McMillan Cottom, "How We Make Black Girls Grow Up Too Fast," *New York Times,* July 29, 2017, https://www.nytimes.com/2017/07/29/opinion/sunday/how-we-make-black-girls-grow-up-too-fast.html.

210 **Monique W. Morris's book *Pushout:*** McMillan Cottom, "Black Girls Grow Up Too Fast," https://www.nytimes.com/2017/07/29/opinion/sunday/how-we-make-black-girls-grow-up-too-fast.html.

210 **"Left to navigate school…":** McMillan Cottom, "Black Girls Grow Up Too Fast," https://www.nytimes.com/2017/07/29/opinion/sunday/how-we-make-black-girls-grow-up-too-fast.html.

211 **Calling the response "creative, appropriate, and powerful":** Crunktastic, "SlutWalks v. Ho Strolls," Crunk Feminist Collective, May 23, 2011, https://crunkfeminist collective.wordpress.com/2011/05/23/slutwalks-v-ho-strolls/.

212 **"perhaps we should line up on the Ho Stroll…sexual rights":** Miller-Young, *A Taste for Brown Sugar,* 201.

212 *The Misadventures of Awkward Black Girl:* Issa Rae Productions, *The Misadventures of Awkward Black Girl,* web series, two seasons, 2011–2013, http://awkwardblackgirl.com; and I. Rae, *The Misadventures of Awkward Black Girl* (New York: Atria, 2016).

212 **interview with Larry Wilmore:** Rae interview with Wilmore, *Black on the Air.*

213 **"Maybe I'm not satisfied…":** *Insecure,* season 1, episode 2, "Messy as F**k," aired October 16, 2016, on HBO, https://www.hbo.com/insecure/season-01/2-messy-as-f-k.

214 **Rae explained her choice:** Rae interview with Wilmore, *Black on the Air.*

214 **Like 50 percent of the women:** C. Northrup, P. Schwartz, and J. Witte, "Why People Cheat: 'The Normal Bar' Reveals Infidelity Causes," *Divorce* (blog), *Huffington Post,* January 22, 2013, excerpt from *The Normal Bar: The Surprising Secrets of Happy Couples and What They Reveal About Creating a New Normal in Your Relationship* (New York: Harmony, 2014), https://www.huffingtonpost.com/2013/01/22/why-people-cheat_n_2483371.html.

215 *Mating in Captivity* **and** *The State of Affairs:* E. Perel, *Mating in Captivity* (New York: HarperCollins, 2006); and E. Perel, *The State of Affairs: Rethinking Infidelity* (New York: HarperCollins, 2017).

215 *"Run away!":* *Insecure,* season 2, episode 1, "Hella Great," aired July 23, 2017, on HBO, https://www.hbo.com/insecure/season-01/2-messy-as-f-k.

216 **As Damon Young wrote on VerySmartBrothas.com:** D. Young, "The Problem with #Team-Lawrence, Explained," Very Smart Brothas, July 25, 2017, https://verysmartbrothas.the-root.com/the-problem-with-teamlawrenceexplained-1822521432.

216 **"A ho phase is…":** Rae interview with Wilmore, *Black on the Air.*

216 **she told me when we talked:** Frenchie Davis, interviews with the author, August 1, 2017, and December 1, 2017.

218 **In 2003, Davis made:** "Fucking Ain't Conscious" Frenchie (Def Poetry), video, posted by rpolanco3, November 11, 2010, excerpt from *Def Poetry Jam,* season 3, episode 5, aired May 3, 2003, on HBO, https://www.youtube.com/watch?v=nGbNKaJcFb0.

218 **a book of poetry:** F. Davis, *Not from Between My Thighs* (self-pub., 2001), https://www.amazon.com/Not-From-Between-My-Thighs/dp/0971438404.

218 **the nation's first study on African American female sexuality:** G. E. Wyatt, S. D.

Peters, and D. Guthrie, "Kinsey Revisited, Part I: Comparisons of the Sexual Socialization and Sexual Behavior of White Women Over 33 Years," *Archives of Sexual Behavior* 17, no. 3 (1988): 201–39; and G. E. Wyatt, S. D. Peters, and D. Guthrie, "Kinsey Revisited, Part II: Comparisons of the Sexual Socialization and Sexual Behavior of Black Women Over 33 Years," *Archives of Sexual Behavior* 17, no. 4 (1988): 289–332.

219 **"clinically trained black females...interview":** Wyatt, Peters, and Guthrie, "Kinsey Revisited, Part II," 327.

219 **"[black] women have broadened their sexual repertoires...intercourse":** Wyatt, Peters, and Guthrie, "Kinsey Revisited, Part II," 316.

219 **"only 26 percent of the Kinsey women...":** Wyatt, Peters, and Guthrie, "Kinsey Revisited, Part II," 314.

219 **"Among ever-married women":** Wyatt, Peters, and Guthrie, "Kinsey Revisited, Part II," 317.

219 **Wyatt, a minister's granddaughter:** G. Pollard-Terry, "A Refined Eye," interview of Gail Elizabeth Wyatt, *Los Angeles Times*, January 3, 2004, http://articles.latimes.com/2004/jan/03/entertainment/et-pollard3.

220 **June Dobbs Butts, another African American sex researcher:** C. Kelley, "Sex Therapist, Witness to Civil Rights Movement to Speak Sunday," *Atlanta in Town*, July 15, 2016, http://atlantaintownpaper.com/2016/07/32886/; "June Dobbs Butts Oral History Interview," interview by F. Abbott, January 29, 2016, Special Collections and Archives, Georgia State University Library, http://digitalcollections.library.gsu.edu/cdm/ref/collection/activistwmn/id/17; and M. McQueen, "June Dobbs Butts, Pioneer Work on Sex Therapy's New Frontier," *Washington Post*, October 9, 1980, https://www.washingtonpost.com/archive/local/1980/10/09/june-dobbs-butts-pioneer-work-on-sex-therapys-new-frontier/7db54898-4411-45a8-9035-19b7543db4ff/?utm_term=.654db922f5a0.

221 **"Sex Education: Who Needs It?":** J. Dobbs Butts, "Sex Education: Who Needs It?," *Ebony*, April 1977, 96–98, 100.

221 **"Sex and the Modern Black Couple":** Dobbs Butts, "Sex Education," 128, 130, 132, 134.

221 **"Americans snicker at sexual references...discomfort":** J. Dobbs Butts, "Inextricable Aspects of Sex and Race," *Contributions in Black Studies* 1, no. 5 (1977): 53.

221 *Difficult Women:* R. Gay, *Difficult Women* (New York: Grove Press, 2017).

CHAPTER EIGHT: LOVING THE WOMAN WHO'S UNTRUE

225 **Tim wanted to let me know more about himself:** Tim, interviews with the author, 2016, 2017.

234 **Jenkins is a tenured professor of philosophy:** Profile, "Carrie Jenkins," University of British Columbia website, accessed February 11, 2018, https://philosophy.ubc.ca/persons/carrie-jenkins/.

234 **Her 2008 book *Grounding Concepts*:** C. S. Jenkins, *Grounding Concepts: An Empirical Basis for Arithmetical Knowledge* (Oxford, UK: Oxford University Press, 2008).

234 **What Love Is: And What It Could Be:** C. Jenkins, *What Love Is: And What It Could Be* (New York: Basic Books, 2017).

235 **When we spoke:** Carrie Jenkins, interview with the author, August 7, 2017.

235 **"On the mornings when I walk...easy and comfortable":** Jenkins, *What Love Is*, ix.

236 **Jenkins told me she spends one night a week:** Jenkins, correspondence with the author, August 15, 2017.

236 **She describes herself:** Jenkins, interview, August 7, 2017.

237 **"Get herpes and die":** M. Weigel, "'I Have Multiple Loves': Carrie Jenkins Makes the Philosophical Case for Polyamory," *Chronicle of Higher Education*, February 3, 2017.

238 **One article about Jenkins:** D. Baer, "Maybe Monogamy Isn't the Only Way to Love," The Cut, *New York*, March 6, 2017, https://www.thecut.com/2017/03/science-of-polyamory-open-relationships-and-nonmonogamy.html.

239 **Indeed, a hacked email:** K. Snyder, "Hollywood Sets Up Its Lady Superheroes to Fail," *Wired*, June 14, 2015, https://www.wired.com/2015/06/hollywood-sets-lady-superheroes-fail/; and J. Bailey, "Will November's Diverse Blockbusters Kill Hollywood's Teenage Boy Obsession?" *Flavorwire*, December 4, 2013, http://flavorwire.com/428023/will-novembers-diverse-blockbusters-kill-hollywoodsteenage-boy-obsession.

239 **viciously racist, misogynist trolling:** N. Woolf, "Leslie Jones Bombarded with Racist Tweets After *Ghostbusters* Opens," *The Guardian*, July 18, 2016, https://www.theguardian.com/culture/2016/jul/18/leslie-jones-racist-tweets-ghostbusters.

239 **"I have wildly optimistic days...":** Jenkins, interview, August 7, 2017.

241 **like thirty-three-year-old Mara:** Mara, interview with the author, 2017.

241 **"When it comes to sexual autonomy...aren't":** Alicia Walker, interview with the author, September 25, 2017.

242 **"very married, publicly married...":** Michelle, interview with the author, 2017.

247 **Robert, sixty:** Robert, interviews with the author, 2017.

248 **"That's a honey of an anklet":** *Double Indemnity*, directed by B. Wilder, screenplay by B. Wilder and R. Chandler (Hollywood, CA: Paramount Pictures, 1944), film.

248 **Peter the Great, who beheaded his wife's supposed lover:** D. Ley, *Insatiable Wives: Women Who Stray and the Men Who Love Them* (Lanham, MD: Rowman and Littlefield, 2009), 8.

249 **Justin Lehmiller found in a survey:** J. J. Lehmiller, *Tell Me What You Want: The Science of Sexual Desire and How It Can Help You Improve Your Sex Life* (Boston: Da Capo Press, 2018); and J. J. Lehmiller, correspondence with the author, October 25, 2017.

250 **her Nerve.com article:** K. Ma, "Take My Wife, Please: The Rise of Cuckolding Culture," DateHookup.com (originally Nerve.com), March 3, 2010, https://www.datehookup.com/singles-content-take-my-wife-please--the-rise-of-cuckolding-culture.htm.

251 **On her hotwife lifestyle blog:** A. McCall, "Hotwife Feedback," Combined Blogs, AlexisMcCall.com, January 30, 2017, http://www.alexismccall.com/combined_blogs.html.

251 **McCall defines a hotwife as:** A. McCall, "Hotwife Sex vs Adultery," Combined Blogs, AlexisMcCall.com, June 14, 2017, http://www.alexismccall.com/combined_blogs.html.

252 *Insatiable Wives:* Ley, *Insatiable Wives*.

253 **"I initially thought...":** David Ley, interview with the author, June 27, 2017.

253 **"his presence lingers in her":** Ley, *Insatiable Wives*, 17.

254 **in a study of gay men into cuckolding:** J. J. Lehmiller, D. Ley, and D. Savage, "The Psychology of Gay Men's Cuckolding Fantasies," *Archives of Sexual Behavior*, published online ahead of print (December 28, 2017): 1–15.

254 **"It seems that when your relationship is codified and legalized":** Ley, interview, June 27, 2017.

254 **"For the grass to be greener...just grass":** Ley, *Insatiable Wives*, 113.

254 **"To some of these people, a black guy is...":** Ma, "Take My Wife, Please," https://www.datehookup.com/singles-content-take-my-wife-please--the-rise-of-cuckolding-culture.htm.

254 **Mireille Miller-Young, the historian and porn scholar:** "Black Stud, White Desire: Black Masculinity in Cuckold Pornography and Sex Work," in A. Davis and Black Sexual Economies Collective, eds., *Black Sexual Economies: Race and Sex in a Culture of Capital* (Champaign: University of Illinois Press, forthcoming), 1–11.

255 **"You sometimes get these situations...":** Ley, interview, June 27, 2017.

256 **As Alexis McCall puts it:** McCall, "Hotwife Feedback," http://www.alexismccall.com/combined_blogs.html.

CHAPTER NINE: LIFE IS SHORT. SHOULD YOU BE UNTRUE?

257 **"men and women basically want...very similar"**: Tammy Nelson, interview with the author, July 5, 2017.

258 **"to add excitement to my life"**: "The Top Five Reasons Married Moms Cheat," *Divorce* (blog), *Huffington Post*, February 27, 2014, https://www.huffingtonpost.com/2014 /02/27/married-moms-cheat_n_4868716.html.

258 **In a 2011 Kinsey study:** K. P. Mark, E. Janssen, and R. R. Milhausen, "Infidelity in Heterosexual Couples: Demographic, Interpersonal, and Personality-Related Predictors of Extradyadic Sex," *Archives of Sexual Behavior* 40, no. 5 (2011): 971–82.

258 **In her Good in Bed survey:** "Good in Bed Surveys, Report #1: Relationship Boredom," GoodinBed.com, https://www.goodinbed.com/research/GIB_Survey_Report-1.pdf.

259 **Tilda Swinton comes to mind:** K. Roiphe, "Liberated in Love: Can Open Marriage Work?," *Harper's Bazaar*, July 13, 2009, http://www.harpersbazaar.com/culture /features/a400/open-marriages-0809/.

259 **Arline Geronimus:** A. Geronimus, "What Teen Mothers Know," *Human Nature* 7, no. 4 (1996): 323–52.

260 **the famous T-shirt test:** C. Wedekind, T. Seebeck, F. Bettens, and A. J. Paepke, "MHC-Dependent Mate Preferences in Humans," *Proceedings of the Royal Society B, Biological Sciences* 260, no. 1359 (1995): 245–49.

260 **Leslie Vosshall, a neurobiologist:** Leslie Vosshall, correspondence with the author, October 26, 2017.

260 **Another study of Hutterites:** C. Ober, L. R. Weitkamp, N. Cox, H. Dytch, D. Kostyu, and S. Elias, "HLA and Mate Choice in Humans," *American Journal of Human Genetics* 61, no. 3 (1997): 497–504.

AFTERWORD: FEMALE CHOICES

264 **Virginia was married once:** Virginia, interviews with the author, 2017.

INDEX

ABOUT THE AUTHOR

Wednesday Martin, PhD, is the author of the #1 *New York Times* best-seller *Primates of Park Avenue*. Her book *Stepmonster*, unique in its feminist approach to stepmothering, was a finalist for a Books for a Better Life Award, and she has written for the *New York Times*, *The Atlantic*, *The Forward*, the *Hollywood Reporter*, the *Sunday Times* (London), the *Daily Beast*, and *Refinery29*, among others. She has appeared on *The Dr. Oz Show*, *Good Morning America*, *Nightline*, CNN, and the *Today* show. Wednesday earned her doctorate in comparative literature and cultural studies at Yale and lives in New York City with her husband and their two sons.